MW01614921

Touch the Sky

...the story of a Mom, a Wife, an Airshow Pilot and Wingrider

by

Sandi Pierce Browne

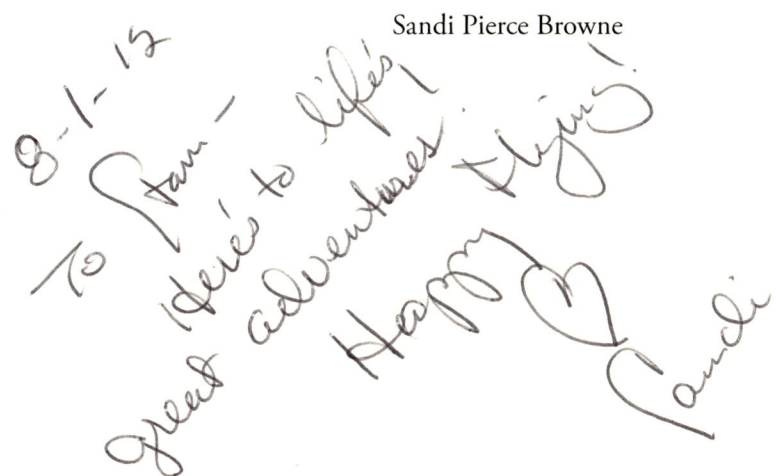

8-1-13

To Stan —
Here's to life's
great adventures!
Happy Flying!
Sandi

Heartlines
PUBLISHING GROUP
ROCKWALL TEXAS

Cover Design by Bud Gray

Library of Congress Control Number: 2010910061

ISBN: 978-0-615-38594-5

PRINTED IN THE UNITED STATES OF AMERICA

BY THE VOOM GROUP, INC. • 1825 E. PLANO PKWY. • SUITE 250

PLANO, TX 75074

To my precious daughters
Wendi Linn & Chandelle

CONTENTS

Hilton Head, South Carolina

I lowered my head to fight the wind. Beneath me, my sneakers poised on the center section of the top wing of a circus-painted biplane. Blood-red sunburst rays zapped from under my feet to the wing tips on either side. Standing like a hood ornament on an automobile in a windstorm, I rode as a passenger atop an old biplane a few thousand feet in the air. Any minute, the plane would loop, roll, and fly upside down. The thought terrified me.

Why was I doing this? Why did I agree to ride outside an airplane flying aerobatics? I thrived on challenge, but this was ridiculous. Scared or not, I couldn't back out. It was too late. So many dreams and so much work had brought me to this moment. A reluctant sightseer along for the ride, my gaze swept forward to the front of the wing and my stomach tightened. The biplane rode waves of South Carolina sky with ocean and beach flashing underneath. I raised my head and the wind ruffled my cheeks as it continued to push me into the steel brace at my back.

In an effort to distract myself, I inhaled the ocean air pummeling my body. Like a sentry scanning the horizon, I gazed at the ground from my new observation tower. The deserted Hilton Head airport lay below and to one side. A few airplanes rested on the ramp and sea birds were the only patrons. In the midst of my musing, the plane hit a downdraft and we dropped a few feet. Heart aflutter, I grabbed the seatbelt linked about my waist, the belt that attached me to the airplane. I held onto the metal fittings, thankful for the cool hardness that was my lifeline. I found myself remembering my mom's words. "You're a mother of a precious four-year old. Are you crazy?"

Alone atop the beast of a biplane, my mom's misgivings blended with my own fear and panic, threatening to engulf me. Calm down, Sandi. You're an airshow pilot; you've done scarier things than this.

It was a lie. Nothing was scarier than being on top of this wing, sans parachute, with only air around me. The phrase *blown away* took on a new meaning. I grinned at my joke and wind gushed into my mouth. I clamped my lips together and realized that smiling needed to be an internal expression for passengers on airplane wings.

I passed my fingers along the edge of the cloth helmet I wore, tucking in a curl that whipped my cheek. I ran my hands down my jumpsuit and stopped at the seatbelt holding me. With a tug, I snugged it even tighter. Could I back out, return to the airport, and accept a coward's embarrassment?

Now or never, I let my right foot trail behind the wingstand a signal to my pilot that I was ready to begin. Ready as I would ever be.

AUGUST, 1966

1

FIRST FLIGHT

Tim's Airpark, Austin, Texas

"Yell 'Clear prop' through the open window," he said. Heart thumping, I turned my head to look at the man sardined next to me. We sat side by side in an airplane cockpit smaller than the inside of a sports car. What a strange way to interview for a job.

"You don't want to start the propeller rotating with someone nearby," he said, "so you open the window." He paused until I turned the clasp and freed the window on my left. "Now yell 'CLEAR PROP' and look for anyone in the way of the propeller."

I looked through the windshield, scanning around the front of a high wing airplane, reminding me of a large aluminum kite. Across the ramp, several guys of varying ages lazed near the door of the aviation operation, coffee cups in hand. Snippets of laughter and conversation drifted over to the airplane. Were they laughing at me? I could understand why; twenty-one-year-old girls didn't take flying lessons. Most girls my age were either married or pursuing guys at college. Similar to my friends, I had traveled a familiar trail, marrying my high-school-sweetheart-turned-law-student. I completed three years of college and lacked a degree, but had a fourteen-month-old baby. It seemed a good trade-off to me.

Just two hours before, I had driven north across Austin to Tim's Airpark for a job interview as a secretary-receptionist. I left my daughter at the babysitter, mailed a letter for my law-student husband, and hurried to be on time for my appointment. Laid off during a round of office pruning, this job was important.

My prospective airport boss and I had gone through the normal interview process. Where have you worked? Do you like people? What do you plan on doing when your husband graduates? None of the questions were unusual. I was surprised when my potential boss, a man my father's age, said, "Call me Jim." I couldn't imagine addressing an older man by his first name.

"Sandi, have you ever been up in a small airplane?"

"No," I forced myself to say his name, "Jim." I rushed to let him know I wasn't anti-airplane. "I did fly once in an airliner, Trans-Texas Airways, a DC-3 I think."

Jim nodded, "Nice ship."

"My dad was a private pilot and so was my brother…Jim. I was little when they flew and they never took me up."

Images cascaded across my mind; my father flying with friends and then my brother taking piloting lessons. I enjoyed the car rides with my parents to airports to watch planes on lazy Sunday afternoons after church. My mental pictures of pilots featured heroes, men flanked by wives and girlfriends, talking airplanes, competing in their pilot stories, and looking as if they knew some secret we earthbound females didn't understand.

Jim's voice broke into my reverie, "Time to change that. We can't have a secretary who doesn't know something about aviation."

"What?" I said. What was this man saying?

"Time to go fly. I'll give you an introductory flight lesson. Let's see how you like boring holes in the sky."

The fear in the pit of my stomach crept upward. Fly? He couldn't mean me. I imagined my mom saying, "Sandra, stay away from airplanes. They're dangerous." I set my questions and my mom's admonishments aside. I needed a job and if I had to take to the skies as part of the process, so be it.

Like a willing puppy, I followed the ex-Texas-Ranger while he demonstrated how to check the airplane before we took to the skies. Dazed, I stayed close nodding my head as if I understood, though I found it hard to concentrate.

I watched in amazement as he maneuvered his over six-foot frame into the small craft. I was short and wore the plane more easily. How strange I felt, crammed thigh-to-thigh beside the local Wyatt Earp in a fragile looking flying machine about to blast off into the hot August sky. Perspiration beaded on his balding head and his knees pushed against the instrument panel.

"Now open that window, there to your side," he said and waited for me to follow his command. "Now yell, 'Clear Prop' and close the window."

I opened the window and said, "Clear prop," looking to his face for approval to quell my mounting tension.

"No, no. No one can hear you." He flung the door beside him open and bellowed, "CLEAR PROP!" He looked at me. "Now you." Hot summer air filled the plane. At least, it was fresh.

Did he expect me to open my door? My stomach lurched. No way, I'm not going to pop out of this flimsy tin can. Would he leave his door gaping in the air?

I hesitated as I tried to figure out what Jim wanted me to do. He noticed my confusion. "Just yell out the window. We don't want to chop anyone up."

I bent to the window I had previously opened and gave it my best yell,

"Clear prop!"

"Great, now turn the key all the way to the right, and rest your right hand on the throttle." He pointed to a knob on a silver rod to my right.

I did as I was told, and the propeller turned. The engine caught, chugging, a heart beating erratically. The fuselage vibrated and the noise of metal creaking came from behind. My apprehension grew as this Model-T of an airplane popped and groaned. Maybe Mom was right. Airplanes did sound dangerous. His hand pushed mine forward. "Give it a little gas to make it run smooth."

I breathed deeper when the engine noise rounded out and the vibration stopped. We sat snug behind a wraparound window separating our little world, the cockpit, from the panorama of airport life. To our right, a man stood on a ladder next to a high wing airplane at the gas pumps. A low-wing airplane passed in front of us, and the guys on the porch stopped talking to watch it go by. What fun to be part of this pilot world.

The excitement of a new adventure began to overrun my fear, though I still wished Jim would close his door. He said to rest my left hand on the wheel, to keep my right hand atop the throttle jutting from the middle of the instrument panel, and to steer the plane on the ground with the rudder pedals at my feet.

I grabbed the wheel and turned it right. Nothing happened. I felt my stomach lurch, and knew, I couldn't do this.

"Relax. Let go of the yoke, the control wheel," he said. "You steer airplanes on the ground with your feet. Push on the right rudder pedal. See what happens."

I put pressure on the right pedal and the plane slowly inched its way to the right as we moved forward. A heavy push on the left rudder and we moseyed back to the left. Back and forth we went, me pressing the rudder pedals, grabbing the wheel, and trying to learn how to steer this crazy vehicle, while his calm voice droned on. My feet, hands, and brain were so occupied I had little time to worry about the impression I made or my chances of being hired. I heard Jim talking on the radio, but I was too busy attempting to move the plane in a forward direction to pay attention.

I taxied, weaving past the gawking guys on the porch, past the rows of airplanes, and beside the burnt brown grass of a Central Texas summer. It took a while, but we made it along the asphalt highway to the end of the runway. The challenge of airplane tasks kept me busy and my fear receded from my thoughts.

He handed me a plastic-covered piece of paper, and told me to use the checklist. Not understanding, but happy to comply, I read, "Check the controls for free and proper movement."

Jim patiently explained how to turn the wheel and look outside at the wing to make certain things were working properly. He spoke the unfamiliar language of aviation with words falling on me like rain on a metal roof, hitting briefly then running off and dropping away. I had little idea what the phrases meant as we went step by step down the checklist, yet I enjoyed their sound.

At last, he slammed his door shut. "Rest your hands on your wheel and your feet on your rudder pedals. On take off, I'll be flying with my set of controls, but I want you to follow through with me. In the air, we use the ailerons and rudder to turn the airplane and go up and down."

Oh my God, what are ailerons? Elevators? Those words were in the checklist earlier, but I didn't remember what they meant. Never mind, the man next to me would take care of everything.

At last, I was going to fly in a small airplane. I had no protective mother to ward off the dangers of the world, no well-meaning friends to tell me

I was crazy, and no husband present to say this wasn't a good idea. It was just me, an airplane, and a potential boss ready to initiate me into the sky. I began to doubt I could pull this off.

Jim lined the plane up along the centerline of the runway and pushed the throttle into the panel. The engine grew louder as the plane gathered speed, as did the fuselage sounds. Rivulets of air spilled across the windshield.

"Watch the airspeed, Sandi. There, on the instrument panel." I searched for something that looked like a speedometer, but got lost in the engine noise, the groans of the plane, and the image of the airport zooming away beside us. My hands dropped from the wheel. In what seemed only a moment, I heard Jim say, "Now with a little back pressure on the controls, we are flying."

And we were. The plane felt stable in the air as if a giant hand had reached down and pulled it skyward. I was John Glenn riding my rocket into space, leaving earth and all its concerns behind.

"Now, you take the controls." Jim's words brought my attention back from sightseeing out the window. What did he mean? I was along for the ride, a willing spectator, but only that. My potential boss had other ideas. He told me to put my left hand on the wheel, and thus began my first lesson in flying.

In spite of bouncing around in a hot afternoon sky, the next thirty minutes sped by. Jim taught me to look outside to see how the plane was flying in relation to the distant horizon. Was the nose too high or low? Were the wings level? This aviating was a complicated adventure, but one that captivated me. I tried to absorb all he said and promptly forgot most of it. I lost myself in trying to control the plane. It demanded my total attention, and yet, I couldn't keep the nose straight or the wings level with any consistency. Never had I been so challenged, and I reveled in it.

I relished the crisp sky, the small people and buildings beneath us, and especially the way the earth trailed off in the distance, as if it were painted. I liked being a part of an impressionistic scene, a smudge of an airplane in a blue-white brush-stroked sky, with some unseen artist perfecting the canvas. Sure, the plane was noisy and we were crowded like best friends on a carnival ride, but in this first short flight, I discovered something I hadn't realized was missing in my life. I couldn't define what it was but I liked it and wanted more, much more. Now, I needed the secretarial job not only for income, but also as a means to get back into the air.

2

THE SKY BECKONS

The phone rang as I opened the door to our rental house. Laden with groceries, I struggled to the kitchen, dropped the bags and grabbed the black receiver. "Sandra," my mom said. "I was hoping you were home."

She still called me Sandra, although I had started using Sandi when I went off to college. "I'm here, barely. Just got in from a job interview."

"How nice. Tell me all about it. Is it in the medical profession?" My mom was a dental assistant and anything involved with medicine fascinated her. She would have been ecstatic if I had become a nurse.

"No medicine. In fact, Daddy will probably like this job more than you. I'd be a secretary at a small airport on the north side of town." The silence swelled with her unspoken thoughts. It wouldn't last long. My mom was full of opinions, often expressing them. I hurried to add, "Now Mother, there's nothing wrong with working at an airport." I cradled the phone under my ear, and stooped to move the grocery bags from the floor to the counter.

"You know how I feel about airplanes. I was never so glad as when your dad quit flying, after the heart attack. I thought I'd die when your brother got his license. Thank goodness he doesn't fly anymore. Can't you find a job somewhere else?"

"Jobs aren't easy to find right now." A little fib wouldn't hurt. Mom didn't mind the idea of airplanes, I reminded myself as I put the eggs in the refrigerator; she just didn't want anyone she loved up in one.

I loved my mother, but she carried an image of herself as director of our family's movie while she had raised independent children wanting to write, direct, and produce their own stories. Tension flared when our actions didn't match her desires.

"I know you," she said. "You'll be up in one of those planes before you know it, just like your father and your brother." I decided not to tell her about my introductory lesson. As she rambled on, I thought about my brother Tommy and wondered why he had quit flying. Nine years older than me, my brother was movie-star handsome and athletic, with a rising career in the advertising business. I had always wanted to be like him, but, in my mind I never measured up. Our family defined me as the "smart one," not glamorous as I wished to be.

I was putting the folded paper grocery bags under the sink when my mother's words caught my attention, "Flying is dangerous. You're a mother and a wife, you belong on the ground. How many women do you know who fly airplanes?"

I struggled to think of one. At last, I said, "Amelia Earhart."

"Yes, and she died." I heard my mom's harrumph, and imagined my four-foot-eleven-inch mother sitting at her kitchen counter mentally shaking her finger at me.

"Well, I'm just going to be a secretary," I lied again, "and we need the money. How are things in Dallas?"

"Don't try and sidetrack me. Have you thought about your daughter?"

"Her dad's picking her up on his way home." I smiled to myself as I sidestepped her real question.

"No, I mean how can you think about a flying job when you have a child?"

When irritated with my mom, I would daydream of a life raised by the perfect mother, either biological or adopted, just not the one I had. This was one of those times. "Oh, Mother." I recognized the whine in my voice and the familiar stomach tightening that often accompanied our mother-daughter talks. "It's just a secretarial job. I have to go now. They'll be home soon, and dinner's not ready."

"Sandra, don't take the job. You're smart, think about what I've said. I know you can find something else. I love you, honey. Remember, you're the light of my life."

"Bye, Mom. Love you."

I hung up the phone. Friendly fire had just shot me down from the stratosphere in which I had been soaring. What had I been thinking? Mother was right. With the exception of Earhart, I had never heard of, much less known, another woman pilot. I hadn't seen one woman earlier at the airport. Flying cost money, something my mom hadn't mentioned, and my law-student husband and I had none to spare. Self-doubt roared back into my thoughts.

I prepared dinner and consoled myself. I could learn to fly when I was older. Yes, I would fly when my daughter was grown and my husband an established lawyer. My life would be more financially stable. I would be more mature, better able to understand the difficult concepts I had heard this morning.

Anyway, I reminded myself, the job paid poorly, and the airport was located on the opposite side of town from our house. I'd have to work weekends. I sighed and tried to buoy my sinking spirits. I can learn to fly later. Yes, I'll learn later.

Like a lover's memory beckoning beyond reason, the thought of the job and the world it offered encircled my mind. As I slid meatloaf into the oven, the memory of my flight returned. It had been so much fun and I wasn't certain why. Part of my enjoyment was the way flying had demanded all my attention to coordinate my mind and body. It was a skill like tennis, only much more complicated, like driving a race car or motorcyle.

My thoughts turned to how peaceful and perfect the earth looked from our airplane observatory. Jim, my potential boss, and I flew above the fray in a modest little ship. People could be arguing below, but I saw only the beauty. After the flight, I had felt so confident. In spite of my many mistakes, I was somehow bigger than life for flying off into the blue. Nope, I decided, this aviation stuff was for me.

Maybe my husband could take care of our daughter on weekends, in between his studies. What difference would it make which two days of the week I spent with her? One day when we had more money, we could buy an airplane and I would fly us on great vacations. Perhaps my husband would also become a pilot. This job could be an opportunity for our family.

Compelling reasons for working at the airport built a fortress against my misgivings. By the time the front door opened, I was determined to call Jim the next morning and say yes. Could I convince my husband?

SEPTEMBER, 1966

3

THE LOCAL HERO

How should I ask Walt Pierce, the local hero of our flight school, to fly with me? I thought as car horns honked angrily around me. Tempers were soaring on Interstate 35 through Austin. Traffic slowed to a standstill, and I was late for work, my job at Tim's Airpark. Late on a day I needed to be calm and inviting. Instead, I was frustrated and upset. Why would anyone, much less Walt, want to help me?

"Wish they all could be...California Girls" blared over the radio. I reached up and turned it off. I liked the Beach Boys, but I didn't need the distraction. I sure wasn't a California girl with blonde hair and tanned firm body. I felt certain any of the pilots at the airport would fly with one of those. I was a young, married woman who worked as a secretary for a flight school and was seeking serious flight instruction, not sexual advances.

The bumper-to-bumper traffic inched forward while I chewed on my problem. What words would convince the top instructor at our flight school to take pity on me, a beginning student?

I had started work three weeks earlier at the airport and this morning, the morning I intended to ask for help, I was going to be late to work. I hit the heel of my hand against the steering wheel. Would he do it? Would he help me out?

Walt Pierce, an older man of twenty-six, taught people to fly upside down in a Citabria, a cute little high-wing airplane with a tail wheel and turned up nose. With so much experience, I feared he wouldn't want to waste his time with me. A former airline pilot, he performed at regional airshows in his own airplane, taught aerobatics at our flight school, and spent any spare time flying charters, or if he had to, giving dual instruction to students. I had heard him tell Jim, my boss, that he only wanted to teach aerobatics, no beginners. Nope, for certain, he wouldn't do it. Oh, he'd be nice, let me down gently, but he wouldn't fly with me.

Tall and slender, Walt reminded me of a dark-haired Lindbergh. He ambled through the day with few words, often sprawling across a chair between flights while the other fliers gathered round, amusing him with their aviation adventures. He had always been pleasant to me, once or twice even asking about my flying lessons.

I thought about my current flight instructor, the one I wanted to change. Early on, he offered to teach me at no charge. With my employee discount, I was able to rent a small Cessna for $6.00 an hour which still strained our budget, but got me in the air. After only three hours of dual instruction, I had realized the free flight lessons, though a nice offer, weren't working. I longed to be in the air while my friendly instructor wanted to drink coffee and impress me with his aviation exploits. I had watched the other instructors interact with their students and knew there was more to flight lessons than telling tales.

My plan was to talk Walt into instructing me for one lesson. The other pilots deferred to him, the big man on our little campus. If he flew with me once, perhaps the instructors would take me seriously. Walt seemed nice enough, and I hoped, might help me out. Still, my three hours of logged time were so insignificant compared to his eight thousand hours in the air. Not bad, I reminded myself, for a girl about to turn twenty-two next week.

At last, the traffic opened up. I rushed into the flight school, throwing my things on the desk behind the counter. This was my new work place and I was very much at home. Here, I greeted people, scheduled airplanes and instructors, and answered the busy phone. I listened while pilots, sprawled on couches and chairs, regaled each other with stories of near misses, perfect days, and great tailwinds on trips in airplanes. They drank their coffee, flipped through dog-eared aviation magazines, and jumped into the storytelling when openings appeared.

I hurried to make the coffee before they started arriving, before Walt came to work. If I pled with him, would he take pity on a struggling would-be aviator?

Coffee brewing, I straightened the magazines, picked up trash in the pilot area, and knew in my heart I had to ask him that day. If I didn't, I might never get enough courage. After all, the worse he could say was no. At that thought, my spirits sagged.

Flying already meant a great deal to me. My first lesson had been only four weeks ago, but already on my days off, I read aviation books and dreamed of a future as a pilot. At any excuse, I would drag my daughter to the airport with me to watch the airplanes. I had already begun studying for the private pilot written examination while doing my weekly ironing.

The airport was a magnet pulling me close. At night, I excitedly shared my day's activities with my husband before he went to work. He was busy with law school plus a part-time job, and it was easy for my head to stay in the clouds, touching down only to take care of my family.

Yes, I would ask Walt this morning. I'd explain I only needed him to fly with me once or twice. That would be enough.

On the way back from emptying the trash, Walt sauntered to the counter and glanced at the scheduling book. He wore his usual plain shirt with olive drab pants. Military-shined black Wellington boots, aviator sunglasses, and large watch with many dials, all broadcast "pilot." I scurried back to my desk.

He took off the glasses and smiled his lopsided grin. "You must be a Texas dervish. I never saw any one move so fast." I smiled to myself; if he only knew.

"That's me, all right. I ran late this morning and then got caught in traffic. The babysitter took longer. I was afraid Jim would be here, tapping his foot, and you guys lined up waiting for coffee." I ran out of breath. Well, that certainly made an impression. He'd never fly with me.

"Whoa, slow down," he said. He turned the scheduling book around and ran his finger down his column of students for the day. He would walk away any minute. What should I say?

"You have an accent," I said. "Where were you raised?" Okay, Sandi, now's the time. You can do it.

"No," he said, "You have the drawl. I'm from New Mexico where we speak clearer than you Texans." He moved toward the coffee pot.

"Walt." My voice came out weak and crackly, but he paused to look back. "I've wanted to ask, could you, I mean, would you…" I gulped a breath. "Would you be willing to fly with me? Just one hour would be neat." I rushed on. "The instructors aren't taking me seriously, and I thought if you flew with me…" I was begging, but it was worth it, "…if you flew with me, just one hour, they would know I'm sincere about being a pilot."

He listened with little expression as my words fell over each other. "I mean, I really want to learn to fly, to fly really well. Someday, I'd like to be a flight instructor or something." Did girls become flight instructors? I didn't know. I hadn't seen any.

I saw crinkle lines form around his eyes as he came back to the counter.

Without saying anything, he looked at his schedule. He glanced up and said, "You want to have a lesson every day on your lunch hour? Maybe 12:15?"

I was shocked. He had said yes, yes to much more than I had asked. "Yes, noon would work. Oh, yes, but, but I can't afford to fly everyday." I was on a budget, a budget not including airplane rentals and fees to high and mighty head aerobatic instructors.

"Three days a week?" I nodded and he wrote my name on his schedule. He dropped the pen and said, "We'll start today."

"Oh thank you, thank you." I hated to ask, but needed to know how deep into debt I was about to go. "How much do you want me to pay you?"

As he ambled away, he said, "We'll talk about it later."

OCTOBER, 1966

4

OBSESSED WITH FLYING

"For the first time in my life, I feel like I've come home," I said and sipped the diet Tab soda. I relaxed on a rusted metal lawn chair, enjoying the October hint of fall in the air. Walt and I lounged on the porch outside the flight school, the same place my laughing observers had watched my preflight just a few weeks ago. Now I was one of them, officially an airport bum, someone who hung around the airport drinking coffee or sodas and talking airplanes, part of the group who grew silent when nonpilots approached. Since the day I had asked Walt to fly with me, I had flown with no one else.

Being in the air felt familiar and comfortable, as if I had returned to where I belonged. Unfortunately, my marriage and home were not so peaceful. All my husband and I seemed to do since I had begun flying was fight. Finances were tight, and while he might have understood spending too much money on clothes, he could not understand money going for airplanes. Disliking the tension, I stayed longer and longer at the airport. I had found my niche in the erector set of life and discovered a passion I did not know was missing. Giving up flying was not an option I even considered anymore.

Before flying, I would have said my life was on track with a husband and child, but now I wasn't certain. I had enjoyed hearing about my husband's law school studies. Now, it was his turn to share my world of airplanes. Busy working a night shift, going to classes, and studying, he had little time for a wife obsessed with aviation. We shared our daughter, but our marriage found itself on rocky terrain.

I pushed away my disturbing thoughts and said, "Great way to spend my day off, taking an hour of dual and getting ready for my long solo cross-county flight. It's hard to believe I'm going to College Station, Houston, and back, all alone in an airplane."

Walt tilted his wooden chair against the wall, resting on the back two legs.

I knew he listened to my babbling, though he drank a coke and kept his eyes on the runway, mesmerized by the dance of airplanes breaking free, flying round the home nest like baby birds, and floating back to mother earth.

"I'm so glad I took this job." I smiled at him and he nodded in return, our little communication ritual. My glance lingered. Was he interested in me, beyond student and teacher? There were sparks, I could feel the delicious sexual tension coming from a shared interest. Was some undercurrent pulling me out to an unknown sea? Perhaps it was only the flying, but it felt like more. I didn't know or even care. I only wanted to fly.

"Do you suppose all those Sunday afternoons at airports as a child makes flying seem so familiar to me?" He didn't respond. "I have a picture of me standing on the tire of my daddy's airplane, an old Aeronca, when I was four or five."

Eyes still on the traffic pattern, he said, "The Aeronca Aircraft Company became Champion Aircraft which now produces the Citabria, your precious Tinkerbelle." I awaited his tidbits of aviation information like a puppy at a cook-out.

When Walt became my instructor, he encouraged me to change from flying the Cessna 150 to the 115 horsepower Citabria the flight school used for aerobatic instruction. The Citabria, airbatic spelled backwards, featured a tail wheel instead of one on the nose. It had a stick instead of a control wheel, and fabric covering a steel frame. The nose jauntily faced skyward and the wings sported a festive blue and white sunburst pattern. It was no wonder the pilots called her Tinkerbelle, she was magic. I began flying Tinkerbelle and now considered her mine.

"Just think," I said, "My dad owned one of the parents or maybe grandparents of my airplane."

"Tinkerbelle is an airplane, Sandi, and belongs to the flight school, not you." His gruff voice didn't fool me; I knew he liked the Citabria also.

"I know, I know. I just like to pretend she's mine. Maybe if I sprinkle some fairy dust?" He ignored my chattering. My words often spewed out, while his were spoken as if drawn from a miser's bank account. "Who would believe I already have fifteen hours of flight time?"

"I do. I was there." He chuckled, smiling his unique grin, a grin showing off-center front teeth. "Maybe you belong in the air, like me."

"Yeah, maybe," I said.

I knew I wanted to be just like him, a Zen monk of aviation; calm, centered, one with my airplane. I looked back to the runway and noticed the sun's glint bouncing off a turning propeller on a landing airplane. The plane hit the ground with a thud, bounced back into the air, and thumped its way to a stop. I cringed, remembering similar landings I had made, and the ones I knew were yet to come.

"I haven't seen many women pilots," I said.

Walt's chair plopped to the floor. He pivoted to look me straight in the face. "There are a lot of women pilots, fine pilots. Women ferried big bombers in World War II." For a moment I could see those brave young girls hating war like I did, but excited to fly forbidden military airplanes.

The sound of his voice popped my fantasy. "Some of the greatest airshow pilots have been women, Betty Skelton and Caro Bailey in little Pitts Specials, Kaddy Landry in her big bull Stearman."

I nodded my head in response to his pep talk, but somehow just couldn't imagine me ever being able to fly like the women he mentioned. Was I lacking inner strength, the confidence to make my life what I wanted? The more I read about pilots, the more I heard tales of courage and ability to remain calm no matter what the circumstance, the more I lost in comparison to them. I was so emotional, and these pilots demonstrated calm. Where did they get such outward confidence? Was it testosterone or only arrogance? Still, I did feel older, more mature since I had soloed three weeks before. I grinned. Of course. I was now a woman of twenty-two.

Walt leaned his chair back against the wall. "Someday, I'm going to have a 450 Stearman and make my living in the airshow business. I'll sell my TCraft, even though it's been a great airshow airplane. I'll get me a big, smoke-belching Stearman."

Here he goes again, I thought with amusement. Even this taciturn aviator talks when it comes to his flying dreams. I had heard him share this fantasy with students, other flight instructors, and with nearly any pilot who would listen. The reserved man from New Mexico had a vision, and it comforted me to be a friend of someone so certain of what he wanted. An image of my husband drifted through my mind. He knew exactly what he wanted, to be a lawyer. Did lawyers have flight instructors for wives?

A page had turned in my life and I felt removed from the old story, but not quite into the new chapter. Six weeks earlier, I had defined happiness as mother, wife, baker of cakes and cookies, and center of emotional support for the family system. It had seemed more than enough. I thought I would live a life similar to my mom's and her mom before her, only better. I wouldn't make their mistakes. I'd be a better mother, a better wife, and do things right. Things had changed, and I was different. For the first time, I knew exactly what I wanted. I longed to be a professional pilot, spending my days in the air, but I still wanted to be married and a mother. Sadness enveloped me as I thought of my marriage now in turmoil. I had no idea how to combine a career and family.

A child of my times, I was raised in the fifties by a traditional mother who didn't go to work until I was in junior high school. My image of families didn't include professional women, women with careers instead of jobs. Women's liberation was a new concept for me, something people talked about back East and maybe at big universities here in Texas. Still, underneath a traditional exterior, my inner self bubbled with drive, abilities, and a need to create. I so wanted to have a life of challenge, to prove to myself and the world, I could fly with the best of them.

I stretched, moving slightly to a more comfortable position on the hard chair. A soft breeze caressed my skin as I brought my attention back to Walt's voice. He continued to drone on about smoke systems, the modifications he would make to his fantasy plane, and how he might raise the money for his ideas; idle pilot talk after an enjoyable flight.

"You could be part of that dream," he said.

My attention zeroed in. What was he saying? This was different, new words in the familiar litany of his story. "I'm not kidding, Sandi. I'll need a girl wingrider. You could be her."

"What's a wingrider?" What a dumb thing to say. He'll think me a dunce, but I had no idea what he meant.

"It's a person, a gal like you. You'd ride up on top of the plane. Wave at the crowd while I fly my airshow routine."

"I could do that." Where did those words come from? Maybe the fearless-aviator image was sinking in. I congratulated myself for sounding more like the pilots I knew.

"I mean it. You have what it takes. You could be a pilot in the show, fly a solo routine, maybe do a dual with me, and be the wingrider."

My world burst open as if overstuffed with potentials, possibilities, and opportunities. Me with fifteen hours, fly airshows? I searched his face for a sardonic grin or teasing look, but he was serious.

"Would I fly Tinkerbelle?" I asked.

"You'd have a much finer aerobatic airplane."

Impossible, an airplane finer than my little trainer? Images of me flying around Texas in Tinkerbelle filled my mind. I liked the idea. I'd get a blue jumpsuit to match the paint scheme, maybe find some sneakers in a matching color, and even glue little silver stars on them. I could dress my daughter in a matching jumpsuit, and she could go to the airshows with me. Oh, the possibilities.

Troubling concerns soon replaced my initial exhilaration. What if I didn't have what it took? I might never be a good enough pilot for such a magnificent dream. My dad hung out at airports and told the stories, but he never became a commercial pilot, much less an airshow pilot. Was I so different than him? It was a glorious quest, but maybe not mine.

I pasted on my best public relations smile. "Oh sure, I could do that," but my heart doubted.

Walt's invitation into his airshow dream rocked my inner world and caused me to rethink my life. He was my mentor, someone I was lucky to have in my flying life, a friend who now offered much more.

"Sandi," he said. "Flying is the most important thing in my life. I lived near the airport as a kid."

"Roswell?"

"Yep, Roswell. Rode my bike down there most days. Washed and waxed planes for rides. Listened to the old timers talk. Got in an airplane any time I could. One day, the Cole Brothers Airshow came to town. From that moment on, I was going to be an airshow pilot."

Wow. He was really talking to me, sharing. Using my learned girl-skills to keep guys talking, I said, "How'd you get the money to learn to fly?"

He smiled. "The local pilots took me under their wings. Taught me what they knew. I soloed an Aeronca as soon as I turned 16. I got my mom to sign the papers and I joined the Air Force as soon as I was old enough."

Our relationship deepened from that moment. Our time together still centered on flying, hours talking with me, his devoted student, asking questions of him, my most esteemed master. We flew early in the morning before my workday started, and I began lying to my husband. I didn't ask what Walt was telling his wife.

In one early morning's flight lesson, he said, "Today's the day. You're going to learn to loop an airplane." Everything stopped. My breath, my pulse, even my thoughts seemed suspended.

"Are you sure? I'm only a Student Pilot." He had to be an idiot. Didn't he know I talk a good game, but I wasn't good enough? Maybe some day.

He pulled a miniature airplane out of his pocket and described the mechanics of flying a loop as if I were simply learning to turn an airplane a different direction. "Don't worry," he said, "I'll demonstrate the loop first, and then I'll talk you through several of them."

My stomach clenched, but suddenly, it hit me. Next to the fear sat something else, something I had felt before when I was a debater in high school and college. Excitement hovered alongside the fear. My exhilaration and fear fueled a rocket that propelled me forward. Amazed at my own reaction, I climbed into the front seat, where the pilot-in-command flew. Walt sat directly behind me in the instructor's seat.

"Secure the seat belt tight so you won't slide around during the maneuvers," Walt said.

I pulled it as tight as I could.

"Also, set the altimeter to zero instead of the field elevation. We want to be able to glance at the altimeter and know how high we are. Head northeast, and climb to 4,000 feet above the ground."

My muscles clenched. Can a chest explode with conflicting emotions?

"Find a nice long road to use as a reference point."

Climbing to altitude, I lined the plane up over a farm road shooting north to the horizon with no time for looking at the miniature life alive below me.

"I've got the plane," he said, then whipped us right and then left as he looked for traffic, all the while commenting on what he was doing. I tried to focus as he lowered the nose of the airplane and pulled back on the stick. Positive g-forces, the effect of gravity, pushed me down into the seat. My tension eased as I paid attention. This man knew what he was doing and I enjoyed being a passenger while he flew aerobatics. It was fun.

"Follow me through," he said.

I rested my hand lightly on the stick as we flew straight up into the sky, upside down, and then zoomd earthward, at last bumping through our prop wash where we had begun the maneuver.

"That bump let us know we came back to the same altitude. Now, it's your turn. Line up on the road."

Walt's words pushed me over a cliff. I gripped the stick in my right hand like a lifeline while my left hand seemed frozen on the throttle.

You can't do this, fear whispered inside me and I agreed. Riding through aerobatics while Walt flew was one thing, but for me to loop the plane was quite another.

Walt's calm instructor-voice coached over the engine noise, "Now make your clearing turns and look for traffic."

I knew how to turn Tinkerbelle and look for airplanes. Anxiety flooded through me with each beat of my heart, but my hands stayed busy flying the airplane.

"Now, line up on the road. Lower the nose until you get 140 miles per hour." Centering us over the road was easy, and lowering the nose as if I were trying to lose altitude was something I had done many times. Wind whistled across the windshield like it always did when we flew this fast. I increased the pressure on the stick to keep the nose down and the speed building.

"Check your altimeter," he said. "What's your altitude?"

A quick glance at the altimeter. "3,700 feet."

"Pull back on the stick with a solid pressure, not a jerk. As the nose of the airplane comes up, add full power."

A small inner voice whispered, you can't do this, but I obeyed my teacher in the back seat and pulled back on the stick.

"You're losing the horizon in front of you," he said, "so look to your left wing."

My stomach lurched as the earth in front of me vanished. I stared into blank space.

"Look left," Walt's voice reminded me from the back seat.

Turning my head left, I again saw the earth with my left wingtip making a circle around the horizon. The airplane quieted as the speed died down.

"Loosen up on the stick a little. Fly an arc over the horizon, not an egg." I released some of the back pressure on the stick and my body immediately fell against the seat belt. What do I need to do? I screamed inside.

"More back pressure. You relaxed too much." Walt's calm voice reassured me. "You want to stay with positive g's in this maneuver."

With increased back pressure as instructed, my weight transferred from the seat belt back into the seat, although we remained upside down. The wingtip changed its curve on the horizon.

"Throw your head back, and look through the greenhouse. See if you're lined up on the road."

I pivoted my head and looked up through the greenhouse, the Plexiglas roof covering the cabin. Sure enough, the ground appeared above and behind my head. I flew at an angle to the road over my head, but had no idea how to get the airplane's flight path back to the straight asphalt line.

Walt said, "Now come back on the power, use the rudder to line up with the road, and get us back to straight and level flight."

Airplane nose down, we dive bombed toward earth with Tinkerbelle bucking like a horse. I panicked. What should I do?

The throttle moved under my left hand as Walt said, "I'm pulling back on the power. Gently bring the nose up as you straighten the wings."

The plane slowed down, and I regained control. Back to straight and level, we flew towards a silo off to one side of the road now below us, where it belonged. My breathing returned to normal, and my panic at feeling out of control settled.

"Next time, pull the power back. Start getting the nose back to level sooner." Walt said. "I'll talk you through it."

Something inside me trusted that he would. Hadn't he been calm when we accidentally flew inverted and had negative g's on top of the loop? Hadn't he pulled the power back, correcting my high speed run toward the ground? I relaxed, having faith not in myself but my aerobatics instructor.

Then I realized what I had done. I had flown my first loop. It may have been a crummy loop, but it was mine. I had broken my personal sound barrier, and Chuck Yeager couldn't have been more thrilled. Flying the loop was…fun, scary, but fun.

"Check your altitude," Walt said.

Another glance at the altimeter, and I discovered a loss of nearly a thousand feet. OK, it wasn't perfect, but I had flown Tinkerbelle upside down and around. I recovered, I was alive, and the plane was fine. You're some student pilot, I told myself, and half-way believed it.

"Climb back to 4,000 feet, and do it again," he said.

Let's see what I can do this time. I resolved to make the plane do what Walt said, well…at least, more of what he said.

The days rushed by with work, family life interspersed with cross-country flights needed for my private pilot license, practicing loops, and learning how to do spins and barrel rolls.

Few nonmilitary pilots are taught aerobatics. An advanced pilot who might want to learn such skills would have to find an airplane built to withstand the stresses of aerobatics, and then, would search for an instructor capable of teaching them the intricacies of performing gymnastics in the sky. For me, a student pilot, to learn even these simple maneuvers was phenomenal. Our flight school had both the airplane and a qualified instructor interested enough to teach me.

At home in the sky, the freedom of twisting and turning reminded me of dreams where I soared safe and protected. The challenge of staying oriented while maintaining the proper airspeed and position of the airplane in relation to the horizon was heady stuff. High above the ground I would occasionally fall out of a maneuver and tumble earthward. At first, the fear seemed overwhelming as my stomach lurched, but slowly I gained confidence. I learned how to recover from my mistakes that resulted in the plane being in very unusual positions. Tinkerbelle and I would then climb back up to starting altitude, clear the area, and try the maneuver again. I, who never had liked carnival rides, thought flying aerobatic maneuvers cool. People of my generation might be protesting and declaring themselves liberated, but Tinkerbelle and I etched figures in the sky.

In between students, Walt hung out in the office talking with me about aerobatic airplanes, the intricacies of different maneuvers, and about aerobatic competition versus airshow flying. Our airport bums watched with knowing glances and amused smiles. They also began to pay attention when I told my pilot stories. At home, my husband no longer listened to my aviation exploits and I quit sharing them.

Before long, I was filled with giddy and excited feelings: the rush of adrenaline, the can't-wait-to-go-flying, heart pounding stuff of romance novels. I had fallen in love with flying, and maybe, with Walt. How could this be happening to me?

I bounced out of bed in the morning, hummed the Air Force song throughout the day, and dreamed of owning my own airplane. I was in love, all in caps please. Lust, love, and flying all swirled into a modern montage of two equal human beings pursuing their careers together. Of course, I didn't have equal experience, I certainly didn't feel equal, but my dream was to be on par with him, to be good enough. Walt expected me to do it.

It was the sixties and though the feminist movement had begun, it hadn't yet reached it's fullness in the Southwest. I grew up in a culture that encouraged anyone born and raised in the great state of Texas, man or woman, to reach for dreams people from other parts of the country might not even consider. However, most Texas women I knew funneled those dreams and ambitions through the men they loved. We might pretend we were weak, but we knew better. It wasn't a question of equality; we thought we were smarter, stronger, and more capable. In spite of that confidence, until my generation most Texas women were teachers, secretaries, or nurses. With those cultural genes pumping my bloodstream and the encouragement of Walt, I rushed like a fighter pilot into aerial combat. At the same time, part of me held back, knowing I was going against tradition.

Why hadn't I, the honor society student in high school, gone to law school? Other fellow debaters, even girls, had. Perhaps dark crevices of unworthiness, inadequacy, or other unnamed fears enslaved me or at least limited my vision. If so, my desire to fly pulled me forward in spite of any rough subconscious terrain. I had begun my process of liberation.

Walt gave me the opportunity to use my abilities and to channel my high energy. He asked me to share his flying dream. No one had ever offered such an equal partnership before. I thrived in ways I never imagined.

Between family and flying, my whirlwind life allowed little time for introspection. When I did pause for a moment, a pesky voice inside me whispered, would you love Walt without the flying?

I pushed the irritating thought aside, consumed with intense passion and a youth permeated with Hollywood movies and romantic notions. Walt was my flight instructor, mentor, and coach. He and flying were inextricably linked in my psyche. How could I love one and not the other? Wedding vows and family responsibilities ignored, I flung myself into the open arms not only of aviation, but also my personal aerobatics guru.

One day I left my husband, took my daughter, and moved into an apartment nearer the airport. I rode such a tidal wave of emotion combined with certainty of direction that neither my solid Christian upbringing nor my personal sense of right and wrong stopped me. I had no doubts. If Jesus were around and flew, I figured he would agree. I was twenty-two years old and I grabbed my destiny. I vowed to not become my parents who stay married fighting, criticizing, and miserable. Marriage would not trap me.

Too immature to see the connection that bound my parents beyond their words, I rushed headlong into my passion. I did not think about a world not as forgiving as Jesus. However, I did know I would regret not going with Walt on this flying journey. Unfortunately, I did not look beyond my emotions and gave little thought to the consequences of my actions.

NOVEMBER, 1966

5

PAPA TIGER FRANK PRICE

"There's Frank." Walt pointed to the north end of the runway where a bright yellow biplane framed against the blue sky, pivoted quickly and dive bombed the airport. Puffy white smoke etched its journey and trailed its descent.

Walt and I sat outside the fixed base operation, awaiting the arrival of Walt's mentor, Frank Price, founder of the American Tiger Club and lovingly called "Papa Tiger." We were flying south to Crystal City, Texas in Tinkerbelle, alongside Frank, for an American Tiger Club airshow and aerobatic contest. Walt and I both were competing in the aerobatic contest. I had misgivings about my flying in the contest, but was excited to see my first airshow where Walt and Frank, among others, would perform.

We jumped to our feet. With a quick flip, Frank's biplane rolled upside down only a few feet above the asphalt runway. I gasped as the plane flicked from inverted to inverted, stopping at distinct points around the roll. A fire-engine-red sunburst paint scheme graced the top of its wings, making it easy to see when the plane was upside down. Still inverted, the plane climbed to traffic pattern altitude and turned to downwind leg. It chugged along in the pattern as if all planes came in for landing inverted with the pilot on his head, hanging against the seatbelt.

Was this what Walt expected me to do? Is this what airshows were all about?

A cloth-helmeted figure stuck out of the open cockpit with only air between it and the runway. I knew what it felt to hang by a seatbelt inverted, and shivered thinking of only air sandwiched between me and the ground.

The plane dropped lower, descending closer and closer to the runway. At the last minute the yellow biplane rolled upright, and in seconds, its wheels kissed the ground.

"Isn't Frank something?" Walt said. "I told you about him competing at the first world aerobatic contest in Czechoslovakia in 1960."

We watched the yellow bee of an airplane as it slowed down on the runway. Walt continued, the happy docent discussing a master artist. "Frank talked the military into taking his 1929 Great Lakes on one of their transports to Europe. It was a one-way trip, so he had to barnstorm and crop dust to raise enough money to get him and the Great Lakes home, this time on a ship."

Walt was well into his story, a story I had heard before, as Frank taxied toward the gas pumps. "Frank wanted America represented at the first world contest. So, this crop-duster pilot from Waco, Texas, with little money, and no official sanction from anybody just showed up. The Czechs were not happy with 'crazee American.'"

We moved towards the stunning ship now parked. "Isn't it gorgeous?" Walt said. All I could do was nod. "It's a Bucker Jungmeister, the Stradivarius of aerobatic aircraft, built by the Germans in the 1930's. Frank's modified it with a Lycoming engine."

Walt rushed forward to greet his hero. I paused, taking in the magnificent beast in front of me as if it were a work of art. The brilliant yellow with red trim paint sparkled in the sun. In addition to the sunburst pattern atop the wings, red scallops graced the leading edge on the bottom of the wings, stripes decorated the engine cowling and ran down the fuselage, and a red checkerboard design festooned the tail.

A single-place airplane, the Bucker's lone cockpit sat above the bottom wing with the upper wings sweeping back on either side. The landing gear thrust forward, and the plane looked about to leap from the ground. Like Tinkerbelle, the plane sat with its nose in the air. At least, they both were tail-wheel airplanes.

I felt so small, so inconsequential. I, a student pilot only able to fly three aerobatic maneuvers, was meeting the first American to compete in the World Aerobatic Competition.

A bear of a man emerged from the cockpit, shaking off the airplane like a too-tight coat. His substantial paws tugged at the stretched elastic around the bottom of his worn leather coat. Rawboned and big, this pilot in an oil-stained white flight suit turned gray seemed twice the mass of Walt, though they were of similar height. I stood apart, my usual ebullience dampened by the splendor of the biplane in front of me, the physical roughness of Papa Tiger Frank Price, and the awe-inspiring flight demonstration I had just seen. I wanted to slink away to some safe haven where nothing would be expected of me.

Walt motioned. "Come meet Frank."

Frank's hawk gaze swept across me as he extended his hand. I stepped forward and smiled. His hands, his presence, his voice enveloped me, and the gathering crowd. His voice boomed out, a Texas accent with a slight lisp. "So, you're the newest member of the Tiger Club. Like to fly upside down, do you?"

I murmured an assent.

"It's a good thing, if you want to keep up with this guy." He chucked my lover on the shoulder. "Walt here helps me teach my aerobatic students."

Frank turned the spotlight of his attention on me. "You excited about the contest?"

I stammered, "I'm just a beginner. I only can do a loop, a spin, and a barrel roll."

"It's where we all started," he said and turned to Walt, "You teach her the new Aresti System?"

Frank spoke of the shorthand system used for judging aerobatic contests that Count Jose Luis Aresti of Spain had developed and was coming into use in America. It featured an imaginary box in the sky in which the competition flight had to be centered with aerobatic maneuvers being flown with precision and scored according to difficulty.

"You bet," Walt said. "She's been working on keeping the lines straight between maneuvers. I told her it's the future of aerobatic competition."

"He's right," Frank said. "Before Aresti developed his system, contest judges just decided who was best, and they were the winner. Couldn't help but pick their favorites. Last year's competition in Crystal City was only the second time the system had been used on our side of the water."

Frank heard a noise behind him and turned to see the gas boy dragging the fuel hose and a ladder up to the front of his plane. Confused, the young man was trying to figure out where to begin.

"No, no boy," Frank said. "I'll do the filling, you just hand me the hose." He glanced at us and shrugged. I felt like the gas boy looked, overwhelmed by what I had seen, not sure what to do, and doubting my place in the picture.

Later that day Walt and I flew in Tinkerbelle, tucked close to Frank's right wing, a teenage bird in formation next to Mama or in this case, Papa. Frank, all helmet and goggles, looked our direction, a toothy smile the width of his face flashing in the sunlight. Walt made small corrections, a touch of aileron to move closer, a little pressure to slide out a bit, always staying in the same spot next to the Bucker's right wing.

No matter how much I enjoyed riding waves of air beside the Bucker, worrisome images of performing poorly in the upcoming contest kept coming to mind. Able to absorb only so much negativity, my thoughts fled to visions of flying an open-cockpit airplane like Frank's. I pictured me wearing helmet and goggles with wind whipping strands of my exposed hair. I imagined looking out on my snazzy paint scheme on the wings, one above and one below the cockpit. The helmet would crush my hair, but it would be okay, a mark of an open-cockpit pilot. Maybe I'd get a short Amelia hairdo. Right hand on the stick, I'd push left over to inverted, and... and...and there my daydream lurched to a stop. I'd be upside down with nothing between me and the ground, only my seatbelts holding me into the airplane. It wasn't a pleasant thought.

Along the way, other Tiger Club members joined our flight. Our gaggle of airplanes at last reached South Texas, and we all zoomed down the Crystal City runway behind the Bucker in a welcoming fly-by. Tinkerbelle bucked with speed as Walt kept us close to Frank's right wing.

The Bucker pulled up vertically and disappeared from my sight. I heard Walt's voice on the radio. "Two out."

In the next instant, I was pushed into my seat staring at an empty sky. We pivoted left, entering downwind leg for landing.

The weekend became a blur of interesting people and airplanes, pilot stories, parties, a trip to Mexico, and my looming participation in my first aerobatic contest. Walt borrowed Leroy Braxdale's Stearman to take me for my first open-cockpit biplane ride. After that flight, I vowed to one day have my own open-cockpit biplane.

On the first day of the contest, small clumps of pilots from across the United States gathered under wings of airplanes, in the lobby of the flight school, outside on hard benches and lawn chairs. They talked about the new Aresti system of judging, ways to modify oil tanks so they worked upside down without damaging engines, and shared stories of bad weather, high altitude, and aircraft failure. Though competitors, these fellow Tiger Club members were brothers and I, the little sister who one day hoped to grow up. Immersed in the mosaic of shared memory, I still burned with anxiety about my upcoming contest flight. I longed to be accepted as part of such an amazing assembly, but felt like a gatecrasher at a family reunion.

Walt conversed with his friends, sharing ideas about airplanes and aerobatic maneuvers. By his side, half-listening, I smiled at the red-checkered shirt he wore, a promotion from Ralston Purina. He might be enthused, but my nerves were on edge. A volcano about to explode, I rushed away to phone Austin to check on my daughter. This was the first time I had been gone from her for any length of time. It felt strange and I missed her.

The conversation with the babysitter did not go well. Her silence filled the spaces with unspoken thoughts, and, although my daughter was fine, I sensed the babysitter was unhappy with me. I interpreted her quiet spaces as judgments about my performance as a parent. Part of me agreed with her imagined criticism. What was I doing miles away, competing in a contest for which I wasn't qualified, with a babysitter at home judging me? Good mothers stayed home, as had my mother and my grandmother before her.

Rather than return to the pilots and their stories, I sauntered over to Tinkerbelle to prepare for my upcoming competition flight. In the midst of my preparations, a man of medium height, baseball cap atop his head and camera around his neck, trotted across the ramp.

As he approached, he held out his hand. "I'm Johnny Myers. Walt said I'd find you with your plane." I shook his hand and introduced myself.

"Sandi, I fly aerobatics, but I also write for the Austin newspaper and I want to get your picture and some information for a story."

"About me?" I pointed across the ramp at a group gathered around Frank. "There's your story."

He smiled. "They're just old farts. Now you, you're the story." He pulled out a pad and pen from his rear pocket. "I understand they call you Tinkerbelle."

"No, no, the airplane is Tinkerbelle." I hesitated, not knowing what to say next. What did he want from me?

"Just relax, I won't bite. Tell me how you got involved in flying acro. What you plan on doing with your flying?"

"Someday, I'm going to be an airshow pilot." I smiled, thinking of my ride in the Stearman the day before. "And I'll own an open-cockpit airplane."

He jotted something in his pad, asked another question, made more notes, and then asked more questions. I relaxed, enjoying sharing my thoughts and opinions. What great fun, talking while a reporter listened. Later, I willingly climbed into Tinkerbelle where he took my picture; a picture he said would be in the Austin newspaper the next week.

After climbing out of Tinkerbelle, his questions grew further apart and he had his head down as if in thought. He looked up and said, "I hope you won't mind me saying something?"

I gave him an encouraging glance, though part of me tensed at the tone of his voice.

His head dropped again as if searching for something on the ground. "I know Walt's wife. She's a nice person." He looked up at me. "The problem in the marriage is Walt, not her."

The air seemed sucked out of the environment, and I forced myself to breathe. "What do you mean?"

"I mean, you're a good kid. You deserve better." He looked into my face, and then quickly added, "Walt's a great pilot. A nice guy, but he doesn't do well in the husband department."

I said nothing.

"I just don't want to see you hurt."

At last, I found my voice. "I don't know what to say." I cleared my throat. "I've got to get ready to fly. I think I'm up pretty soon."

I heard the jingle of coins in his pocket. "Sure. Hope I didn't upset you." He started away, and then turned back. "Have a good flight."

My legs felt as if they were crumbling underneath me. I sat on the ramp under Tinkerbelle's wing, leaning against the blue Fiberglass wheel pant that streamlined the tire.

The reporter was wrong. Walt had shared all the problems with his marriage and sure, some of them were his, but really, she was the problem. If Walt and I married, it would be different. After all, we had so much in common, we both loved flying and we wanted the same things. Maybe the reporter was envious.

One of the competition officials strode up and yelled, "Start your engine." He pointed out to the runway. "You fly after the Clipped Cub taxiing out."

I got to my feet, and put the reporter's disturbing comments away, as if locked in an imaginary chest. I was an expert at concealing bothersome things and promised myself to consider his words later.

Walt came running across the ramp as I taxied out of the parking space. He opened the door, and I felt the cool rush of prop blast. A light kiss, and he said, "Good luck, Tiger. You'll do great. Have fun."

Yeah, right. The United States Tiger Club was watching, and he wanted me to have fun.

In spite of misgivings, something did settle inside of me as I climbed to altitude. I flew the upcoming maneuvers in my mind, reminding myself of the airspeeds, altitudes, and all the things I needed to remember. By the time I lined up on the edge of the imaginary box that made up the aerobatic flight area and wagged my wings, left then right, to let the judges know the start of my competition sequence, I was enjoying myself.

The first maneuver was a precision one-turn spin to the left. Emotions stuffed, I glanced at the altimeter and pulled back on the throttle, the nose rising to maintain altitude and the straight line necessary at the beginning of a maneuver. The engine and wind noise died down as Tinkerbelle slowed, then shuddered into a stall. I kicked full left rudder and the plane broke into a spin. Like a dancer avoiding dizziness, I used reference points on the ground to mark the turn.

The plane rotated and I called out loud, "Half." Slight right rudder, then at one quarter turn more full right rudder, and I popped the stick forward. The nose of the plane stopped slightly to one side of the imaginary flight line. Little early in recovering, I critiqued myself as I eased back to the center line of my imaginary box.

I shot vertically toward the ground as I gathered speed, and then pulled the elevator back, pushed into my seat at over 4 g's, four times my weight. I took a deep breath and told myself to relax as I flew a short straight line, then pulled up into a loop. Down the backside of the loop I accelerated, keeping enough speed to establish a straight line and enter the barrel roll.

If I waited too long I'd be out of the box, the aerobatic area, in which I had to fly the sequence. A quick glance at the altimeter, two thousand feet, and then over to the airspeed, which showed 130 miles per hour. Up and around, I formed a barrel in the sky, staying solid in the seat with positive G forces. I flew another straight line and then a wing wag to tell the judges I was finished.

I had done it. I'd finished my first aerobatic contest. I may have flown only three maneuvers, but I did them. I landed, thinking of ways to improve before the next competition. Walt, all smiles, gave me a thumbs-up and, like an Air Force crewman, guided me into the parking spot.

Suddenly, the reporter's words flooded my mind and my stomach lurched. I whispered to myself, "It'll be different. Our relationship will be different."

APRIL, 1967

6

NATIONAL AIRSHOWS

Luck Field, Ft. Worth, Texas

"Harold, I want you to meet my wife, Sandi." Walt said to Harold Krier, another of his heroes and star of Bill Sweet's National Airshows. "We just got married this weekend. Sandi's an aerobatic pilot." Only seven months earlier, I had interviewed for a job and taken my first airplane ride. Now, I had a Private Pilot's license and was Mrs. Walt Pierce. A tornado had swept across my life and things were still spinning.

A slow smile spread across the older man's suntanned face. His hair was streaked with gray and I guessed him to be an old man, somewhere in his forties. He said, "Why'd you ever take up with this guy?"

Although Harold joked, it was a good question, one that had plagued me since my very messy divorce two months earlier.

The day of my divorce, the courtroom had resembled a television set minus Perry Mason and the throngs of on-lookers. I expected a simple hearing. It did feel awkward to have two lawyers between me and my estranged husband, but I had no concern other than to get the divorce completed as soon as possible. I was glad my soon to be ex-husband was hidden behind his attorney.

He was hurt and angry with me. How could I blame him? Livid when the picture of me appeared in the Austin newspaper, he was barely civil when picking up our daughter for visits. I knew I was the one who had made a mess of our marriage. Devastation lay around me and I was consumed with guilt. Yet even though I felt remorse, I didn't want to return to my old life.

The divorce hearing proceeded with legalese discussions of the little property we owned and our myriad bills. Our lawyers talked, the judge responded, and the hearing moved along. I regretted that my law-student husband was an innocent bystander caught in a gale force of nature, but this was simply a necessary next step for me.

The atmosphere in the courtroom changed when my husband's attorney said, "My client, the father, seeks custody of the minor child."

My heart pounded as if a hired killer had lined me in his gun sight. I tried to comprehend the proceedings, but my mind simply couldn't wrap around the situation. The lawyer started naming reasons I was not a good mother. A good mother wouldn't leave her child to fly away. A good mother wouldn't live with a lover. A good mother would be more stable. A good mother would...would not...and it went on and on. I felt like a wanton woman from biblical times, each accusation a stone tearing at me.

Some things he said were true. I was young with many issues and personality defects to be resolved by life. In contrast, my husband was presented as noble and pure, a dedicated law student wronged by his immoral wife. Unable to deal with reality playing out before me, I emotionally checked out. I became an audience member rather than a participant in the tragic play of reality.

It made little difference that I was a kind person who had worked to help my husband through school. As a good Baptist girl, I didn't do drugs, drank little, and wasn't a smoker. Most importantly, I loved my daughter with my life and had taken care of her while separated. My husband was a full-time law student, unable to raise her. No one seemed upset that she would be torn not only from her mother, but also her father who intended to send her to live with his parents in Dallas.

Maybe they were right. Maybe I wasn't a good person. How could I pretend moving in with my lover was the moral thing to do? Perhaps I was unfit to be a mother. Caught in my moral dilemma, I lacked the will to fight.

I sat dazed while around me the attorneys argued back and forth. The judge spoke, and I had trouble following his words. "…custody of the minor child, a daughter, is awarded to the father."

Surely, they didn't mean to take my child away? The courtroom swirled with activity, but I didn't move. I was vaguely aware when the judge left the courtroom. My attorney said something, but again, I couldn't focus. Instead, a pain welled within me and loud moaning wails of a wounded animal bounced off the walls of the near-empty courtroom. This time, my emotions couldn't be locked away in some dark chest. I hurt in ways I never imagined.

Shaken, I quit my job, packed my belongings, and followed my daughter to Dallas where she lived with her other grandparents. I moved in with my parents and looked for work. I still loved flying, but could think of nothing but my missing child. My self-esteem, that had flourished in an airplane, now lay around me in jagged pieces of guilt and sorrow.

At first, my ex-husband remembered my hysteria in the courtroom and wouldn't let me see my daughter alone. That changed as her grandparents became confident I was stable. I worked in the daytime, paced the floor at night, and fought a pervading sense of failure. On weekends, I rushed to get my daughter. Although I lived in the same community where I had been raised, I avoided people and had little desire to return to church with my parents. Fortunately, my daughter seemed not to suffer, happy to go with me, but also happy to be with her father's parents whom she loved also.

Walt visited me on weekends, bringing an airplane for me to fly when he could. When at last, his divorce was final, we married.

"Hey, Sandi." Walt shook my arm, pulling me from the remembered nightmare of my divorce. "I just told Harold that one of these days you're going to be my wingrider. You know Harold has a Great Lakes biplane and carries a wingrider?"

A weak smile crossed my face as I tried to shake myself free from memories. Harold shook his head and said, "Kinda windy up there on top of that wing, isn't it?" He looked at Walt. "It'll be great to have you two on the circuit."

"We have a booking in Odessa this summer. It'll be Sandi's first airshow."

"Riding the wing?" Harold asked.

"No." I struggled to come present. "I'm flying a solo act in a borrowed cub and Walt will fly the TCraft. No Stearman yet, so no wingriding." Harold knew that fact, but was being nice to budding airshow pilots.

He asked Walt, "Will Roy Schleymeyer fly acro in one of his sailplanes?"

"Yep, couldn't have an airshow in Odessa without Roy." said Walt, "Jimmy Franklin's supposed to fly his Waco. He's been doing aerobatics quite a while, but I think it's his first show also."

Harold nodded, "Good kid. I heard he just bought Pappy Spinks' UPF-7. You two want to take a look at my new bird?"

We ducked under the rope line separating pilots from fans, and followed Harold to his airplane. The Chipmunk's paint glistened in the April sunshine, its low-wings jutting out longer than I expected. With a combination of adoration and attention, we trailed Harold around his airplane as he explained the work he had done. He and Walt talked inverted fuel systems, four aileron conversions, and the upcoming airshow season. The more Harold talked, the more amazed I became as he freely shared his knowledge and time with two wannabes.

Mind wandering, my thoughts returned to my time in Dallas. After the divorce, Walt had been supportive when I scheduled an appointment with a renowned child-custody lawyer. He knew I loved my daughter and wanted her to live with us. "What do I need to do," I asked the expensive attorney, "to get my baby back?"

"Find a job," he said. "Stay in one place, give up flying, and maybe, just maybe, you can regain custody of your child." He leaned back in his chair. "It doesn't help that your ex-husband is a law student and will soon be an attorney." He went on to warn me to expect child custody battles until my daughter was old enough to choose where she wanted to live.

Walt had comforted me in my angst, but I knew he didn't really identify with my inner torment. His world revolved around airplanes and flying. He loved me and wanted me happy, and if that included my child, he supported my efforts.

I shrugged off troubling memories. After all, this was a new day, my wedding weekend. I watched my new husband, the man I loved and for whom I had changed so much, and his hero discuss the intricacies of day-to-day airshow flying while in the background Bill Sweet's Midwestern voice echoed across Luck Field. In front of us, World War II aircraft staged a mock battle over the runway. Late April in north Texas was already hot and my bare arms resembled boiling lobsters. Why hadn't I worn a long-sleeved shirt to protect them? I reminded myself that actions have consequences and some of them are not so pleasant. It was a hard lesson I was beginning to learn, as I felt much older than my twenty-two years.

I was excited about my new life flying with Walt, but sadness had etched a new facet into my personality. The repercussions of my divorce created ghosts that haunted me day and night. I missed my child and I felt myself sinking into quicksand made up of regrets and self-condemnation.

I wasn't yet comfortable in my new world of airshows and airplanes, yet no longer the wife of a law student. Occupying limbo, somewhere between the old and new life, I wandered my world as if someone had drained my life-blood as I grieved the loss of my daughter. I found respite only when distracted by the minutiae of piloting an airplane. At night, after Walt drifted to sleep, my tears came and I would slip from bed to face my demons. Exhaustion eventually would set in, and at last, sleep.

I blamed myself for not having the daughter I loved, but took it out on Walt. A layer of crankiness covered my normally sunny disposition and at times I doubted if he would stick with me. Even as I pushed him away, I clung to him and our dream with solid determination. I vowed to create the dream, no matter the difficulties. If nothing else, I needed to provide some meaning for my suffering. Stoically, Walt continued to encourage my flying and was kind to me in spite of my increasing bad temper.

It was the perfect wedding present for us to spend time with Harold on the performers' side of the rope. Just a few steps away normal people, not aerobatic pilots like us, rushed to buy cold drinks and hot dogs at concession stands. Mothers slathered suntan lotion on their children's exposed arms and legs while Bill Sweet's excited voice over the public address system caused them to look skyward in wonder

"Thanks, Harold." Walt said. "For all the info. Tell Charlie hello for us."

We smiled and bid Harold goodbye before turning back into mere spectators.

"Isn't Harold a great guy?" Walt said. "I'm sorry you didn't meet Charlie Hilliard. He's my age and a super pilot. He started flying aerobatics in a J-3Cub, like you're going to fly in Odessa. Of course, his had clipped wings and a bigger engine."

Walt kissed me lightly. "I love you. I'm so glad you're my wife."

"I love you, too." I said, suspecting my love for this man was more than he would ever realize. Certainly, I had given up more to be with him than intended.

Enough troubling thoughts. It was my wedding weekend and I intended to enjoy it. My mood lifted as we wandered the airshow grounds and talked airplanes. Harold and Charlie flew amazing airshow sequences nearly brushing the ground. Patriotic music, parachutists, and display aircraft filled my senses, living little room for my unhappiness.

"Ladies and gentlemen," Bill Sweet's voice blasted from a nearby speaker. "Turn your eyes to the end of the runway. Watch as Margaret Ritchie and her clipped-wing Taylorcraft defy death. She's taking off now, watch, WATCH the bright orange and black Tcraft accelerate. Oooooohhhh myyyyy! Look at the 'Flying Grandmother' from California go."

A pumpkin-colored airplane stayed low to the ground, gaining speed. The smoke popped on just before the nose came up and the plane slow rolled to an inverted climb. Mesmerized, I watched a woman airshow pilot perform for the first time. I had caught sight of the older, attractive woman signing autographs earlier in the day, in a jumpsuit that matched her airplane. It was hard to imagine her baking cookies for grandkids.

Her modified BC12-D Taylorcraft looked a lot like Tinkerbelle that I had flown in Austin, similar to the L-2 Tcraft Walt had modified for his airshow performances.

"She's climbing up…up…up into the sky," Bill's voice blared. "Here she comes…zooming toward us. Don't cover your eyes, kids. Everybody wave at grandma as she goes by."

This pilot acted like no grandmother I ever knew. Mesmerized, I watched her fly a sequence of aerobatic maneuvers staying positioned in front of the crowd. I wanted to be such an airshow pilot and to tell my grandchildren stories of my adventures. I wanted a career and a family.

What if I couldn't have both?

SEPTEMBER, 1968

7

SHAWN DELL

McCollum Airport, Marietta, Georgia

I lowered my pregnant body onto a couch facing the windows to watch the airplanes in the traffic pattern. A local instructor sat with his student at a table near the coffee pot, discussing an upcoming cross-country flight. I hoped to have students myself, after I had the baby and took my flight instructor's check-ride scheduled next month. Sighing, I settled into the soft fabric, a little concerned I might not be able to get back up. I laid my head against the couch for a quick rest. Walt was flying with a student in the school's Stearman biplane. I was so happy to be pregnant, in spite of my body that resembled a whale.

Pilots have a fluid life, flying from place to place as a part of their work. This was our third move in a little over a year as Walt chased flying jobs that paid better and brought our airshow dream nearer. He flew while I worked in a variety of jobs as secretary, receptionist, Hertz counter girl, and brief stints as a temporary worker, all the while flying as many hours as possible. I thought of my friends back home after college. Most had stayed in one house, one town, and one job. No, I didn't want their lives. Maybe my daughter was better off without me? This pregnant pilot felt worn out.

We had moved to the southeast when Walt took a job flying the Lockheed PV-2, a World War II bomber, in low-level fire ant eradication work on government contract. His experience with the airline combined with crop dusting time made him perfect for the job. He flew three contracts a year and I had gone with him, always building my flight time. In Savannah, Georgia, I had flown with newly returned Vietnam Vet, Steve Oliver, and checked out in his Cessna-140. It was a fun life. In between contracts, Walt ran an aerobatic school just north of Atlanta. We had saved enough money to buy a Stearman to convert for airshow flying. Still looking like a cropduster, it needed a bigger engine and was a long way from airshow ready. I now flew the Tcraft, but also had dreams for converting to clipped wings and a bigger engine. We needed money to make our dream of airshow flying come true.

Walt flew with aerobatic students while I performed secretarial duties and towed banners across the Atlanta sky. I had gotten my commercial pilot's license and made a little bit of money with towing banners, that is, until eight months pregnant. My big stomach now got in the way of the controls. If I moved the seat back to make room for my belly, then I couldn't reach the rudder pedals. If I reached the rudder pedals, then the stick ran into my stomach. I took it as nature's way of telling me to quit flying for a while.

I felt the baby kick and my whole being smiled. There, there, my little love child, you'll be out soon enough. Your mommy loves you. Would we have a girl or a boy? It mattered little; I just wanted my baby.

It seemed impossible that only two years earlier, I had my first flight at Tim's Airpark in Austin. Here I was, a commercial pilot and earning at least a part of my income flying.

The aviation life had cost me dearly. Thoughts of my daughter in Texas, living with her dad and his new wife, eclipsed my contentment. Like a haunting melody that plays itself over and over through the mind, my thoughts returned to my lost child. We had moved so often that I saw my daughter less and less. Currently living near Atlanta with little money to get to Texas, I knew my lifestyle would never be as stable as my ex-husband's would. Regaining custody did not seem hopeful.

I looked out the window of the flight school, searching the sky for the return of Walt and his student. The sky buzzed with Cessna trainers, but no sight of the aerobatic school's biplane.

Attempting to relax the muscles in my back, I closed my eyes and breathed deeply. My mom's words popped into my mind, "Sandra, your 'real' mother loved you so much that she gave you up for adoption." Our family myth had me, a surprise war baby, as a gift bestowed by a too-young unmarried mother on my family. I felt my adopted family's love for me, but I always questioned what "giving someone up" really meant. My child's mind had not understood letting go. That child believed you held on tight to what you loved and didn't let anyone take it away. Did my lost daughter miss me? On this early September day in Georgia, I couldn't decide what was right. Should I have quit flying and done everything to regain custody of her?

I opened my eyes to distance the thoughts, idly watching the airplanes practice landings in the pattern. Was it a greater love to let a beloved child go to a more stable life or fight in court with a deeply wounded ex-husband? The debater in me looked at both sides of the issue, but had no clue to the answer. I only knew that at night I still was restless and unable to sleep, captured by continued grief. At least, I had quit letting my anger and unhappiness spew over Walt. It wasn't fair but my rage had seeped into everything we did for a while. I guessed I wanted him to feel as miserable as I was.

Turning my attention back to the traffic pattern, I saw the large blue and yellow biplane above the lush green Georgia countryside, following a small Cessna in the traffic pattern. I rolled out of the chair, hoisted myself up, and waddled over to the window for a better view. I considered going outside to join a group of pilots who sat watching the planes, but the sticky Georgia heat kept me close to the air conditioning.

I envisioned Walt in the front cockpit, talking on the microphone to the student who sat behind him. I imagined him sharing airspeeds and power settings, mentioning reference points on the ground, and giving instructions on landing the skittish biplane.

I envied the student. There had been no way to lug my pregnant body up onto the lower wing of the biplane and lift myself into the open cockpit, even if the control stick had cleared my belly, which I doubted. I sighed, ready to have this very welcome baby.

The Stearman made a ninety degree turn to the left and flew the base leg of the pattern. I settled into a straight-back chair near the window. Relieved to get off my feet, I watched the biplane make another turn and line up on final approach to landing.

The big bird soared over the fence at the end of the airport, crossed the lights at the beginning of the runway, and plopped down on the asphalt strip. It bounced back up, finally settling onto the runway. The Stearman's nose darted right and then returned to the center. The biplane rolled straight ahead for a few seconds before it headed right, a horse taking control from the rider. The plane bolted to one side of the runway. Sparks flew as it tore down a landing light and headed to the grassy area with a ditch just beyond.

I jumped up, moving out the door as fast as I could. The Stearman went nose first into the ditch. I ran as the plane pivoted up on its nose, engine and propeller chewing the ground with its tail pointing skyward. A litany began in my head. Walt, please be okay, please be okay, please be okay.

My insides felt like fire and my legs could no longer carry my pregnant body forward. I stood in the middle of the ramp holding my belly, watching to see if the upside-down ice cream cone stuck in the ground would catch fire. The Stearman's fuel tank was in the center section of the wing, a little above and forward of the front cockpit where Walt sat. Had it ruptured on impact? Would the fuel spill and look for a spark with which to mate? Don't burn, I willed, please don't burn.

In eternity-moments, I watched to see if the wrecked Stearman would burst into flames. At last, a van driven by the gas boy pulled up. "Get in," he said.

I limped to the open door and pulled myself into the passenger seat. We sped down the taxiway. Was Walt okay? I rubbed my stomach, hoping to stop the burning feeling. Would his plane catch on fire?

At last, I saw Walt with his student standing to one side of the injured bird. The van squealed to a stop across from the wreck. I wanted to run to my husband, but my strained muscles refused to budge. Shape up, kid, no tears now. My Superman walked toward me, helmet and goggles in his hand.

Walt bent through the van's open window and kissed me. I mumbled, "You okay?"

Nodding, he motioned to what looked like a mammoth airplane monument with its tail facing heavenward. "The right brake locked on landing. Off we went." He smiled his crooked grin. "I guess it'll be a while before you get to fly that Stearman."

It was a surprise I didn't go into labor that night, but one week later our daughter, Shawn Dell, burst into the world. We named her for the chandelle, an advanced flying maneuver, and sent out yellow student pilot certificates announcing her birth. Two days old, we lugged her to the airport in a white wicker baby basket. That day and most days after, we took turns caring for our darling baby while the other one flew.

Shawn snuggled into our lives, bringing light to dark caverns inside of me. One child does not replace the loss of another, but at least now I had a reason to be up at night. I rocked her, sang nursery songs, and studied for my looming flight instructor check-ride. I was happy at last, living a new life with my own family. I knew that my other child had a new mother and a loving family to care for her. And I had another daughter.

By November I had earned my flight instructor rating, a job teaching students to fly, and was open to new adventures.

8

PARACHUTING ADVENTURES

Cline Field, north of Marietta, Georgia

"Sandi, you're first." Ed Lowder, our parachute instructor, called out. It was Thanksgiving Day. Walt and I stood atop a platform four feet above a grassy area. Shawn slept peacefully in her portable playpen in a shaded area, oblivious to the activity around her.

Ed said, "Remember what you practiced on the ground. Knees and feet together, knees slightly bent, land on the balls of your feet, roll to the side of your calf, thigh, butt, and last, your upper back."

I glanced over at Walt. It was time to make a practice landing off the platform and after that, our first parachute jump. Diving into the sky did not excite me. I liked to fly airplanes, not leave them. What if I hurt myself? Is this what condemned prisoners felt on the gallows? A man came up to Ed and asked him a question, and I hoped for a reprieve.

Cline Field, a skydiving area north of Atlanta, nestled in a forest of pine and hardwood trees. These tall sentinels protected our little skydiver village. It was a crisp day in the north Georgia woods, a welcome relief from the thick wet air swirling around McCullom airport all week. Skydivers parachuted off this airstrip away from congested air traffic. Next to the grass runway, a Cessna 180 sat nose high, tail wheel on the ground, ready to carry jumpers, including Walt and me, into the sky.

To my right, colorful parachutes scattered, laid on strips of canvas to protect them from the ground. Several men and two women knelt beside the chutes, folding, patting, inserting lines into heavy-duty rubber bands, packing the large canopies into their containers with great care. Children played amidst the colorful chutes, their backs to tables laden with food, nearby coolers filled with beer and cold drinks. Spouses and girlfriends lolled in chairs pulled into the November sun. I looked over to Shawn's playpen. The pink-blanketed bundle had moved, but seemed still asleep. She was an easy baby, comfortable when we toted her to the airport, or to restaurants, and now, even at this skydiving field.

One more time, I questioned how I had let Walt talk me into this. I loved the guy, but this was ridiculous. He had gotten on a "We need to skydive" kick, and one day, had said, "If we ever have a wing fail during aerobatics, we need to know how to use our parachutes."

I didn't want to think about wings falling off airplanes, much less having to jump out to save my life. Although logical, his argument was not one I wanted to hear. I had this nagging suspicion he wanted me to parachute in our future airshows. I was not interested in skydiving at airshows, but flying, flying like grandmother Margaret Ritchie. That's what I wanted to do. Still, maybe making one or two jumps with him wasn't a bad idea. Based on the result of my first marriage, I knew it was a good idea to continue to do things with your husband. Maybe the family that parachutes together, stays together? Unless one has a chute that doesn't open. Why did I think of that?

Below the platform, Ed continued talking with the man. Our instructor was average in height and build, running his parachute ground school with the authority of a military man. Had he been an Army parachutist? I didn't know. He was in his thirties and older than us, but still full of enthusiasm.

Ed appeared so normal, not like the crazy jumpers I had heard so much about in pilot stories. This man didn't look like he would pull the keys from an aircraft as he exited, leaving the pilot to a dead stick landing with no way to restart the engine. I shivered, identifying with the pilot not the skydiver, and imagined having to make a landing on a short grass field with no power in case I came in too low.

Ed didn't seem like jumpers I had heard about landing at civic club breakfasts and then dropping their jumpsuits, streaking naked through shocked crowds. I had sat outside airport flight schools and heard these tales, stories sworn to be true by pilot friends. Nope, Ed didn't strike me as that kind of parachutist.

It amazed me that Walt and I, proud aerobatic pilots, were getting ready to jump out of a perfectly good airplane. Up to this point, we had always been what parachutists called "whuffos," nonskydivers who asked, "Whuffo you jump out of them airplanes?" In spite of my misgivings and fear, this Thanksgiving we were going to make our first parachute jump. I guessed we were creating a new family tradition. Part of me wanted to create the tradition of watching Walt jump, while on the ground, I watched Shawn sleep.

"Sandi."

I looked down.

Ed said, "Jump."

'She who hesitates is lost' ran through my mind. I stepped forward and leapt from the platform. Knees and feet together, then boom, I was on the ground and rolling. I got to my feet, feeling pretty proud of myself. I brushed grass from my baggy jumpsuit designed for a six-foot man. Feeling like an aristocratic lion licking its coat, I was grateful to have jumped off the lousy platform without breaking anything. I turned to watch my gangly husband jump to the ground, arms flailing, then brought close to his sides. Maybe my short compact body was an advantage.

"You two are ready," Ed said. "It's time to jump."

I checked on Shawn who still slept in her playpen, pink cap hiding her wispy blonde hair. A content baby, she had adjusted to days at the airport and evenings in her carrying basket at the local pizza parlor with us telling pilot stories and drinking beer. She was proving to be a good skydiving baby. How could she be so peaceful while her Mama was about to leap from a skyscraper without a safety net?

Ed helped me into my parachute, fastening the harness around my chest and legs. He smiled as he clipped the reserve parachute to the harness on my chest. I looked over at Walt who stood to the side doing nothing. "Hey," I called. "Where's your chute?"

"I'm going to fly the airplane," he said.

"What?" I said. What did he mean, he'd fly the airplane?

"I'm going to fly the plane," he repeated as if talking to a stupid student.

I was furious. Here I was, my five foot two and one-half inch body nearly unable to walk with parachute gear hanging all over me, all because he wanted us to do this together. How could he wimp out on this shared experience?

"You're a rat," I said, and thought far worse things. "Let me get out of this gear. I'll fly the damn plane. You can jump. Right now I feel like pushing you out—without a chute."

He just grinned and remained silent.

I wanted to hit him and run over to my sleeping baby. I wished she would cry, so I could get out of jumping. My anger and fear coalesced into a strong resolve to show up my husband. I might be afraid, but I wouldn't let anyone know it. Nothing, I decided, would stop me from making this parachute jump.

Walt's cute grin didn't win me over this time. I became a little dictator. "Go check on Shawn once more before we take off. Betty, the brunette sitting near the playpen, said she'd watch her until we get back."

Annoyed, I turned back to Ed. "I guess it's you and me."

Ed just grinned. I waited for him to say something sarcastic about Walt. Instead, he went over the instructions and checked my gear to make certain all was secure. We walked to the jump plane which, at first glance, looked like a normal airplane. On closer inspection, I saw a gaping hole where the door had been removed. Under it, a large metal step extended. The plane was stripped down inside with only the pilot's seat remaining. Walt climbed into that seat and started down the checklist.

Two other jumpers lumbered into the plane, and behind them, I struggled to lift myself into the doorway. Ed finally gave me a boost and I made it into the plane with him following. He hooked my static line to a "D" ring on the floor of the plane and pulled to make certain it was secure. My stomach felt like a seasick sailor in a raging sea. Why had I agreed to do this, and now, that…that…chicken-of-a-husband was flying the airplane.

Ed reminded me that when I jumped, the static line would reach its end and the small mesh pilot chute would release, pulling the pen and then the parachute from the container. Omigod, what if it didn't work?

I was angry at Walt, but it still felt good to have him flying. At least, I wasn't concerned about an unknown pilot and airplane problems. This was not my normal pilot world. I sat backwards on the floor of the stripped-down Cessna 180 with no right door. Like a kangaroo, we bounced along the grass, metal creaking and wind rushing in where a door belonged. My hair itched under the skydiving helmet and I moved it with my gloved hand. Immersed in engine and wind noise, we climbed to 3,500 feet above the ground with my stomach flip-flopping as I mentally rehearsed the upcoming jump. I worried over the details, reminding myself of the procedures if my main chute didn't open.

Ed's voice reverberated in my mind. "If your main chute doesn't open, cut it away as quickly as possible and then pull the ripcord on the reserve parachute on your chest." He smiled and said, "Piece of cake for an upside-down pilot like you."

In the air, Walt flew us over the drop zone while Ed, half-hanging from the door frame, peered to the ground below. Directly over the landing area, he dropped a piece of yellow crepe paper and watched as the streamer drifted to the ground. He then signaled course corrections to Walt to compensate for the wind drift.

As we circled for my jump, Ed said, "Stand-by. You ready?"

What was I going to say? Nope, I think I'll wait until tomorrow? I nodded and gave him a confident thumbs-up.

"Go." He motioned for me to get on the step. The cumbersome parachute gear was heavy and although I tried, I barely moved. Incoming air pushed me back into the airplane. Ed picked me up and I swung outside the plane, putting both clunky boots on the step beneath the fuselage. I leaned over the strut where my gloved hands held tightly. I worked my way out the strut until my hands were between the taped marks and my feet trailed behind me. The wind blew across me, and even though I still held onto the strut, I felt like a bird surfing sky. Did birds have stomach aches?

Arching my body as I had been instructed, I looked to Ed. He motioned, and I let go. Before I could remember to count, I felt a tug and looked up to see a circular orange and white parachute. Overhead, my canopy was fully open, dropping me gently towards earth. No twisted canopy, no frantic trying to pull a reserve chute, no death fall to earth.

Instead, I peacefully drifted through a blue, blue sky.

Free of my burdens and fear of an unopened parachute, each breath of brisk air seemed deeper, more satisfying than on the ground. The crystal green hills rolled into a brilliant sky, vivid and perfect in my heightened perception. I hung protected under orange and white nylon, floating, rocking gently, more an observer than participant. I fumbled the glove off my right hand and tucked it behind the reserve chute strapped across my chest. I reached out to touch the sky around me. It felt like air, the same as on the ground or in an open-cockpit plane, simply air. The change was in me, not the sky. Unencumbered, without an airplane, I rode currents of air like a bird drifting over land. Alone, yet connected to everything. I was at peace.

Above and over my shoulder, I saw a colorful rectangular parachute with a figure hanging underneath. Although we had no communication, it was nice to be sharing this experience with Ed nearby.

The drop zone was ahead, an open field amidst a forest of evergreens and leafless trees. My pleasure in the moment fled as I realized I was coming in low, too close to the trees now beneath me. My pilot senses screamed that I wasn't going to make the drop zone. Maybe the parachute floated further than an airplane?

The tree tops rushed closer and closer. I remembered Ed's instructions "turn into the wind before touch down" and reached up for my toggles, the handles that pull on the risers and turn the canopy. Similar to an airplane, I turned into the wind for landing. A ballerina in combat boots, my toes skimmed the green and brown tree tops while a symphony of people called to me in the distance.

"C'mon baby," I whispered. "Get mama home." At the last moment, I remembered to pull my legs together, as Ed had instructed, and slammed into a green pine jungle.

I fell through the branches, expecting to crash into the ground. Abruptly, I jerked to a stop and bobbed fifteen feet over the shadowy loam below. My canopy was caught on the limbs of arrow-straight Ponderosa pines and I hung suspended, a baby swaying gently in its swing. Then swoosh, I settled to the ground, covered in orange and white nylon. I thrashed about, struggling to find my way out of my colorful canopy tent.

Bruised pine and dank forest smells permeated the air. Off with my remaining glove, my helmet, and then I gazed upward. I looked beyond the torn branches to a now unoccupied sky, my sky. It seemed to tease me. Relief flooded over me as I paused alone, breathing in my personal forest. In only minutes, my skydiving buddies found me.

Parachuting was great fun. It wasn't like flying an airplane upside down. For me, nothing compared to that, but still it was fun. I was ready to jump again. No football games for me on this gorgeous Thanksgiving afternoon.

I was still furious with Walt for not sharing the parachute experience that he had talked me into. I laughed when I heard about his surprised look when Ed pulled the keys from the Cessna's ignition, and then jumped out. Walt had landed on the tiny skydiving field amidst a Georgia forest with no power.

1969

9

CROPDUSTING IN BOMBERS

Charleston, South Carolina

It was 5 a.m., time to begin the preflight on the silver World War II bomber towering thirteen feet above me. I stifled a yawn and reminded myself to pay close attention. These old airplanes always seemed to have something falling off or breaking. I was officially Walt's copilot on the PV-2 on a fire ant eradication contract. What a coup to be the first woman hired for the job, but for me, the mission was making money. At least that's what I told myself. Truth was, it was exciting to crop dust in a bomber, to fly a man's airplane with men.

These old Lockheeds were first built for submarine patrol in the United States and then used by the Royal Air Force as bombers. The plane in front of me had wings and a tail wheel like Tinkerbelle, but the similarity ended there. It stood two and one-half times taller than me with a seventy-five-foot wingspan and weighed over 22,000 pounds empty. Its big fat belly slung low to the ground and the tail with a mammoth horizontal stabilizer sported two vertical fins and rudders. Before this job, I was teaching students to fly in Atlanta, sitting behind a four-cylinder, hundred horsepower engine. The PV-2 flew with two engines with 18 cylinders each and between them, developed over 4,000 horsepower on take-off.

I smelled the salty ocean air and hoped the mist around me would lift soon. The coastal fog covered our airplane world where ten planes parked in two rows facing each other across a secluded ramp area. We flew from the Charleston Municipal Airport and Air Force Base, a combined civilian and military facility, but traffic and buildings were obscured this early morning.

I untied one edge of the canvas cover that protected the windshield and overhead hatch. A whistling melody drifted my way from a fellow copilot who also performed the morning rituals. Had we been a scene in a movie, spectators would have guessed it was a bomber base in World War II with the captains off at the morning briefing, copilots making certain planes were safe, and everyone concerned about making it back home.

Home? What was home? We had moved so often and always rented. I smiled, thinking of my darling Shawn, back in Atlanta. She was my home. The day I left, she had crawled down the hall towards me with her fine blonde curls held by a bow the color of her corduroy jumpsuit. I was running late and in a hurry. I picked her up and planted a kiss on her still-squirming body. I said, "Mommy loves you," and pointed her back up the hallway. Like a wind-up toy, she took off for the rear bedroom while I gathered her things to take to the baby-sitter.

What was I doing on this damp ramp in Charleston with my baby away from me? OKAY, OKAY, I reassured myself. You're away from her, but she has a wonderful babysitter. Shawn was staying with an older woman and friend whose husband was one of the student pilots I instructed. She had been happy to keep Shawn until I found a sitter in Charleston. So far, no luck. My work hours were brutal and not many people wanted to keep a child from early in the morning until after dark at night. Still, I hadn't given up.

When I had left for this job, I tried to explain to Shawn I would be gone for a while. After kissing her rosy cheek, I set her on the ground where she made tiny sounds of happiness as she played with her toys, unaware I was leaving. Perhaps, she wouldn't miss me, at least not much. With that thought, I returned to my work not wanting to think of the implications of my daughter being happy without me.

I unknotted the last rope holding the cockpit cover and slid the stiff canvas to the ground. Salty water dripped from its edges as I folded and then stowed it inside the rear compartment door. On an airliner, this door would lead to the passenger seating area. In these converted PV-2s, the compartment was filled with a large aluminum storage tank that blocked the inside entrance to the cockpit. Pilots entered and exited the airplane through a hatch over the captain's seat atop the airplane.

In place of bombs, our planes carried Mirex, ground up corn cobs treated with a chemical, to kill our "foes." The enemy was a tiny fire ant infesting the southern part of the United States. Only the environmentalists were returning fire, although rumor had it that a farmer in South Georgia had opened fire with his shotgun at one of our competitor's planes dropping ant bait over his farm.

On this soggy morning, I did my usual jumping and stretching to reach handholds and steps, designed for tall men, to get up on the wing and into the cockpit. I checked to make certain the switches were off before the necessary turning of the propellers. At that moment, I had no thoughts of killing fire ants or whether the environment would suffer; my only concern was the safety of the plane for the day's flight and making enough money to come one step closer to our airshow dream. We would fly airshows and have Shawn with us. She would wear cute outfits and be the youngest member of our airshow team. It was a good dream, a family dream, a way to have the things I so desired.

Working my way around the airplane, I became the detective, looking for unseen dangers that might remain hidden without a preflight inspection. Flying copilot had created my usual butterflies of fear and excitement at the challenge of learning something new, but I felt safe with Walt as my captain.

By the time I finished, the sky had turned from deep charcoal to light gray as if someone had turned a rheostat on a light switch. I walked toward the on-site USDA trailer where the captains were gathered around Lyle Rosendahl, chief pilot for our Ralco employer. Ralco was based out of Cheyenne, Wyoming and flew fire fighting work in the west and crop dusting that required large areas to be covered. They also kept a maintenance base in Bainbridge, Georgia where the crews worked on the bombers between government contracts. Killing the little fire ants had turned into a profitable aviation business.

Later that morning, we taxied away from our parking spaces into position in a line of bombers that made their way to the end of the runway for take off. I felt snug inside the cozy cockpit. A bulkhead was at our back, an instrument panel in front, and the throttle quadrant nestled between the two of us. No room to take a stretch break or any other kind of break. I looked at Walt, my captain, aware of my love and deep respect for his flying ability.

Enjoying my copilot duties, I talked to ground control and received clearance to taxi to the run-up area at the end of the runway. The woman copilot was of interest to the men in Charleston control tower. Once, when taxiing close by the tower, Walt pointed out someone looking through binoculars at us. Walt laughed and said, "He must be interested in World War II airplanes." I lived in a time when no women flew in the military, no women flew airliners, and no women were in the space program, yet here I was co-pilot on this ancient bomber.

I reached up to turn on the Decca navigation recording system which would verify our flight path for the USDA. These representatives of the government tracked most aspects of our operation. They watched the loading crew transfer ten thousand pounds of fire ant bait into our planes and checked to see how much we had on return. They recorded when the dispersal system went on and off and kept print-outs of our flight paths. Flying in this program was challenging and exacting.

In addition, everything about the PV-2 was hard work, from the on-going maintenance to simply making crop-dusting turns in the air. Unlike modern large airplanes with servotabs and systems designed for ease of operation, the PV-2 required physical strength and stamina. So far, with help from Walt on the crop-duster turns, I was able to do the work.

The control tower cleared us to go and Walt taxied the plane to the center line of the runway. We had enough fuel for a four hour flight plus the fire ant bait which made take off a critical time for our heavily loaded bird. Both engines roared. We lumbered down the concrete runway with 4,000 horsepower straining to gather enough speed to lift all 33,000 pounds of loaded airplane into the air.

On either side of the cockpit, the radial engines with their giant paddle propellers generated a din, more than our headsets and ear plugs could handle. Walt was in command and flying the airplane. My job was to monitor the airspeed indicator, giving him a hand signal when we reached take-off speed, since he couldn't hear my voice over the noise around us.

The airplane accelerated when, without warning, the left wing dropped. My glance darted to the windshield. The airplane's nose pulled hard left with our engines full blast and propellers chopping the air.

Walt yanked the throttles to idle and yelled, "Cut the mixtures."

I tugged the two mixture knobs back which cut off the fuel to the engines. With all switches off, the cockpit went silent. We looked out at a tilted world. Our giant bird's left wing lay near the ground and we sat at an angle. Stunned, an image of war-movie bombers bursting into flames filled my mind.

Walt motioned to the hatch over his head. We had one mission, to get out of the airplane before it caught fire. We snatched off our headsets and unhooked the seatbelts. Opening the cockpit hatch, Walt burst out of his seat. Heart-in-throat, I watched as he rested his hands on the sides of the hatch and pulled himself onto the top of the airplane. Up and out of my seat, close behind him. Too close. A size-eleven boot kicked me in the mouth, leaving a gash. Blood dripped onto my clothes.

Ignoring my injury, I erupted out of the hatch, half-ran down the wing and jumped to the ground. I trailed Walt to the front of the tilted wing, aware the plane could burst into flames at any moment.

No gas fumes hung in the air, so I knew the gas tank must not be ruptured. The left wing of the big silver bird rested close to the ground. Gone were the wheel and tire and only a nub remained holding the left side of the airplane off the runway. Debris littered the ground.

A huge Air Force C-5A, much like a giant skyscraper with wings, roared low over our heads. Walt shouted over the noise, "Couldn't land, because of us." It was then that Walt noticed my bleeding lip, but became distracted when cars, some with flashing lights, appeared from all directions. They surrounded us as if we were on America's Most Wanted list. I laughed, so happy to be alive and next to my husband, with only a bloody lip.

The chief pilot, mechanics, on-site men from the USDA, and various Air Force personnel all had an opinion on how to get the airplane off the main runway now closed to military and commercial traffic. Pieces of the blown-apart wheel lay in the grass over to one side. Under the stress and strain, the ancient World War II wheel casting had disintegrated on our take off roll. Since Charleston had only one runway suitable for their C-5A traffic, the Air Force threatened to bulldoze the crippled PV-2 from the runway if it wasn't moved quickly. It took an hour and strong talking, but a rental crane finally arrived, lifted the wing, and the mechanics installed another wheel and tire.

Two hours after the accident, Walt and I climbed back into the same airplane, now fitted with a different wheel and tire, and taxied to the parking area. My heartbeat had returned to normal, but my thinking was quickened. Images of what might have been overlapped with what had happened. The take off had been fine, then, before the next breath, everything changed. While the mechanic inspected our PV-2 for damage I calmed down, but the seriousness of flying was slowly infiltrating my romantic notions.

That afternoon as we flew that same airplane, we droned across the flat Charleston countryside. We dropped bait on those treacherous little fire ants while I hoped that, back in Atlanta, Shawn played happily unaware her parents were away. I snuck glances at Walt, this man with whom I flew shoulder-to-shoulder, loving him more than ever. He was my captain, my teacher, my husband, the father of my child, and most of all, my friend. There was no place else on earth that I would rather have been.

As the physical demands of the airplane and job filled my days, I thought less and less about the accident and told myself my problems were over, everything was fine. My cut had turned into a scab on my lip and a great pilot story.

One morning, the clouds and visibility were below the minimums required for flying on this contract. Copilots still did the preflight and pulled through the props before they had a cup of coffee. I stifled another yawn. I hadn't adjusted to getting up so early in the morning. Most of the guys slept a half-hour later, but a gal needed extra time to put on makeup and curl her long hair. I might be oily, dirty, and beat at the end of the day, but at least I started out looking like a woman.

I stood in front of the right engine of our PV-2, staring at the large three-bladed propeller as if it would turn without my help. My thoughts were on Shawn still in Atlanta. I had found no babysitter and it was probably just as well. Our friends in Atlanta understood and assured me she was happy. I hoped she was busily exploring her world. Here in Charleston, her parents were stressed out and had little free time with days starting early and ending late.

After a hard day of low-level flying, the captains would wander off to talk to the USDA reps and drink beer. We weary copilots walked out on the wings of the old bombers, knelt down by the engines, and hauled up heavy buckets of oil to fill the reservoirs. Once the oil-guzzling engines were replenished, the captains often reappeared to help secure the canvas cover over the plane and declare the day done. At last, we tired copilots guzzled down the best-tasting beer of our evening as we gathered in front of the planes to comment on the day's flights. The pilots, as a group, traveled in communal cars to local restaurants where they devoured vast quantities of food before hurrying to the motels and bed.

The next morning, it all began again. At least, we were making good money. By the end of the month with both of us flying, we could buy that low-time Wright R-975 engine for the Stearman. It wasn't the Pratt and Whitney we wanted, but it would work and was less expensive. We needed the 450 horsepower to carry a wingrider and turn the Stearman into a real airshow airplane.

"Get with it, Sandi," I said aloud and placed my shoulder against a propeller blade. With all my strength, I pushed it forward as fast as I could move it. I then stepped back, jumped up and grabbed the descending blade, using my weight to pull it down. Each engine had to be rotated through nine blades. It sounded easy enough at first, but was a challenge for someone short like me. Some of the captains occasionally gathered, coffee cups in hand to watch my morning exercise routine. The other copilots were men, all taller and stronger than me. They simply pushed the blades around. This morning, I began my huffing and puffing without an audience, but it wouldn't last long. By the time I finished the first engine; a crowd of four had arrived, including Walt and my new captain, Bob Greer.

Chief Pilot Lyle had decided Walt needed to fly with a copilot getting ready for a checkride with the FAA. Captains were required to have special type-ratings to command airplanes as large as these, and Walt was the only pilot on the crew qualified to recommend the candidate. The other captains had not been interested in flying with a woman copilot, even one they liked. I worried I might be headed back to my flight instructing job. At last, Bob Greer stepped forward. "I'd be honored," he said, "to fly with Sandi. I like women." Had it not been for Greer, as we called him, my bomber-flying days would have ended that day.

The sun peeked through the haze as I crossed over to the second engine with my entourage following. They were an unusual group. Other than Walt, they looked like Marlboro men in different stages of life. Most wore faded jeans, scuffed boots, and tattered cowboy hats. My captain, Greer, was in his early forties, medium height with a weathered complexion and a world-embracing smile. He had flown tankers, fought fires in the West, and liked bush-flying in Alaska. He reminded me of an old-time mountain man without the beard.

Greer smiled and said, "How're you doing, darlin'?" He turned to the group, "I'm the only captain on this here job that can call his copilot darlin'." They all laughed. Greer casually asked me, "Need any help?"

"Nope, I've got it covered." I jumped up and grabbed the propeller blade. No way would my captain preflight his airplane. The men watched with interest as I finished preparing the plane for the day's work.

Fog lay over the surrounding lowlands where we were scheduled to fly later. The crew stood outside the government trailer, drinking coffee and sharing pilot stories. We talked of near misses, close calls, mishaps, and even my accidental parachute into the trees. Walt took a lot of ribbing about chickening out on the parachute jump, although most of the guys identified with him in the story.

Lyle, the chief pilot, pulled his pipe from his shirt pocket. Several of the others took out pipes, even the ones from Georgia who wore dark blue jeans and cowboy boots with unworn heels, and joined Lyle in a smoke. I wondered how many of them had smoked pipes before this job. The rich smell of blended tobacco filled the air while we all contemplated our individual universes.

"Hey, darlin'," Greer broke the silence. "Were you in a bit of a hurry to get out of the airplane?" Everybody, including Walt, laughed. Greer continued, pointing to the scab on my lip, "How does it feel to be married to a man who kicks you in the mouth?"

Grinning, I almost felt like one of the guys. At last, the fog cleared and everyone took to the air.

Greer and I had been flying two hours at tree-top level across the coastal land south of Charleston. Up and down twenty-mile long swaths, we flew at 160 knots using an experimental navigation system, called Hi-Fix, which guided and tracked our flight path. It was different than the system the other PV-2s used. Whichever one of us was flying kept a needle centered by picking reference points on the ground and making small corrections with the elevator and rudder. Above my head, the monitor recorded our flight path, which the USDA would later review. If our needle had strayed fifty feet, they called it a "skip" and the swath would later have to be flown again. The program had its bugs and some days we sat on the ground waiting not only for the weather to improve, but for the equipment to work properly.

This day was no different than the many other days I had flown. Beneath us, wetlands spread in all directions with the ocean off the right wing on the far horizon. We turned off the dispersal system over big pools of water to protect the marshland environment.

It was hot, as usual. The sun bore down on the cockpit and I wiped sweat blended with makeup from my face. We wore earplugs and headsets with boom microphones for communication. Still, the overpowering engine noise was like standing between freight trains roaring down parallel tracks. Greer and I used hand signals to communicate in addition to talking over the intercom.

Each of us took turns flying for long segments of time. When I flew, Greer had to help me hold the elevator up when I made the steep crop duster turns at the end of each swath. The PV-2 was a big bomber, not a small crop dusting airplane. It was heavier, flew at faster speeds, and required strength to make the extreme turn-around necessary to line up properly on the next imaginary row. Without his help, the nose would lower and the airplane would lose altitude.

At the end of each swath, I would flip the bait application switch off and then pull the nose of the airplane up while making a seventy degree turn to the right. Greer would have his hands on his set of controls and assist me in keeping the elevator back. I was strong, but not strong enough to do the turns alone. We flew outbound approximately twenty seconds or a total of four swaths on the navigation system. We needed this distance to have enough space to make the teardrop turn back in to the next lane over the land we were covering. I then would bank the airplane steeply to the left, turn inbound and allow the nose to drop as the plane descended back to the proper altitude. If all of this worked, the plane would be lined up next to the last swath we had flown and the navigation needle would be centered. Flipping the bait-switch on at the proper time, we would settle down for another run, always keeping the needle centered and flying at tree-top level over the countryside.

On and on the flight continued, two pilots immersed in inner thoughts, united in a common outer goal of keeping the needle centered and holding a set altitude above the ground. We flew hypnotized with engine noise, landscape and duties blending into a tapestry of aviation life. An aviation wag once said, "Aviation is hours and hours of boredom, punctuated by a few moments of stark terror." How true those words would be this day.

Greer was flying, hands on the yoke, eyes forward looking at the land ahead. I was lost in my thoughts, idly watching the needle record our flight path when I heard a loud thud. The airplane shuddered and the nose yawed to the right. My stomach tensed. Panic gripped my insides. What was wrong? Had we hit an unseen radio tower? I looked out my side of the aircraft and saw the heavy aluminum leading edge of the wing crumpled outboard of the engine, in front of the aileron. Black feathers and blood covered the jagged aluminum now crumpled back to the spar.

I pressed the microphone button and said, "Buzzard." I turned to look at Greer who hadn't made out what I said. I motioned for him to pull the headset from his ear. I cupped my hands together, leaned across the throttles and yelled as loud as I could, "BUZZARD."

"Shit," he said lips moving but sound drowned out by engine noise.

Mind racing, I looked at the instruments...then out to the wing...over to Greer…and questioned what this would do to the airplane. Could we fly at a slower speed for landing? Would we stall and crash off the end of the runway?

Greer had sweat on his brow, nothing unusual in this heat. How serious did my captain think our situation? Personally, I thought it was pretty damn serious as we limped back to Charleston airport.

Greer signaled me to call approach control. Grateful to cover my concern with activity, I flipped the switches to transmit on the proper frequency and said, "Charleston Approach, PV 57Charlie, inbound for landing."

Greer hadn't instructed me to declare an emergency which, again, was no surprise. In one of our many pilot talks around the airplanes, all of the captains had agreed it would have to be a by-God-real-emergency to get the FAA involved in their flying. Anyway, the FAA and airport paperwork took way too long to fill out.

Approach control handed us over to the tower who cleared us to land short of the crossing runway where an airliner would be landing. Landing on a shorter runway at the end of a flight presented no problem if we were low on fuel and the fire ant bait was close to empty. This day was different. Could we stop a more than half-loaded aircraft before the intersecting runway? I looked at Greer to see what he wanted me to tell the tower. He nodded okay.

Greer kept the speed higher than normal as we descended for landing. I talked to the tower and wondered if we would crash. I put down the landing gear and had a vision of running into an airliner. I completed the landing checklist and wished there was some action I could take. In emergencies, the pilot-in-command is very busy flying the airplane while copilots do what they can to assist and think of all the bad things that could happen.

Our airspeed fell off as Greer brought the bomber closer to the end of the runway. I saw the control wheel shake in his hand. Greer rammed the throttles forward to gain speed. Slowly, the plane accelerated and inched higher. The bird strike had crammed the leading edge of the wing back to the spar and disturbed the flow over the aileron. This time, Greer called the tower, "Charleston, PV 57Charlie going around. Request landing on long runway."

"57Charlie, permission granted. Is there a problem?"

"Negative. 57 Charlie's loaded. We need the long runway." Greer's calm voice did not reflect the concern I knew he felt. Pilots in emergencies prefer to be the one flying and I was no exception. My legs were jumpy and my hands twitched to take the controls, even though Greer had far more piloting experience and ability to get us back on the ground in one piece. Copilot duties complete, I could only wait and watch.

Greer used extra speed on the next approach. As we neared the runway, he slowed the airplane but kept a higher speed to keep the aileron from buffeting. At last, he flew the main wheels onto the runway at 140 knots, over 161 miles per hour and 60 knots over the normal stall speed. We barreled down the concrete on the front two wheels, like a race car at Indy, and used most of the long runway before turning off. I relaxed, breathing more deeply as we taxied to our parking area.

The beer tasted sweeter to me that night at dinner. Greer told our story and our fellow pilots listened to each word, filed away the useful information and, I knew, inwardly questioned how they would have handled the situation had it happened to them.

Greer broke the tension when he said, "She just yelled, 'Buzzard' like birds hit us every day. Yep, she's my darlin' copilot." As usual, we all laughed. This was our pilot world, a world where we learned from each

other's experiences, where we lived close to danger, always making light of
that nearness to death

After dinner, Greer took me aside and said, "Sandi, I don't know if I
can continue to fly with you. How could I be responsible for the death of a
mother of a small child?"

"Oh, Bob." I touched his shoulder. "You have kids at home and still
do this kind of flying. I'm just a pilot making a buck." He nodded and I
wondered what he was thinking.

The next morning, Greer and I were atop the PV's right wing. We
both had screwdrivers and took out screws set one inch apart that held
the leading-edge aluminum piece to the spar. Ralco's mechanics from the
Bainbridge facility were driving in a replacement leading edge they had
removed from a spare airplane.

That evening at dinner, the guys asked what we had done all day. I said,
"Greer and I spent the day screwing on the wing of our airplane."

1970

10

MOTHER AND FLYING

Monroeville, Alabama

"Yes Mother, the parachute I use is safe, even if it is only modified Army surplus."

"Parachuting is dangerous," she said. "What if something happened to you?"

It was March and I was in southern Alabama making one of my every-so-often phone calls home. My mom had been worried since the first time she heard about my parachuting. I understood, but found her concerns irritating. There was no pleasing her. No matter what I did, something was always wrong. She had wanted a daughter who accomplished great things and yet, nitpicked me to death.

"I'm not jumping a lot, anyway," I said. "I just called to let you know that I was in an article in last Sunday's Atlanta paper." The publicity should get her off my back. I knew she and my dad would read the article and paste it in the scrapbook they kept on my flying adventures.

"Did you save me a copy?" she said.

I smiled, imagining my parents proudly showing the scrapbook to their friends. So far, it was a small book, but one day I hoped to fill it with airshow publicity. "I saved you a copy. The article is about girl parachutists in the Atlanta area. I'm one of the ones they featured. They also mentioned our airshow flying."

Her silence communicated her displeasure more than words. Like a bulldog, once my mother took hold of a position, she rarely let go. "Sandra," she said and paused.

I hated her calling me Sandra. It set my nerves on edge. Why couldn't she recognize I was Sandi now? She knew I had been Sandi since college. But no, my mom had to call me Sandra. I felt my shoulders tense.

"Sandra," she said again, "Are you sure what you're doing is safe? Flying upside down and now parachuting. That's no way for a mother to be."

I wanted to scream that times had changed. You're an old woman of fifty-nine, Mama. Modern women can do what they want. Mothers can be who they want to be. Instead, in the calmest voice I could muster, said, "Mama, you know I love my daughter and she's doing really well."

"Where are you anyway?" she asked at last.

I relaxed slightly. Maybe we could have an easy conversation, talk about non-controversial subjects. At times, I felt sorry for my mom. She had always been ambitious for me. Many times in my life, she had said, "Sandra, you're going to do something special in your life. I just know it." She never considered it might include jumping out of planes or flying in airshows.

"We're in Monroeville, Alabama visiting our friends, Ann and Jennings Carter. He's a duster pilot, owns Carters' Dusting Services. Walt's been sleeping in the office bedroom and installing the new engine on the Stearman. Carter helps Walt when he can." I rushed on, "The engine is wonderful with twice the power of the old one."

"I've never heard of Monroeville." Mother was a big-city gal who believed living in Dallas in the "Great State of Texas" was the only place to be.

"Me neither. It's about ninety miles north and a little west of

Pensacola. Harper Lee lives here. You know, the writer. She wrote *To Kill A Mockingbird*."

"Yes. It was a great book and even better movie. I like that Gregory Peck."

"Well, our friend Carter is Harper Lee's cousin and, as a kid, played with her and another cousin, Truman Capote." I hoped to impress my Mom with the fact that I now traveled in the sphere of celebrities, even from small towns in Alabama.

"How interesting, what does he have to say about his famous relatives?"

I was silent. She wouldn't understand. I belonged to the skies and neither politics nor famous writers stayed long in my field of vision. Stories about the Bucker Jungmann, a rare biplane that Carter owned, or what it was like to be a duster pilot, interested me more than hearing childhood adventures with cousins turned into authors, unless they wrote flying stories. My single-minded focus was centered on becoming the best aerobatic pilot I could while making a living in the airshow business.

I stammered, "Nothing. We just talk flying." I stopped, not knowing what to say. My world was flying and my mom was actively opposed to it. I might brush against exciting, worldly things, but I didn't really care about them. Yet if I didn't call, my mom worried, and I loved her. I wanted her to be happy with me and love what I did.

Mom's voice rescued me. "Did you quit your flight-instructing job?"

"Oh no, I just took a few days off. Shawn and I were lonely for Walt. We hopped on a bus."

I decided not to tell her how much I missed being with Walt and how he had lured me to Alabama with a promised aerobatic flight in Carter's Jungmann. From the first time I had seen Frank Price fly the Jungmeister in Austin, I had wanted to pilot the quick-rolling biplane. The Jungmann was a two-place version of the Jungmeister and our friend Carter owned one. Obviously, a trip to Monroeville was indicated.

"I'm glad you rode the bus. I'd hate to think of you driving alone with a toddler across Georgia and Alabama."

She was probably right about driving our worn-out car cross country, but why couldn't she recognize my abilities? I was a commercial pilot, capable of flying passengers all over the United States, in fact, they would pay me to fly them. Me. Alone. No other pilot. Certainly, I could drive a car three hundred miles to see my husband.

"Can I talk to Shawn?" she said.

"She and her dad went to the hardware store. No breakfast before they left, so they'll be back soon."

I stirred the boiling rice on the small stove in the kitchen. The crop dusting office was a prefabricated home with most of the square footage in what would have been a living room, now used as an office. A kitchen with eating area, bathroom, and bedroom occupied the remaining space.

"Do you want me to call you back when she gets here?" I said. The bubbling rice reminded me of how broke we were. All of our money had been spent on the engine and the mount, so now we ate rice for breakfast and peanut butter sandwiches other times. The prudent thing would have been for me to stay in Atlanta, save the bus fare, and fly with as many students as possible.

"That's okay," Mom said. "How is my baby doing?"

I smiled. At last, something my mom and I agreed upon. "Not a baby anymore. She's walking all over the place and getting into everything. She talks up a storm, lots of gibberish with real words mixed in. I wish you and Daddy could see her." I heard my mom sigh.

"Atlanta is a long way from Dallas. We'll come visit one of these days. I do wish you two would get a home and stay put. It'd be better for Shawn." Mother rambled on about raising a child in a stable environment.

I tuned her out and opened the small refrigerator, looking for margarine.

"When are you two going to settle down?" she asked.

Never, I wanted to yell. I slammed the refrigerator door. At least, Shawn had a mom and dad who loved each other and their work, more than I could say for my parents.

I could hear the resentment in my voice. "Mother, Walt and I are trying to earn enough to modify our planes so we can fly airshows. We've found clipped wings to put on the TCraft and it needs a bigger engine, but there isn't enough money to buy them. The Stearman still needs a smoke system, wheel pants, cowling, and lots of other things."

"I know, sweetie," she said, but I knew she hadn't really heard me. "Things are rough for you right now, but remember, you can do anything you set your mind to do." Her encouragement touched me. It was rough financially at the moment, but she was right that Walt and I could accomplish our dream.

Then she continued, "I just worry about Shawn."

It was my turn to sigh. "You know I love Shawn, so very much. Once we get into the airshow business, we'll live in one place." I rationalized that it was only a small fib to ease her mind. I really had no idea where we would live or what it would be like to be in the airshow business.

"Oh, I forgot to tell you," I said. "We've come up with a name for our airshow. We're going to call ourselves 'The Flying Pierces' with the flying written upside down." I waited for a response and finally said, "Isn't it a great name?"

"Sandra, are you sure you want to be an airshow pilot? It's so dangerous.

You have a child. You could be hurt or killed."

"Oh, Mother." She just didn't understand, and I doubted she ever would. Resigned, I said, "It's not as dangerous as you think. Gotta go. Tell Daddy I love him. And you, too."

I hung up the phone.

JULY, 1970

11

ATOP THE WING

Hilton Head, South Carolina

I must have been crazy to agree to ride outside an airplane flying upside down low to the ground, or water, as this day's show would be. I shivered in spite of the South Carolina heat. What sane person would want to be a wingrider? It was the first day of the Beaufort Water Festival, an airshow where we had booked The Flying Pierces wing act two months ago. I still had not ridden atop the Stearman's wing.

Walt calmly drove the car as if nothing unusual was about to happen. How could he appear so unconcerned? We had accomplished the near impossible, putting together enough money to buy the Stearman and bigger engine. It seemed like validation of our efforts when Helen Holland, an airshow promoter and wife of airshow pilot Jim Holland, called in May. Helen had read the women-parachutists article in the Atlanta Journal and Constitution and wanted to hire us for the Beaufort Water Festival. Walt would fly a solo act in the Stearman, the two of us would do the wing act, and I would make a water parachute jump on the last day of the show. The famous Charleston airshow pilot, Bevo Howard, was also scheduled to fly his historic Bucker Jungmeister.

"Yes," we had said. Yes, yes, yes!

It would be our initial airshow as The Flying Pierces. We would have to hustle to prepare for it, but we knew we could do it. The smoke system had yet to be installed, neither Walt nor I had ever flown the wing act, and I only had twelve parachute jumps and hadn't made a jump into water. Daunting tasks all, but none of that mattered. We, the soon-to-be renowned Flying Pierces had booked our first airshow.

I rolled the rental car's window down, and breathed in warm air burdened with humidity. "How much farther?" I asked.

Walt's attention stayed focused on the road. "We're nearly there. It's tough staging this far away from Beaufort, not that we have any choice. Can't land on water."

Flying aerobatics over water challenged the best pilots. Depth perception was difficult, and possible engine failure caused tremors in the most valiant hearts. I thought of the Stearman with me atop the wing landing on the water and my stomach clenched as if punched by Cassius Clay. If the plane flipped, I would be one crushed wingrider.

Walt had told me the troubling story of the first wingrider on a Stearman's wing. The Cole Brothers Airshow decided to carry a wingrider on Marion Cole's airshow Stearman. The first Stearman wingrider climbed atop Marion's plane and hooked cables from the airplane to his harness. He then slid his feet into braces attached to the top wing. This was in keeping with 1930's technology designed for a Curtis Jenny with a ninety-horsepower engine and a top speed of 90 miles per hour. The Stearman had 450 horsepower and did aerobatics at much greater airspeeds.

Marion took off on a practice flight with the wingrider. As the airplane accelerated, air forced its way over the wingrider who blew backward. His ankles snapped like twigs. I hoped nothing of mine would snap. The Cole brothers invented the wingstand, installing it before Marion's next practice session, with a new wingrider. Airshow pilots since that time used steel wingstands to brace people standing atop their wing. Thank goodness, someone had figured out the problems before us.

My mind flitted to thoughts of Bevo Howard, aerobatic great who flew the famous Jungmeister that came to the United States aboard the Hindenburg. Walt and I had met him in Charleston on the fire-ant contract where Bevo owned the Beechcraft Aircraft Dealership at the airport. A southern gentlemen through and through, he rarely spoke of his aviation exploits, instead performing amazing feats in his historic airplane similar to the one Papa Tiger Frank Price flew. How could we be flying an airshow with the famous Bevo Howard?

"Didn't Shawn look cute?" I said, in an effort to distract myself. "All dressed in her red, white, and blue outfit? She'll have fun today with Helen." I paused long enough to say a prayer that Shawn would enjoy the water festival and not be a burden to Helen, the promoter of this airshow, who had agreed to take care of her while we flew. I inclined my head toward the open window. The wind blowing through my hair helped dispel images from my mind of a Stearman landing in water.

We had been so confident the day Helen called, never doubting we had plenty of time to prepare for the Beaufort airshow. How hard could it be, we'd laughed, to install a smoke system and work out the bugs in the airplane? Costumes and harness for the wing act should be easy. Walt had already built the wingstand. We knew we'd have lots of time to practice and get comfortable with our new act. It was true the plane would perform differently with a person on top of the wing, but that was no problem. And we'd save the last two weeks for practice flights.

Life, as it often does, proceeded at its own pace. Parts came in slowly. Everything cost more than we thought. Now here we were the first day of the show and I still had not ridden on the wing. Our current plan was to fly a practice flight, and then land to debrief. The official airshow flight would follow in two hours.

We pulled into the airport, carved from a seaside forest of pine. I jumped from the car, relieved to have something to do. I put on my heavy black jumpsuit while Walt prepared the Stearman. The July heat pressed against me, and drops of moisture dampened my back. Dense east-coast clouds scattered across the summer sky as errant seagulls from nearby beaches congregated to one side of the airport ramp. I chuckled. My first wingriding fans were going to be birds.

Only a few miles away I knew that people clad in swimsuits dug their bare feet into cool sand and walked along the Atlantic's edge. I imagined others lounging under umbrellas or in beach chairs, reveling in the sunshine and enjoying the refreshing ocean breeze. Reading a book on the beach sounded much better than what I was about to do.

Walt stopped a moment. "We'll do a brief practice session, so we can see how the plane flies with you on the wing. We'll land, then talk about it, and get ready for the airshow performance. Remember, it's a long flight from Hilton Head to the show site at Beaufort, not as far as driving. Still, conserve your energy."

"How am I supposed to conserve energy?"

He retreated into a mental world where he contemplated problems such as these. Physically, he stood beside me, but his mind was far away. At last, he said, "On the flight over and back, try to rest on the wingstand. We know the wind is going to be strong, so just relax into it as much as you can."

Unbidden, my mother's fearful admonitions played like a tape recorder in my mind. I imagined a devastating crash with the airplane under water and Shawn crying for her Mommy and Daddy on the shore. I could take it no longer. Stop. Stop this nonsense.

Walt's voice cut through my mind chatter. "Sandi, you'll be fine today. Wingriders have been around since the 1920's. People have flown on Stearman wings for a long time."

He wandered off to finish the preflight. I tugged at my custom red harness, made of parachute webbing, fit across my upper body and fastened at my waist. It would hold me to the airplane when we were upside down. At least, that was the plan. Modern wing acts used metal wingstands that supported the wingrider's back and harnesses with cables fastened to the wing a fact for which I was very grateful. Often the safety equipment would be hidden under clothing or colored to blend, from the public's eye.

Walt was right; many people had done this before me. We had a working smoke system that chugged out billows of puffy smoke. I was able to scramble to the top wing of the Stearman and back to the ground without hurting myself. Both of these things were major accomplishments. Still, we hadn't flown me atop the wing, no loops, no rolls, no figuring out airspeeds, and no inverted fuel system. I longed to say, "No way," to Walt, but couldn't. It might not be as pretty or professional a performance as we wanted, but The Flying Pierces would fly the wing act at the Beaufort Water Festival later that day.

In spite of the warmth, I shuddered. With a strong resolve, I reminded myself that the next day I would make my first exhibition parachute jump. I only had twelve parachute jumps and knew I shouldn't parachute at an airshow, much less into water. Where were government rules when you needed them? Anyway, that jump would happen, and be inconsequential compared to the wingriding.

Maybe mom was right. Maybe I did belong at home, baking cookies for Shawn, doing whatever it was regular wives did. I couldn't imagine

Lindbergh feeling this way.

I looked at Walt for reassurance. He stood behind the cockpit on the left side of the airplane, checking the oil level in the baggage compartment turned into an engine oil storage tank. Closing the aluminum door, he wiped his hands on a red shop rag and stuffed the frayed cloth into his back pocket. He looked my direction. "Ready?"

"Sure," I said, but knew I would never be ready.

Walt acted as if this upcoming flight were nothing unusual while fear wrapped like tentacles, strangling me, crushing my chest, and whispering in my ear, "Don't do this."

"Now remember," Walt said, "I'll climb to altitude over the airport. We'll do a loop, a hammerhead turn, and a few rolls. If everything is okay, I'll make a pass down the runway." He rubbed my shoulder. "It's going to be fine. We'll do a simple routine. You wave at the imaginary crowd. Before you know it, we'll be back on the ground."

Sure. Easy for you to say. Sit in a cockpit while I'm strapped outside on top of the wing.

I walked to the back of the Stearman's wing next to the cockpit, the ground reassuringly still under my feet. My gaze moved upward, stopping at the wingstand that towered above the center section that held the airplane's fuel tank. Biplanes have a center section that sits above the fuselage with upper wing panels extending on either side. From a distance, the top wing appears to be one continuous expanse, although there are three distinct sections.

My first task was to move from the ground to the top of the center section, in the middle of the wing, without falling off the airplane. I had practiced this feat many times and it, at least, felt comfortable.

I reached my right hand to the cockpit opening for balance. I planted my right foot on the black, nonskid, coating that ran up the side of the left wing next to the fuselage. A little hop and both of my feet were on the bottom wing. I wasn't as tall as the World War II pilots who learned to fly in these planes. They didn't have to jump to climb to the bottom wing.

If I had been flying the airplane, I would have swung my foot over into the pilot's seat. Instead, I stretched to grab the handhold in the center section over my head. I raised my leg and placed it on a reinforced spot atop the fuselage in front of the cockpit windshield. I pulled myself up, and now stood on top of the fuselage in front of the open cockpit. My head was above the back of the center section and I towered over Walt, who stood on the wing I had just left.

The next step was trickier. With my hand around the wingstand and one foot on the back of the center section, I half-hopped, half-jumped until I stood behind the wingstand on top of the wing. I ducked under the cables bracing the stand, and slithered forward until I was upright on top of the airplane in front of the wingstand.

The height above the ground was dizzying, and I grabbed the wingstand to steady myself. My heart beat faster looking down, down, down. The fifteen feet from my eyes to the ground felt like a hundred. Is this how divers in Mexico felt when they jumped from the cliffs into water? I felt sick.

Walt followed me up to the top wing. He tightened the seatbelt around my waist, and then hooked the two cables that attached my harness to the airplane. He leaned over and kissed me. "Remember, if this belt failed, these cables would still hold you to the airplane."

Somehow, I was not reassured. I envisioned me flopping in the breeze on the end of a cable, attached to the plane. Not a pleasant scene, but it beat the alternative.

Before he left, he said, "I'll wag the wings before the first maneuver, and you can trail your foot to let me know you're ready to begin."

I gave an automatic nod, struggling to slow my racing thoughts. On went my cloth helmet, down came the military goggles while I made a mental note to find a pair of sexy ski goggles and a showy costume before the next airshow, if there were one. Silly girl, concerned about costumes at a time like this?

Attached to the top of the Stearman, I moved with the airplane as Walt fastened his two seatbelts and shoulder harness in the cockpit. He yelled, "Clear prop."

The large propeller, only six feet away from me, churned the air like a giant fan. A backfire, then the engine came to life, and the airplane trembled under my feet. With the engine at idle, the noise and vibration from the rotating butter-paddle propeller blades was powerful.

The moment was as fresh and uncharted for me, an explorer setting out on a new adventure. Others had ridden atop biplane wings, but I had never talked to such a person or even knew their names. Like Lewis and Clark sailing up the Missouri River, our course was laid out in a general way. Theoretically, we would take off and fly a series of aerobatic maneuvers, but what was it like to stand as a passenger on top of a plane during aerobatics? My excitement for adventure swirled with fear of the unknown. Exhilarated and scared at the same time, the winning emotion remained to be known.

For distraction, I gulped the ocean air, looking at the airport from my new observation tower. We were alone except for the birds, the gas boy, and two airplanes tied down on the other side of the ramp. Black asphalt runway stretched in both directions. Green-blue pines encroached on the sides of the field, threatening to reclaim what once had been theirs.

The plane inched forward. Jerked to reality, I grabbed the cables and steel wire cut into my hands. I'll wear gloves next time. No commitments, Sandi. No commitments to a next time. The Stearman waddled to the end of the runway while my mind produced movies with very bad endings. One featured me standing atop the flight-school Stearman that had crashed in Marietta. My breathing slowed, imagining myself standing outside on that wing, teetering back and forth. A chilling flash of clarity pierced my romantic illusions. Had I been riding the wing that day in Marietta, I would have been flattened.

The engine below roared as Walt added power for take-off. The plane moved forward, gradually accelerating. The wind pummeled my body, attempting to tear me off the wing. Muscles tense against the pressure, hands death-gripping the cables; I hunched forward to keep the top half of my body from blowing back over the wingstand. I was an automobile hood ornament atop a car in the midst of a mighty storm.

As we climbed higher the air cooled, but the wind didn't abate. I tried to conserve my energy by relaxing into the wind while focusing on the magnificent view. Below me, the outline of the barrier island appeared with azure water fanning out for miles, bordered on one side by sandy beaches and marshy wetlands. In the fifties, Hilton Head Island had been purchased for use as a tree farm. Above it, I could see areas where development assailed the forest, and snaking fingers of water flowed into the Atlantic Ocean.

I made small adjustments in my stance as I sought ways to compromise with the wind. Alone, alone on a buffeted world of wing, wind, and sky, I looked at my feet. Scuffed sneakers rested in the middle of a sunburst paint design with blood-red rays shooting out to the plane's wingtips. A passenger planted on the outside of an old biplane that was about to loop and roll and fly upside down.

I was terrified. The pilot in me knew too much. What if the engine quit? Where would we land? Would the plane flip and crush me?

From my eagle's perch, I searched for a strip of clear earth long enough for us to touch down safely. Couldn't land there. Get away from the water. Fly over there, where we could make the airport if the engine stopped. On and on, the inner dialogue instructed and cajoled as my mind tried to control an uncontrollable situation. I stood hunched into the wind with vise-like hands grasping the cables.

My body jerked to the right, and then back to the left as the wings rocked. I clutched the cables even more tightly. What would happen to me when the airplane slow-rolled?

Walt signaled, "Are you ready to begin?"

Shit no, I wasn't ready! Reluctantly, I released my grip, and ran my fingers along the edge of the cloth helmet to tuck in a curl that whipped my cheek, then ran my hands down my jumpsuit and stopped at the seatbelt that held me tight. I gave it one more tug and ran my hand over the hard metal fittings to make certain they were secure. I was ready, ready as ever I would be.

I let my right foot trail behind the wingstand, signaling that I was ready. The Stearman's nose immediately lowered to gain speed. As the speed increased, so did the wind. It hammered, driving me into the wingstand. I hunched further forward to counteract the constant pounding.

Our first maneuver was a loop that would create positive g's, forcing my weight and feet into the wing. At least, I wouldn't be flung outward, away from the airplane. I didn't know if I could take the increased speed of one-hundred-sixty miles per hour needed to perform the maneuver.

I looked downward and my stomach lurched. Nothing, but air, was between me and the ground. The wind amplified with speed. My head bobbed as the wind played prize fighter with my head the punching bag. I lowered it into the wind. Anything to keep it stable.

Wind pressure continued to assail me as the nose of the airplane returned to level. The plane paused for a moment, and then shot above the horizon into a loop. I stared into space. No ground. No ocean. No horizon. Without thinking, I did what any aerobatic pilot would do. I turned my head to look along the left wing to the horizon. The wind snapped my head, and I quickly faced forward. As the airplane slowed over the top of the loop, the beating of the wind slowed. My head dangled toward the ground with only space between me and the South Carolina coast. At this slow speed, I no longer had to fight the wind and had one moment of reprieve.

The speed and wind pressure built again as we rushed down the backside of the loop. The nose of the airplane lowered to gain the necessary speed for the next maneuver, a hammerhead turn. The plane pulled up vertically, and I again stared into space. I fought the urge to turn my head to look at the horizon. Slowing, slowing, slowing, until just above a stall, we pivoted 180 degrees, and flew straight down toward the earth. We needed to gain enough speed to complete the next maneuver.

Enduring the wind required all my attention, and kept my emotion away. With little room for feeling, I observed my weight shifting during the maneuvers, the various pressures of wind, and ways to conserve my physical energy. If a sudden move of the plane scared me, I reminded myself that the cables were strong, the seat belt secured, and the wingstand made of steel. The plane was my stage, and the ground seemed to move around, sometimes below, sometimes above, or to the side of me. Ignoring the view, I focused on keeping my head down into the wind. Saving energy was my goal or I'd be so exhausted I wouldn't be able to climb down to the ground after the flight was over. I banished thoughts of the airshow scheduled later in the day. My goal was only to make it back to the ground.

It was time to fly a low-level inverted pass over the runway where I was to wave at an imaginary crowd. Barreling toward the earth, we stopped at what seemed inches above the ground, but was actually several hundred feet. Walt slow-rolled the Stearman to inverted.

I now hung below the airplane with my head pointing to a ground that looked very near. My unattached feet fell from the wing and swung in space. All my weight was now rested in my shoulder harness and strained the cables that secured me to the wing. Panic came like a tsunami in a Japanese adventure movie. If I were on a roller coaster I would scream, but what to do in this situation? I pushed my feet up and my toes touched the wing. The wind continued to pound and the ground rushed by, way too close to my head. I found comfort in keeping my toes in contact with the wing.

I knew waving to the crowd was a must. Without my arms moving, the spectators at the water festival might not think a real person was attached to the wing, only a dummy lashed to the wingstand. I put out my arm to wave. As the wind whipped it backward, I thought they might be right about the dummy part. Once more, I dragged my arm forward, again the wind yanked it back. This drag-forward-yank-back sequence was the wave to the crowd I would have to use for airshow performances.

At last, Walt rolled upright and we entered the pattern for landing.

Did I really do it? Was I now officially a wingrider? The wind continued to beat my head and body, but inside, a part of me relaxed. I had done it! I rode the wing in spite of my fear. I rode the wing in spite of my mother's warnings. And in that moment, I decided my dream was a worthy one.

In spite of physical pain and my volatile emotions, I had wholeheartedly embraced my imagined life. I became the daring young woman loved by the dashing young man in the celebrated airshow family. Walt and I were Superman and Superwoman with their Superbaby flying into the sunset, inspiring music playing in the background. A love like ours could overcome all obstacles.

The fear? I vowed to do everything to make my job as safe as possible. We'd fly good equipment with excellent maintenance with no more rushed shows like this one. We would devote time and money for practice; flying at least the solo acts most days.

Fear pointed out areas of possible trouble that might need my attention. I knew in that instant that only by facing my fear would life be worth living. My mom was right. Airshow flying was a dangerous career, but Shawn would have a mom who lived her life with passion. I would be a mother, a role model, who pursued her dreams in spite of fear, in spite of roadblocks, and other people's opinions. I chose to live my life in the joy of pursuing my passion instead of fear.

Our wing act later that day at the Water Festival went off without a hitch, though it lacked the polish and professionalism we wanted and were determined to have in the future.

The next day's parachute jump into water seemed insignificant next to the wing act. I parachuted alongside a local skydiving group into the Beaufort Bay, in front of spectators watching from the shore.

The skydivers told me to undo my parachute harness before entering the blue-green water, so that its drag wouldn't pull me under. I treaded water, but hung onto the harness and chute now floating free of my body. The rescue boat came near, and when it arrived, a man pulled me from the churning water. "Hey, we caught us a girl." he yelled to the other boats. That day, I decided my thirteenth jump was my last. Parachuting had been fun, but my life was full of enough excitement.

At the performer's party later that evening, a burly marine, from nearby Parris Island, approached me. He thrust an open copy of Playboy magazine in my face and pointed to the voluptuous centerfold. "That girl should look at you and eat her heart out." My fellow skydiver grinned, patted me on the shoulder, and stumbled off for another beer.

The Superwoman stuff had some real advantages.

AUGUST, 1970

12

FORCED LANDING IN GEORGIA

US Hwy 17, near Riceboro, Georgia

I inched my TCraft, nicknamed Tinkerbelle in honor of the plane in which I learned to fly, closer to the Stearman's right wing. I had inherited Walt's airshow airplane when he bought the Stearman. Tucked in behind the right wing of his candy-apple red, white, and blue biplane, my goal was to stay in the exact same position, no matter what. When Walt's gaily painted plane moved right, I moved right. If the Stearman moved forward, Tinkerbelle moved with it. If it went up or down, I too edged up or down, locked in the same place next to his large biplane.

I looked to the left, flying so that the cockpit area of the Stearman was positioned on an imaginary spot on my window. I reached forward and made a smudge mark on the Plexiglas. Just like all formation pilots, I maneuvered to keep the plane I followed in my sight picture. When Walt's head moved away from the spot, I made tiny corrections. A touch of throttle to move forward. A pressure on the stick. A smidgen of rudder as needed. Tiny moves that aligned his head and cockpit with the smudge mark on my window.

Beneath us, South Georgia forest rolled to the ocean. We weren't high enough to see the water or the construction of an interstate highway that I knew lay between. I wasn't certain of our location, only that we flew

along U. S. Highway 17 and were south of Savannah. Walt was handling
the navigation as I kept my attention focused on his brown leather helmet
and black goggles, I still could see the white cockpit laced with shiny red
upholstery fabric and the wraparound windshield protecting him from the
wind. I glimpsed part of his name, upside down, on the right side of the
plane in giant letters, and a section of the vivid red-with-blue trim sunburst
that shot out the wing. In the background, the highway was a green-gray
blur leading us south to a new home base in Florida.

My shoulders hunched with tension as I struggled to keep Walt's head
correctly placed underneath the smudge in my sight picture. It was exacting
work that required my total concentration, but work in which I delighted.
I felt a kinship with every formation pilot before me. They had flown just
like me, attention focused on the sight picture of the plane they followed,
ignoring the weather, the terrain, and personal concerns. No matter the
difficulty, the formation followed where the leader guided. Such was the
trust for the lead pilot.

My mind flitted to the new life awaiting me in Florida. To make money,
Walt had flown a PV-2 fire ant contract in Central Florida. He came home
wanting to move. Tired of Georgia hills draped with clouds, I longed for
unlimited vistas and sunshine. So, it was off to Florida with lots of sun
and, more importantly, winter airshows. Promoters across the state took
advantage of warm sunny days and plentiful tourists to schedule outdoor
events. The Flying Pierces wanted to be a major part of the Winter Florida
airshow market.

Walt turned his head toward me and smiled. I couldn't see his eyes, but
knew little crinkled lines radiated out from them underneath the goggles.
I smiled back, but stifled the urge to wave. Instead, I kept my hands on
the stick and throttle, making the minor corrections that kept his head

positioned properly in my sight picture.

What a life, what an incredible life we had. It was more than I ever imagined. We were starting to book airshows. I flew my own airplane, not perfect, but with clipped wings, fancy paint job, and a more powerful eighty-five-horsepower engine replacing the original sixty-five-horsepower Continental that Walt had flown. I had a husband who was a cross between Superman and an auto mechanic. He also was stubborn, and although he rarely said no, he conveniently forgot to do those things he didn't want to do. Suddenly irritated, I focused on the smudge spot and Walt's head.

Pay attention, Sandi, which I did for a while. Eventually my thoughts turned to Shawn. She was precious this morning in her yellow and green summer playsuit, waving goodbye as we taxied for take off. She rode with my parents who followed us in their station wagon loaded with our belongings. Daddy was proud of my flying, but had a worried look whenever I talked about airshows. Mother still was having difficulty accepting her daughter, the airshow pilot. Why couldn't she just admit that I was a grownup and this was the life I'd chosen? No one was going to take it away from me. No matter what she, or anyone else, thought about my choices.

Lost in my inner dialogue, the Stearman slid away from me. I jerked my attention back to my flying. Snap to it! I moved the mark on my window back over Walt's cockpit. Good thing I hadn't moved toward the big bird.

Mom and Dad may not have been ecstatic about my airshow flying, but they loved me enough to use their vacation time to help us move. My hand moved without thinking, adding a tad of throttle to bring Walt's head back into alignment in my sight picture. Eventually they'd have to get over it, wouldn't they? After all, Mother was the one who told me I could do anything I set my mind to.

Without warning, Tinkerbelle's engine stopped, and then started again. Startled, I moved away from the Stearman and out of formation.

"Oh no, not again," I said out loud.

My heart thumped as if it were the engine struggling to run. I adjusted the throttle to see if that would free up the fuel flow. Quickly, I checked to make certain the fuel valve was turned to the "on" position. A push on the black mixture knob let me know the maximum amount of fuel should be going to the engine. As my mind considered what might be wrong, the engine smoothed out. My breath returned to normal, although I stayed tense and alert.

Probably dirt in the fuel. I glanced at my watch. Only in the air an hour, I should have had plenty of fuel. The Tcraft had a simple fuel system with two wing tanks that gravity fed into a header tank in the fuselage. Again, gravity fed fuel flowed from the header tank to the carburetor on the engine. If I had fuel in the tank, there wasn't much that could go wrong.

The engine cut out once again, leaving an alarming silence in the air. What could be wrong? Stay calm, Sandi, stay calm! I wished for radios in our planes so I could talk to Walt.

The engine made a half-hearted attempt to run, and then, stopped again. This time, only the sound of air whooshing over the windshield punctuated the silence that hung about me. The propeller rotation slowed down. The Tcraft was now a sailplane soaring to earth in only minutes.

Think, Sandi, think! Remember, your emergency landing practice. Look for a place to land…a clear spot, mostly flat with enough room to stop before hitting one of the many trees below. I scanned the forest beneath me, wanting to panic…to scream. I pushed the Jack-in-the-Box of my emotions closed, and concentrated on finding a landing site. Around me lay miles of trees with a two-lane highway carved through them. No open fields. No nearby airport.

I'd have to land on the highway. The Interstate construction site was a few miles away, but it was too far to glide with no running engine. I brushed away such wishful thinking.

Breathe, Sandi, breathe. I lined up on the two-lane highway below, and focused on keeping my best glide speed. Please God, please keep the cars out of my way.

Watch the speed. WATCH THE SPEED. That's better, but not too slow. That's right, nose down a bit. NO, no that's too fast. I ignored the pulsating tension in my shoulder and neck, pretending the gripping ache in my stomach didn't exist. The plane dropped lower and lower toward the black asphalt surrounded by a sea of green. Grateful that the road was straight in front of me, I worried about the trees that hovered near the edge of the road. Could I clear them? Seven feet had been chopped off Tinkerbelle's wings to improve the roll-rate; still, twenty-nine feet remained. I was trying to land an airliner on a postage stamp. Move! Move cars! Good. Good. Get over further—further. Would my wing hit a car?

Thirty feet in the air, I caught my breath. Silver utility lines hung across the road of my makeshift airport. Do something, Sandi, do something. Should I glide over them and run the risk of snagging the tail wheel, perhaps being pulled out of the sky? Or do I dive under them and maybe catch the lines with the rudder? Hmm, they're about twenty feet above the highway.

With little time to think, I lowered the nose and flew under the wires. I saw them pass overhead through the Plexiglas skylight above my head. I now rushed too fast toward distant cars headed my direction. Forget the cars. Fly the airplane. Back, back a little on the stick to drain off the excess speed, and plop. I was on the ground. I stepped on the heel brakes and Tinkerbelle slowed. I turned the magneto switch off, undid the seat belts, and hopped out of my airplane. I heard the squealing of car brakes as I rushed to the tail of the plane. I had to push the TCraft off the road as quickly as possible, before a car hit us.

A young man, barely more than a boy, wearing worn jeans and a faded shirt seemed to appear by magic. Together, we guided the TCraft to a resting spot under a tree on the side of the road.

"That wuz sum landin," my rescuer said.

I nodded in agreement as the impact of what I had just been through hit me. The tension left my body and suddenly weak, I leaned against the side of the airplane to steady myself. The boy talked to me, but inside I kept shouting, I'm on the ground. I made it. I landed on this busy highway and didn't hit the high lines, a tree, or a car.

Air moved around us each time a vehicle passed. Any one of them could have smashed into me. Images of a mangled TCraft with me inside flashed in my mind, and my breath hesitated.

"Ma'am." I noticed my helper had pulled a peach out of his pocket and offered it to me. I took the yellow-pink gift, aware of its incredible beauty. I stood next to my airplane on the side of a Georgia road with a teenage boy offering me a Georgia peach.

"What happened?" he asked.

"The engine quit." I said, unable to focus on anything but the softness of the peach and the way the fuzz felt against my fingers.

"Why?" he said, "Why did it quit?"

The boy's voice blended with the sound of the cars whizzing past. Dappled shadows of sun painted the ground while above, a canopy of green shaded our world. I heard myself answering the stranger, "I've been having fuel problems since we made the engine run-upside down." I saw his puzzled look, but didn't have the energy to explain why the engine needed to run inverted. "I had to land on an interstate outside of Charleston three months ago, but it has run perfectly since then. That is, until today."

Vaguely aware how strange this scene must be, I spoke without emotion as if nothing unusual had happened. Numb, that's what it was. I was numb.

He shook his head as if he couldn't believe what I told him of landing on roads all over the South. To this young man, I was Neil Armstrong landing on the moon. I didn't share how many times Walt and I had been through the fuel system, the calls we had made to Frank Price and Harold Krier, or the mechanics we had consulted.

The boy didn't know and wouldn't understand how the Stearman and Tcraft were originally built as Standard Category airplanes, but had been licensed under the Experimental Exhibition Category that allowed us to modify them for airshow work. Unfortunately, there were no books on how to make airplanes do the kinds of things we wanted them to do.

I raised the peach to my nose and smelled its ripe sweetness as a breeze swept through the trees.

"Hey, look up there." He pointed skyward to the other side of the road.

I heard the deep-throated roar of a radial engine, and rushed from under the trees to see Walt flying low, directly across from us. As the Stearman passed by, Walt yelled something unintelligible. He made another pass, pulled the engine back to idle, and shouted again. Neither the boy nor I understood. At that moment, buying radios for both airplanes moved to the top of my priority list.

One more time, the Stearman circled and made a pass low over the trees. Walt flew close enough that I saw his hand pointing to the south. Our system of hand signals usually worked in the air, but weren't much use in this situation. He probably intended to head south to the next airport where he would find a car. Hopefully in an hour or two, he might return with fuel.

Tears near the surface, I turned to the TCraft to figure out what happened. I sat the peach inside the cockpit and climbed up on the strut to check the fuel in the right wing tank. It was empty.

Then I went to the left wing and discovered fuel in the tank. What was going on? If I had fuel, why did the engine act as if it were out of gas?

Questions flooded my mind. How far had we flown? Where exactly had I landed? I pulled my aeronautical chart and a jacket from the airplane to protect me from the ground. I turned to thank my helper, but saw him going into a house across the road. Just as well, this strange guest who dropped from the sky wasn't much company right now. I turned my attention to the map, but couldn't concentrate. My internal shaking moved to my hand. I might want to reconstruct our flight path, but my emotions demanded attention.

I jumped when I heard a voice say, "Ma'am."

I looked up to see the youth in front of me, this time, with a bag in his hand. "These are for you."

I opened the paper sack and found more luscious peaches, some with leaves still attached. "Thanks so much." I raised the bag. "And for your help."

He ducked his head, reminding me of a shy two-year old. "Without your help," I said, "I'm not certain I'd have gotten my plane off the road before a car hit me."

"You wanta come over to our house?" He pointed across the road.

"No, I'll wait for my husband. He'll be here in a little while." His smile turned downward. My words rushed out. "I need to figure out what happened. Thanks, anyway."

I sat under a large nearby tree, aware of all the people who had not walked away from forced landings. I wanted Walt. I wanted him to hold me and to say everything was all right. How long would it take him to get here?

I studied the map and decided I must be near Riceboro, Georgia. There was a nearby grass strip at Darien, but Brunswick, Georgia was the closest general aviation field with services. It would be a while before Walt made it back. My parents might even get here before him, which wasn't a pleasant thought. I put the map aside and looked up to discover my helper had left.

I sat that morning under the South Georgia trees, eating a peach and thinking of my recent brush with injury. I had heard pilots tell their stories and they seemed so in control, so confident. Why then, was I still shaking inside like the leaves the breeze ruffled over my head? I had vowed not to let fear stop me, but did that include dodging cars on busy highways?

Relax, you're alive. Your plane's okay. Walt would figure it out. I closed my eyes and drifted into a healing rest.

A while later, the sound of screeching tires awakened me. Dazed, I saw my parent's brown Ford station wagon pull over to my side of the road. Little Shawn jumped up and down in the front seat and pointed my direction.

Later, Mom told me they had been driving along the highway singing "You Are My Sunshine" when Shawn had stopped in the middle of a verse and yelled, "There's Mommy. Look, there's Mommy. And the TCraft!"

"Willa, stop," my dad had shouted. "It's Sandra."

Mom stepped on the brakes, shocked to see me and my airplane on the side of the road.

I rushed to the car, pulled Shawn into my arms, and covered her with kisses. We sat beneath Tinkerbelle's wing, with me holding my daughter close as I told them of my morning's adventure. Shawn squirmed in my lap, but I didn't want to let her go. Mom and dad stole glances at each other as they listened to my tale.

"Anyone want a peach?" I passed around the bag of fruit.

Mother said, "Shawn, come here. Grandmommy will share her peach with you." Shawn obliging climbed from my lap and ran to my mom. "Maybe Granddaddy will get us something to wipe our hands on from the car." She looked at my dad who lumbered over to the station wagon. His thinning hair, excess weight, and the gray pallor of his skin made him look older than his sixty-two years. Surviving my mother's controlling nature, two heart attacks, and a life of unrealized dreams had taken its toll.

We sat for a while in silence, eating our peaches and thinking our individual thoughts. Cars continued to whiz past on the highway. At last, Mother wiped peach juice from Shawn's hands. My parents and I watched as Shawn ran around and around Tinkerbelle, finally sitting near the tail to play in the red dirt.

Mother turned her gaze to me, started to say something, but stopped. She wrestled with her Sagittarius inclination to not pull punches. After a pause, she said, "I'm really glad you're okay."

Me too, Mom, me too, I thought, but said, "Planes still fly when their engines quit."

"I know. I know. That's what your dad has always said." A truck scurried past us on the highway. She inclined her head toward the road and spoke in a quiet voice, "But this is a busy highway."

A part of me wanted to put my head in my mom's lap and let her tell me things were going to be okay. Instead, I jumped up. "Daddy, why don't you look at the plane? See if you can find anything wrong."

"Let's check the fuel in the tanks first," he said, happy to move away from the heavy emotions swirling around us.

I enjoyed sharing airplanes with my dad, happy we had something in common. My mother had always dominated my life, leaving little room for my father. He sported a perpetual cloud that hovered over his head, but it seemed to roll away when he chatted about flying. We moved to the front of Tinkerbelle.

"This is a great airplane, Sandra."

I nodded in agreement.

"They used this L-2 to spot enemy troops and supplies in the war."

"It looks a little different now, Dad."

We shared smiles as we gazed on the old military liaison airplane turned into a perky candy-apple-red, white and blue aerobatic airplane decked out in a sunburst and checkerboard paint scheme. The shiny chrome-plated rocker box covers on the cylinders of the engine peeked through the openings of the engine cowling. The bright propeller gleamed like polished silver on a sumptuous Thanksgiving table.

My dad and I were caught up in airplane stories when Shawn yelled, "There's Daddy."

A Georgia Trooper's car pulled up with Walt in the passenger seat. He smiled his lopsided grin and something settled inside of me. Everything was going to be okay. Walt had landed on the nearby Interstate highway construction site where a friendly Georgia trooper greeted his arrival. He parked the Stearman and left the engine running since it did not have a starter and would be difficult to re-start. One of the highway workers had promised to keep a watchful eye on the airplane. The trooper took Walt to get gas before coming to rescue me.

After discussing the forced landing, Walt and I agreed that it was a fuel starvation problem, one that happened twice after being in the air for at least forty minutes. We decided I would fly the airplane to a nearby grass strip where we would park the airplane until we, meaning Walt, figured out what to do. He climbed up on the strut and emptied the five gallon container of automobile fuel he brought with him.

The time came when I was to fly out of the spot I had so recently been forced into. Part of me wanted anyone but me to fly my plane off that highway, but the bigger part was determined no one but me would pilot Tinkerbelle that day. Ego, courage, or stupidity? I didn't know. My parents' looks of concern were not as powerful as the confident way that Walt looked at me. Motivation is a difficult thing to understand. Perhaps I needed to prove something to myself and others, or maybe was concerned about immersing Shawn in my negative feelings and fears.

No matter. Stomach aflutter, I climbed into Tinkerbelle, buckled myself up, and turned on the switches. Control stick back in my lap, I pushed with my heels on the brakes and yelled, "Ready."

Walt stood in front of the airplane and pulled the propeller through. The engine caught and began running. How long would it run? I hoped for at least thirty minutes, time enough to fly to the nearest landing strip. I had no idea what was wrong with the engine, but I did know the Tcraft belonged on an airport with mechanics and parts, not on the side of a busy highway.

The engine idled, never skipping a beat. Walt and the trooper stopped traffic while I taxied back onto the highway for take off. Heart pounding and with little time for reflection, I ran through my checklist. My parents stood next to their station wagon with Shawn secure in her Granddaddy's arms. She waved to me and I waved back. I pushed the throttle forward and the airplane moved down the highway-airport. Rudder pressure kept it tracking straight. I pushed forward on the elevator and the Tcraft bounced along on its main wheels as if this were a normal take off. Back with the stick, and we popped off the ground with the Continental engine purring.

I wagged my wings goodbye before flying directly to the nearest grass field. Along the way, I listened for unusual sounds from the engine, all the while searching for possible landing sites.

The next day, a local aircraft mechanic installed a new carburetor in the engine. Would this fix the TCraft's fuel problem? How safe was I, really?

JULY, 1971

13

HAROLD KRIER'S GONE

Hayti, Missouri

"Harold Krier is dead," Walt said as he walked toward me.

I dropped the sponge I was using to wash the TCraft into the bucket of soapy water next to Tinkerbelle's left tire. Suds flew into the air. The energy drained from my body and seemed to pool in the pit of my stomach. The July heat in southern Missouri, always oppressive, now felt intolerable.

Walt rushed on. "He was killed yesterday afternoon in Wichita, flight testing the prototype of Pappy Spink's new plane, the Acromaster."

"What happened?" I mumbled.

"They're not certain. Weren't any witnesses. His body was a half mile from the wreckage with a partially opened parachute." Walt shook his head. "The plane's spin chute had been torn off."

"If you're flight testing an airplane," he said, "and can't recover from a spin, then you deploy the spin chute to stop the rotation." Even now as a herald of death, the instructor in Walt wanted to teach me. "Of course, things can go wrong. The spin chute might be torn from the airplane if the structure isn't strong enough. A mini parachute opening on an airplane puts a lot of pressure…" his voice trailed away "…on the tail."

We stood looking at each other, ignoring the pesky flies, but swatting at an occasional mosquito that had wandered over from the nearby Mississippi

River.

"Remember the first time I met Harold?" I asked in a quiet church voice. "We were at Luck Field in Ft. Worth the weekend we were married." Walt nodded, but didn't speak. "He was so nice to me, taking time to encourage me about my flying."

Harold was dead. Harold, who looked like a nice middle-aged farmer, but was the aerobatic pilot's dream aviator. Harold, a pilot who flew with consummate skill and grace. Not wanting to face the reality of Walt's message, I idly questioned if I should turn off the water. The hose lay untended, water steadily flowing into rivulets and finding its way to the drain in the aircraft washing area.

In my mind's eye, I saw the calm steadiness of Harold as he prepared to fly, the graceful execution of his airshow performance, and his freely-given friendship. I remembered how he had willingly talked to Walt, first about carrying a wingrider and then about Tinkerbelle's fuel problems. Harold, the man who so generously shared his knowledge, even with competitors, was dead.

Walt's voice cut into my memories, "Maybe the plane was in some sort of flat spin and he couldn't recover. Maybe he popped the spin chute, but it was torn from the plane and then he jumped, but was too low."

An insidious notion planted itself in the fertile soil of my imagination. If Harold Krier, a U. S. aerobatic champion, the best of the best, the hero of my hero, was killed flying airplanes, what about Walt? What about me? Quickly, I banished the idea from my consciousness as if a stage curtain had fallen on an unpleasant scene.

"He was flight testing an airplane, Sandi." Walt said. He must have noticed my hesitancy, for he quickly added, "Test pilots fly the edge of the unknown. It's part of their job and dangerous."

It was true, Harold was flight testing a prototype of a new aerobatic airplane, and I was an airshow pilot and wingrider. Flight testing was more dangerous than airshow flying. Still, it occurred to me that Walt might be reassuring himself as well as me.

"Anyway," he said. "Bill Bordeleau called. Harold was scheduled to carry a girl wingrider at the Du Page Airshow in Chicago this Saturday and Sunday. Bill wanted to know if we could fly in Harold's place. Bill said someone from the show will call us."

Bill Bordeleau, an airshow announcer and owner of Continental Airshows was the reason we were in Hayti, Missouri. He had phoned us last winter in Florida and booked both the Stearman and TCraft in several of his airshows around the Midwest this summer. We had flown one of his shows in Memphis a few weeks ago and then come north to Mid-Continent Aircraft, a crop-dusting sales and maintenance facility, located in this small town in the boot heel of Missouri. Mid-Continent had a well respected aircraft maintenance shop that also restored Stearmans to better than new condition. It was a perfect place for Walt to instruct aerobatics and for us to use as a base for our Midwestern airshows during the summer months.

"Do they want me to fly Tinkerbelle?" I said.

"Just the Stearman. They already have a wingrider."

I looked at him in disbelief. "Ole Smokey," our nickname for the Stearman, "has a wingrider and it's me. We're The Flying Pierces, remember?"

"I know, I don't like it either, but Harold was scheduled to fly Patti Deck on his Great Lakes. She's been in Chicago doing publicity and has something of a following; so, they want to use her." He paused and his face went into work mode, brows coming together over eyes no longer aware of me or the surroundings. I imagined gears in his mind rotating into action as he thought through the upcoming airshow.

"Today's Wednesday," he said. "We'll leave for Chicago Friday morning or maybe Thursday afternoon. We need to wash the Stearman."

I listened, outwardly attentive as if I understood what he was saying. In fact, my thoughts were scattered, emotions flitting about unable to light on anything as I tried to make sense of Harold's death. I didn't know him well, we weren't buddies, and I wasn't a protégé, not even a close acquaintance. Much older than me, he was nearer to my parents' generation than to mine. Yet, I had taken him into me as an image, a vision of what I might someday be. Now Harold was dead with Walt flying in his place at the Du Page Airshow.

My mother's words recycled in my mind, "Sandra, it's a dangerous business, you can hurt yourself." I could see her shaking her arthritic finger at me, "You have no business flying around in these airplanes." I thought of Shawn visiting my parents in Dallas. What if it had been Walt and I, instead of Harold. What would happen to her? I longed to curl up in some darkened room and not think.

"What about Harold?" I said.

Walt looked at me as if I spoke a foreign language.

"What about his funeral?"

Walt's expression changed from a professional focus on the task at hand to a young boy's sorrow. Stripped clean of artifice, he looked open and vulnerable. For a brief moment, I saw the New Mexico boy who had followed the career of his hero, Harold Krier, and wanted to be an airshow pilot like him. At last, Walt said, "There's a memorial service in Ashland, Kansas tomorrow. That's where he grew up."

"I wish we could go," I said.

"Me, too." he put his arm around me, and we both knew it was an impossible wish. We were on our way to Chicago for an airshow. There was no time for funerals, even of a beloved hero.

Something fundamental altered inside me that day. Before, I had ignored my mother's fears and cautions. True, I may have chewed on anxious thoughts about my ability to be an airshow pilot, and lived through panic before my first flight as a wingrider, but never did I consider that Walt or I might be killed.

I had assumed that if we flew good equipment, if we practiced enough, if we stayed in control of ourselves and our airplanes, all would be just fine. That muggy Mississippi River day, it became clear to me that the best of aerobatic pilots can be in the wrong equipment at the wrong time. Like a needle, reality pricked my balloon. The balloon didn't burst, but a slow leak developed, changing forever the shape of my romantic notions of airshow life. A part of me grew up that day in southern Missouri.

Outwardly, things appeared the same. I was still happy flying airshows with no intention of quitting. Yet after Harold's death, my airshow performances contained a few feet of extra altitude and a cushion of spare speed for emergencies. I was more cautious before flying in weather, and I slowed down to look, really look, at my airplane during preflight inspections. I paid closer attention to maintenance and would eventually earn my airframe mechanics license. Walt and I always wore a parachute when we flew aerobatics, even though it wasn't required by federal rules. Nothing guaranteed our continued safety, but at least we could make our airshow flying as safe as possible.

I still did not believe I would be killed at an airshow. I never doubted that life held many experiences in store for me. Still it became my goal to stay alive. I never wanted my loved ones to hear, "Well, at least, Sandi died doing what she loved to do."

AUGUST, 1971

14

FLYING AT OSHKOSH

Wittman Field, Oshkosh, Wisconsin

Walt and I roamed airplane heaven. We were in northern Wisconsin at the annual convention of the Experimental Aircraft Association (EAA) where hundreds of airplanes and their pilots had gathered. Around us, acres and acres of unusual airplanes fanned out in all directions. Later that day, we would fly for the first time at the afternoon airshow. Any minute, I expected Paul Poberezny, founder of the organization, to rush up and say, "Who said you could perform in our airshow? Don't you know we only allow the finest, the most respected names in the airshow business to fly Oshkosh?"

I eyed Walt, but couldn't tell if he shared the jitters with me. Outwardly, he appeared his usual calm and collected self; still, he was quieter than normal. We were like country bumpkins at a state fair, only we strolled through row after row of fascinating airplanes. Like the crowds around us, we paused to read information posters hung on propellers and to share a word with the proud owner, maybe builder or designer, of the interesting airplane. Mile after mile of tiny little homebuilts, powerful war birds, gigantic World War II bombers, endless flyable antique airplanes, and innovative experimental designs filled the Wisconsin countryside on and around the Oshkosh airport.

We came to the EAA Convention at Oshkosh because Bill Bordeleau, airshow promoter and owner of Continental Airshows, had encouraged us. Bill had said, "I'll put in a good word for you. Can't guarantee anything, but maybe you'll get to fly the show."

It helped that the-powers-that-be had watched Walt perform at the DuPage airshow after Harold's death. Performers donated their flights at the EAA's evening airshows, happy to support the organization and get the publicity of flying at Oshkosh.

Following Bill's advice, we Flying Pierces had arrived the day before in the Stearman and the TCraft. Before we knew what had happened, we were scheduled to fly the wing act at the afternoon's airshow. Already, both national and international media at the convention were abuzz with talk about our husband-wife wingriding act, and we had yet to perform. What if we didn't live up to their expectations? Would we be disgraced in front of the biggest, most knowledgeable airshow audience in the world?

I shivered. Having grown up in Dallas, how could it be August with temperature in the lower fifties? I turned to Walt and said, "Gotta go. I have an interview with Tracy Pilurs, back at the airplanes. She writes for *Private Pilot Magazine*."

Walt nodded, "That Tracy is quite a woman. Women's Aerobatic Champion and airshow pilot. Built her own Smith Miniplane."

"I can't wait to meet her," I said, waved goodbye and hurried away. I didn't want to be late for my interview with this iconic woman pilot and journalist, rumored paramour of the late Harold Krier.

Walt yelled, "I'll meet you over at the planes in a couple of hours."

"OK," I yelled back.

A cacophony surrounded me as I covered the distance to where our Stearman and Tcraft sat amidst Experimental Exhibition airplanes. Overhead, the popping of small engines interspersed with the whirring, kathunks, and whooshes of the various types of planes that flew in long queues to land at the airport. These lines of incoming planes sometimes extended ten miles south to the town of Fond du Lac. I rushed past one of the many tractors that groaned through the grounds with volunteers walking alongside, picking up rocks and trash that they threw on the towed trailer. The EAA was known for its clean convention grounds.

I didn't want to be late for this interview. I knew so few women pilots, and none who flew airshows. I wanted this unknown woman to like me, to bestow words of airshow wisdom upon me, and hopefully, to become a friend.

I ran down the cornfield row of airplanes where our airplanes sat. Several people stood around my TCraft. I heard one fellow ask another onlooker. "What's this little plane?"

"This placard says it's a Taylorcraft." the second replied.

"Nope, no Taylorcraft I ever saw was tandem. You sit side-by-side in TCrafts."

A silver-haired woman, who I guessed to be Tracy, also studied my airplane. She turned to the two fellows and said, "It's an L-2 Taylorcraft, built as a liaison airplane. L-2s are tandem. In the BC-12D Models, the pilot and passenger sit side-by-side."

The two men nodded their heads and moved on to look at the Stearman.

I rushed up. "Are you Tracy Pilurs?"

She nodded. "You must be sandi pierce, with all small letters. Why in the world do you use all small letters?" I started to respond and she said, "No. No. Wait a minute, let's sit down and get my tape recorder going before you answer that."

She spread a plaid blanket on the ground and motioned for me to sit next to her. Tracy looked more like a grandmother than an airshow pilot and journalist for a national aviation publication. Was she really involved with Harold? Something about her seemed more sophisticated than the man who looked like a farmer from Kansas.

After a few minutes of getting settled, she said, "Testing, testing." Her fingers flew over the tape recorder as she checked to make certain the machine worked properly. Once again, she pressed the "on" button. "Tracy here, with sandi pierce—that's all small letters, of The Flying Pierces Airshow Team—flying is written upside down. We're at the EAA's Annual Convention in Oshkosh, sitting between Walt's big bull Stearman and sandi's petite Taylorcraft. The ground is cool and the temperature falling and it's another frosty summer day in Wisconsin." She turned to me, "God, why didn't the EAA move this fly-in to Alaska so it could be even colder?"

She shrugged her shoulders as if the world were inexplicable and asked, "Now, answer my question. Why all small letters on your name?"

"I probably read too much e. e. cummings," I said and chuckled. No doubt, the lower case poet had an impact on me. After reading his work last winter, I had affectedly begun writing my name without capitalization. I later found that the press loved this. Interviewers always asked about it. Although at times, especially after a few beers in the evening, I admitted to myself that I often felt very small case in an all-caps world.

A feeling of excitement seemed to dance around my interviewer. Her intriguing blue eyes held my gaze and probed my being. I guessed her to be younger than her silver hair suggested. Certainly she was ages older than me, probably in her early fifties, closer to my mom's generation than mine. Yet her skin looked younger than my mom's, smoother with fewer wrinkle lines. Her lilac sweatshirt made her hair even whiter and drew attention to the crystal blue depths of her eyes. The baggy dungarees and loose denim jacket she wore seemed in opposition to her cultured voice and self-assurance.

I wanted to ask her questions. Did you really love Harold? What was it like building your own airshow airplane? What advice would you give to me, a beginner in this business?

Her crisp words piled up like tiny skyscrapers against a clear horizon and, compared to my Texas twang filled with honey and salsa, I felt like an oaf who didn't belong. My stomach was queasy and I knew I had to do something. I asked, "Have you always lived in Chicago?" Maybe if I got to know her better, I wouldn't feel so inadequate.

"Who's interviewing whom?" She said, and stopped the recorder. "I was raised in the Northeast, New York, but I've lived in Chicago for years."

I started to ask how she came to Chicago, but her words stopped me. "Time enough for that later. I'm the columnist, I ask the questions. You're the airshow pilot, you answer. OK?"

The press tags dangling from Tracy's neck and the camera resting against her leg reminded me of my current objective, getting publicity for The Flying Pierces Airshow. She seemed nice enough, just a woman on a mission.

I tried to feel equal to the aviation legend beside me, a difficult task in my current nervous state. After all, Tracy had once been the Women's National Aerobatic Champion and, as Walt had said, was renowned for building a delightful homebuilt biplane called "The Pretty Purple Putty Tat." I remembered the picture I had seen in an aviation magazine of the small biplane, white with purple butterfly sunburst on the wings. It had a control stick covered with fawn-colored mink, and a fake amethyst jewel rested atop the plane's oil cap. No wonder I was excited.

She punched the recorder on. "sandi, what made you become an airshow pilot and wingrider?"

My racing heart slowed as I went into my now familiar airshow spiel. "Love, Tracy, pure and simple. I loved flying and I loved Walt. Before I knew it, I was flying the TCraft upside down in airshows and hanging off the wing of the Stearman."

"Walt must be some powerful guy."

I nodded in response; snuggling into my blue knit jacket, part of our current airshow uniform. It sported a checkerboard design running down the sleeves, my name embroidered on the front, and The Flying Pierces in giant red letters on the back.

The media version of The Flying Pierces Airshow Team was true, not strictly a public relations fantasy. Still, it had metamorphosed into a slick presentation punctuated with appropriate humor and a touch of modesty. My past may have been a raging river overflowing the banks of my life, but the press preferred a courageous warrior who marched bravely into great adventure. I played to their fantasies, which were partially true. I might feel like a hick from Texas, but I talked a good game and performed feats most people were unwilling to do.

"You have a daughter?" she asked.

"We sure do. Her name is Shawn Dell, named for the aerobatic maneuver the chandelle. She's in Dallas with my parents."

Tracy looked at me intently. "Has to be hard to leave her?"

I nodded. "She travels with us a lot, but if we think the schedule will be too demanding on her, she stays with my mom and dad. She really loves them a lot."

Tracy asked about my airplane. "What engine do you have on the TCraft?"

"An eighty-five, but we're going to install a 100-horse Continental this winter."

She smiled, "We pilots always want more horsepower. What about the center of gravity?"

She had asked a critical question. If we put a bigger engine with more weight up front, wouldn't the balance of the plane in the air become unstable and dangerous? I said, "I'll start flying from the rear seat instead of up front where I solo now. With a hundred horses, she'll climb like a homesick angel."

We sat in silence, two pilots lost in dreams of airplanes that rocketed skyward, unfettered by gravity and the mortality of mere humans.

I broke the quiet, "We've already added steel tubing inside the struts for the extra stresses of aerobatics."

"She's a beauty," she said more to herself than me.

For the remainder of the interview we discussed the growth of the airshow industry and the niche The Flying Pierces filled. I shared our future plans to hire a parachutist/stuntman to travel as part of our team. Tracy listened, interjecting occasional questions, always moving the interview along. At last, she popped the "off" button on the recorder. Chuckling with a mixture of childish glee and adult cynicism, she said, "People say you can't make a living in the airshow business. I hope you show them."

Her face had a determined look of taking on the world. "Maybe my article will help. It'll be out in the spring next year."

"Publicity always helps." I said, and then curiosity took control of my mouth. "How old are you?"

A Mona Lisa smile lit her face. "Old enough to be your mother." Her blue eyes looked straight into mine as if about to impart the grand design of life. "sandi, remember," I could see her mental finger in my face, "A woman should never tell her age."

"Why not?" I answered. "I don't mind saying I'm going to be twenty-seven this September."

She laughed. "If I were going to be twenty-seven, I might not mind telling either."

"Oh come on. At least tell me your birthday," I said.

"I was born in December," she answered as if a reluctant witness facing a persistent interrogator.

"My mom's birthday is in December."

"How does she like your flying?" I saw her body relax as the spotlight turned away from her to my mom.

"Not much." I leaned forward and she pulled back slightly. Hmm, I thought, this woman doesn't want to be touched, to have anyone come close. "Mother is happy that I love what I do and she certainly enjoys the publicity, but…but, she worries that I'll be hurt." What an understatement. My mom hated what I did and prayed for a day when I would no longer be an airshow pilot. Fat chance, mother!

Tracy stuffed the recorder into her tote bag. "Non-aviators just don't understand. My husband had no clue why a married woman with six kids wanted to fly. I finally realized he would never comprehend what flying meant to me." She hung the camera around her neck and looked at me. "Of course, we got a divorce," she shrugged, "but you can't divorce your mother."

What made the difference between my mom and the woman in front of me? I guessed they were within ten years of age, and each seemed equally enthusiastic about life. Both were outspoken, words bursting from their mouths that would have been better left unsaid. However Tracy, mother of six, charged into new experiences with courage while my mom was often fearful and anxious. Tracy saw excitement in my airshow flying while my mom imagined only death. On the other hand, my mom freely shared her hugs and laughed about her age while Tracy maintained her distance.

Perhaps it was the mystery surrounding Tracy or her wry wit that captivated me, but, in spite of her guarded stance, I definitely liked her. I hesitated before I said, "I'm a bit overwhelmed. It's all happening so fast." I lowered my voice, "I have the jitters. It's our first performance here tonight. What if we screw up?"

She patted my arm. "The EAA is lucky to have you two fly. My God, sandi, you're performing for free." Her voice seemed stronger although the volume remained the same. "You have the world by the tail, kiddo, and you're doing just fine. You're living every pilot's dream."

She was right. I was living a pilot's dream, a dream for which I had paid dearly with the unplanned loss of a marriage and child. I brushed away the sadness that came whenever I thought of my first child. I was performing at Oskhosh, living my dream. It had never occurred to me that I would be so worried about people's approval.

We stood and folded the blanket which she then stuffed into the tote bag. Tracy looked skyward. "It may rain today."

I glanced at the lowering clouds and sighed. "We can always do slow rolls and inverted passes across the field even with low clouds, but if it rains…" I shook my head, "If it rains, we won't do the Wing Act."

"Why not?" Tracy looked puzzled.

"It hurts too much. The rain feels like needles piercing my skin. The faster the plane flies, the deeper the needles go."

"Then clear skies this evening," she said, and smiled. "Mind if I sit on the flight line with you during the show?"

Without thinking, I touched her arm and this time, she didn't draw away. Hmm, maybe we could be friends. I said, "It'll be fun to have you with us." Tracy gathered her things and I watched her rush off for another interview.

Later that afternoon, it was airshow time. If anything, I was more nervous than before. From the flight line, I watched as people gathered for the upcoming show. I knew they had emptied from the exhibits and workshops, moved away from the concession stands and porta-potties to amble through the gates for the afternoon airshow. They left behind spectators who didn't wear convention badges around their necks which allowed them into the airplane area. Members of EAA gathered in groups and sat on the ground in front of the rows of airplanes. Others lounged under their planes and watched the show. A few select pilots and media gathered around the airshow planes as the airshow performers did preflights, added fuel or smoke oil, adjusted costumes, and got ready to work.

The bellowing engines of the World War II airplanes filled the air with smoke and the sound of blasting fake bombs. The chaos of the war re-enactments matched my inner world. What if these special spectators didn't like us? Would our newly realized airshow dreams vanish if we weren't good enough?

The old bombers flew simulated runs along the runway while fighter planes whooshed around them. Gradually, my attention was drawn into the pretend battle. As Messerschmitts and Mustangs vied for position in the skies, we pilots and wannabes became lost in imaginary battles for our lives. We were Snoopy in mortal combat with the Red Baron in his Fokker Tri-plane or Jimmy Stewart giving his all to defend freedom.

I stood alone in front of the Stearman's wing. Tracy and Walt sat to one side, on the same plaid blanket from the morning's interview, engrossed in conversation and oblivious to the simulated war. I smiled at my husband dressed in airshow-day glory. His blue jacket matched mine and I saw the edge of the small American flag over his left shirt pocket with part of his name showing under the flag. A friend once kidded that Walt probably had his underwear embroidered with his name in red or blue.

I pulled on long silver gloves that matched my silver go-go boots. Goose bumps from the cool air stood up on my arms, and I quickly put my blue Flying Pierces jacket over the shiny red, white, and blue wingriding outfit.

Overhead, World War II had ended and three red biplanes, tiny Pitts Specials, now zipped off the runway in formation, puffing clouds of smoke. Bill Bordeleau's voice blasted from sound system speakers and echoed across the field. "Look overhead. See that dot high in the sky? Any moment now, a jumper will fling himself out of the jump plane."

I saw a speck dropped into the skies from a high-wing airplane. Plummeting earthward, the speck became a person unfurling a flag with red smoke trailing. The national anthem played, and spectators lumbered to their feet. Hats off, they placed their hands over their hearts. Some sang along with the recorded music. I belted out the national anthem and looked skyward where the three red biplanes circled the jumper with the American flag flying behind him. Heart filled to overflowing, my eyes became moist. I was an American, part of the human race fortunate to live in a country where I had freedom to pursue my dreams. Yes, and freedom to worry about failure.

The music ended and though I couldn't see him, I knew the jumper had made a stand-up landing center stage in front of the crowd. Pitts Special biplanes roared up and down the runway through a series of formation aerobatics. It seemed like only a few days ago that I learned to fly in Austin and now I was at Oshkosh, performing with some of the best aerobatic pilots in the world. Bob Heuer, airline pilot and founder of the new International Aerobatic Club, up and coming young airshow pilot Gene Soucy, the Cole brothers, Duane and Marion, Charlie Hilliard, Bob Hoover,

Ed Mahler, Art Scholl, Nick Rezik, Bobby Bishop, the list went on and on, were part of that illustrious group. No wonder I was stressed out.

Walt ambled up to my side. "Time to get ready."

"I guess," I said and looked up at him. "Are you as scared as I am?"

He smiled his crooked grin. "We'll take off after Lyjak lands. I'll stay low down the runway and then climb to 1500 to begin the show sequence."

How could he talk so easily about Bob Lyjak, the renowned Taperwing Waco pilot? Wasn't he as impressed as I was? I took a deep breath and punched his arm. "Can you believe it? We're about to fly at Oshkosh."

"Time to put on the harness," he said, ignoring my comment. I followed him to the left side of the airplane where I took off my jacket and slid my arms into a red harness made of parachute webbing that snugged the upper portion of my body, blending with my wing-riding costume. What if our act didn't measure up? The thought stopped my breath for a moment.

A man, wearing an EAA T-shirt, came up to us and said, "It's time."

Up to the top of the wing, for a second I paused, and then waved at Tracy who stood below taking pictures. Walt followed me atop the wing. He handed me my red helmet and goggles before fastening the belt attached to the wingstand around my waist. Snap went the cables holding the bottom of my harness to the airplane. A final tug on the belt around my waist and Walt leaned down to kiss me.

"Ahhh," I heard from the crowd behind me amidst the snapping sound of cameras taking pictures. I half-turned to wave at the crowd and the many photographers, as Walt made his way back to the cockpit.

The Stearman waddled down the grass in front of the crowd line. Overhead, Lyjak flew his white with red-and-black trimmed Taperwing Waco. I rode atop the wing, head turned skyward watching the pro fly.

Bill Bordeleau's voice boomed from the speakers along the crowd
line. "There he goes folks, Bob Lyjak twisting and turning into the Polish
Centrifuge. Whoooooaaaa, how would you like to be up there with him?"

I chuckled to myself. In most airshow crowds' the response would be
"No," but here at Oshkosh, the answer would be a resounding "Yes! Just let
me loose."

I waved to the people along the crowd line and felt my hair ruffling
in the breeze. Did the crowd really like blonde hair better than my natural
brunette color? Walt had talked me into dying my hair, but I thought he
was the one, not the crowds, who preferred blondes.

Bill's voice broke into my thoughts, "There goes sandi and Walt
Pierce, The Flying Pierces. The only husband-wife airshow team in the
business. They have a cute little daughter named Shawn Dell. That's right
folks, named her after the aerobatic maneuver, the chandelle." Bill's patter
continued as we taxied.

"Hey sandi." I listened more closely as Bill spoke to me over the
speakers.

"You gonna be cold up there?"

With exaggerated moves, I wrapped my silver-gloved arms around my
body as if to give it warmth.

I sent mental thanks to Bill. He was the guy who had helped make this
happen. Thank you Bill, thank you for telling the Oshkosh powers that we
were a good act, a safe act, and a couple of nice kids to boot.

We taxied to the end of the runway and I put on my red helmet,
adjusted the black ski goggles, and tucked stray bits of blonde hair back
where it belonged. As Walt readied for take off, I watched Lyjak coming
in for landing. He whooshed by and the vintage Waco settled onto the
concrete runway. As it moved down the runway, I saw the gold Polish

Crest painted on a red background in the middle of the upper wing.
Walt taxied Ole Smokey to the center of the runway and I looked down
at my silver boots resting atop the red sunburst paint that went out to each
wingtip. I smiled, still feeling a bit like Wonder Woman. Back to reality,
I made a mental note of where the crowd was in relation to the runway. I
didn't want to wave and have no one see it.

The Stearman lumbered forward, slowly gathering speed. I smelled the
acrid odor of burning oil and knew we were blanketing the runway with
white puffy smoke, covering anyone unlucky enough to be on the ground
behind us. I flung out both arms and drug my left arm back and forth
waving to the crowd as I fought the wind pressure. We raced the length
of the runway and then whump. I was pushed into the wing with a force
four times my weight as the Stearman pulled up vertically at the end of the
airshow flight line.

The plane climbed quickly to 1500 feet while I peered like a tourist
at the spectacular view. Below, Lake Winnebago nestled to the east of the
airport. The rain clouds had moved to Michigan, leaving cold air in their
wake, but the adrenaline pumped in my body and kept me warm. From my
birds-eye view, I saw a cluster of general aviation facilities across the runway
from the convention grounds. A tent city filled with campers occupied
the north end of the airport. Fields of automobiles hedged the airport
boundaries and beyond that, an emerald landscape rolled to the horizon
with occasional dots of blue silos. It might be cold, but I liked how the
Wisconsin countryside looked from the top of a wing.

It was true that Walt, snug in his open cockpit, saw the same sights; yet,
I fancied my view more panoramic. It definitely was more exciting. I stood
atop an airplane that seemed so big on the ground, but in the air was like a
small boat bobbing on a vast ocean. Even though I was already tired from

my resistance to the wind that beat upon me, I still enjoyed looking at the world from my perch.

Time to work. My job was to endure to the end of our act and wave to the crowd at the appropriate times. We lined up on the southern end of the airshow flight line and dive-bombed the runway, gaining airspeed and more wind pressure. Slammed back into the brace, I lowered my head into the wind to keep it from being blown backward, and flung out my arms. I waved so people on the ground would see my movement and know I was alive, a human being like them and not an inert dummy. Inwardly I chuckled, certain that a few people on the ground considered me a dummy for being the wingrider instead of the pilot.

Marketing research done on airshow crowds discovered that spectators identified with parachutists and wing acts. Unlike pilots hidden in cockpits, these performers could be seen and their movements discerned. Spectators watched the moving bodies and imagined what it would be like to ride the wing or float earthward under a canopy.

The Stearman looped, rolled, and hammerheaded through our airshow sequence while I struggled against the wind, all the while attempting to conserve my energy. My goal was to climb down to the ground after our act with enough oomph to greet the crowd and sign autographs.

At last, Walt roared toward the runway, leveled out 100 feet above the ground, and rolled the plane upside down. I bounced against my back brace and flung out my arms as I hung below the airplane, weight resting on my shoulder harness. My boots lifted from the wing and I pushed them up to keep them secure against the airplane's surface. I didn't need to have them touching the wing, but it made me feel better. Concrete whizzed above my head as I focused on waving the correct arm to the crowd. The physical beating my body suffered left little room for emotion. I rode the wing most weekends at airshows and no longer considered how close my head was to the runway nor the danger involved in what I did. I had learned that humans can get used to nearly anything.

I sighed as we came in for landing, thankful the beating of the wind had slowed. I rested against the wingstand at my back, and, after we landed quickly unsnapped the cables that attached my harness to the wing. Removing my helmet, I shook my blond hair free. Taxiing along the crowd line to our parking spot, I pivoted slightly to wave at the fans that now clapped and waved back.

We did it! We flew at Oshkosh! I felt like a combination of prima ballerina, conquering matador, and Lindbergh arriving in Paris. When the propeller stopped turning, I unhooked the belt holding me to the wingstand and turned to wave at the crowd, my crowd.

Tracy, over to one side, snapped a picture and then gave me a thumbs-up signal.

*Ole Smokey zooms upward
with sandi on wing*

*Robert Chad LeBeau
makes the American
Flag Jump, 1972*

sandi gets ready to fly her Great Lakes, MiCasa, 1974

sandi flies clipped Tcraft with Juarez Mountains in background, El Paso, 1977

Walt waves to the crowd from the wing of Ole Smokey

GREAT AMERICAN AIR SHOW

P. O. Box 854
Altamonte Springs, Fla. 32701
Phone: (305) 831 - 0803

The Great American Airshow left to right
Lindsey Hess, sandi, Bob Yde (leaning on Pitts), Walt Pierce,
Sky King Kirby Grant, Parachutist Bill Wilkinson, Jim Holland

*sandi signs
autograph after
wingriding act*

*Sandi with opened
parachute in front of
Citabria, Sebring,
Florida, 1969*

Doug Champlin, owner Great Lakes Aircraft Company and sandi in front of her new Great Lakes, Enid, Oklahoma

sandi stop facing backwards on wing and took the picture of Walt in cockpit with Milwaukee, Wisconsin in background

The Mike Douglas TV Show. Mike Douglas interviewing sandi and Walt after they performed the Wing Act live on the show. Sea World, Ohio, 1972

John Patton, Blue Angel narrator, after flight withsandi in Great Lakes. John had taken sandi up in the two place TA4 Skyhawk in background, 1974

*Airshow day, sandi has removed the front
cockpit cover on her Great Lakes*

sandi in front of her 150 hp Clipped TCraft

The Flying Pierces on What's My Line with Larry Blyden,
1972, New York City

Chandelle and sandi decked out for Christmas Parade,
Avon Park, Florida

*Chandelle on the wing of
Mommy's Tcraft*

*Chandelle already
comfortable hanging on
to the strut of Daddy's
Stearman*

*Sandi climbed on top of Ole Smokey and Chandelle was on the
bottom wing of Walt's airplane for a photo shoot, 1989*

*Chandelle, wingwalker, on strut of Walt's Stearman, while Lorraine
Gillette rides the top wing. Sonny Everett's Wildcats Airshow, 1989*

*Wingwalker, Chandelle
Pierce (Shawn) in her
Wildcats' wingwalking
outfit, 1989, Florida*

*Magazine Cover,
National Aeronautics
Association, 1974*

sky diver

MARCH, 1973 • 50¢

THE INTERNATIONAL MAGAZINE OF PARACHUTING

Stuntman/Parachutist Bob LeBeau was suspended from a ladder below sandi's TCraft, opened his parachute and was pulled off the ladder. Sebring, Florida, 1972. Appeared on Sky Diver Magazine, 1973

APRIL, 1972

15

NEW YORK CITY GAMESHOWS

New York City

"Let's have fun fooling the panel," said Garry Moore, the same man I had watched for years with Carol Burnett on television. Like much of America, my family had faithfully tuned to *The Garry Moore Show* and *I've Got A Secret*. And now, Garry was talking to me and the two imposters who would pretend to be me on the game show, *To Tell The Truth*.

It was only April, but already this was my second major encounter with the celebrity world. Just a month earlier, Walt and I had flown an airshow in Sarasota, Florida where William Shatner, Captain Kirk of *Star Trek* fame, was a celebrity announcer. The *Star Trek* series was over, but Shatner had a loyal group of fans in Gulf Coast, Florida who the airshow promoters hoped would turn out to see him. I had watched the series, heard the prima donna rumors, and now looked forward to finding out what Shatner was really like.

At the pre-show briefing, he listened quietly, showed interest in the airshow, and at last, asked about the acts we would perform. Even though he exuded a rugged masculinity befitting a starship captain who "went where no man had gone before," that morning he was simply a performer wanting to provide the best show for the audience. After the briefing, we discussed my wingriding and he laughed and shook his head, making a comment on my sanity.

We performers left the room, walking between reporters and cameras ready to interview the Captain of the U. S. S. Enterprise. I turned back and saw William Shatner, now the Shakespearean actor, taller, more commanding, charismatic, and definitely Captain of the ship.

Now I was in New York City, roaming streets on which Deborah Kerr had run to meet Gary Grant, beat poets changed literature, and fashion models paraded. Dallas, where I was raised and had considered the most sophisticated city in the state, suddenly seemed to be a one-horse town in the wide open spaces of a western movie. How could I, sandi-pierce-all-lower-case, be in the Mecca of stylishness and on national television? I had never been to New York City or even to the state and somehow, I didn't feel ready for it. Part of me longed to be only a tourist. Who was I, anyway? It was a question that troubled me lately. Was I the fearless wingrider and airshow pilot or simply an imposter, pretending like the two women who stood next to me?

Goodson-Todman Production Company had telephoned a month earlier to ask me to be a contestant on their three-year-old quiz show, *To Tell The Truth*. Quiz shows were hot and this was one of the most popular. Of course, I was excited. It was good for business, a new experience, and an opportunity to play tourist in New York City. I kept reminding myself that I had done publicity on local television for most of our airshows; the television camera was no stranger. Yet, inside me this felt very different than our routine airshow publicity. Also, they wanted only me, not Walt. The thought of being alone in New York City doing a national show seemed too much for me to handle, so I invited my mom to join the adventure.

In the studio, the colorful set was painted in swirls of blue, purple, teal, pink, and orange decorated with images of the *To Tell The Truth* logo.

Multiple images of a man standing, one hand raised as if swearing in court but with his fingers crossed, covered the walls and the curtain. The set was nearly psychedelic and very much in keeping with the popular Beatles mania.

Garry Moore, host of the show, had stopped to greet us before the filming began. He was short with receding reddish-brown hair and a touch of gray on the sides. He wore a muted-brown patterned suit with a green and black tie and looked the same as he had appeared on my television set. His friendly smile made me feel more at home.

"You ready?" he said. My imposters and I nodded.

I couldn't tell his age; only that he was much older than me, but still seemed young in spirit. He sported a fatherly smile when he said, "Which one of you is the wingrider?"

"I am."

"Some people are really crazy," he said and shook his head. He walked to the edge of the curtain and turned back for a moment. "Have fun!"

Have fun? My first appearance on national television and he wanted me to have fun?

The sound stage was smaller than I expected. Lights cluttered the floor and hung from above. Large cameras on dollies stood in front of us. Hard New York accents filled the air in contrast to the delightful sherbet-colored set. People scurried around the stage intent on doing their jobs.

I felt as soft as my Texas drawl, different from and out of sync with the action. It reassured me to know that my mom sat beyond the confusion, hidden in the darkness and anonymity of the live studio audience who had been herded into two sections of elevated movie-theater rows. Their conversations swelled in volume at the excitement of being part of a national quiz show, even if only as spectators. I smiled, thinking that my mom probably knew everything about the people next to her and had shared all my triumphs since grade school with them. She seemed to know who I was, why didn't I? I felt like the great pretender. I pretended bravery when I felt anxious. I had pretended to not mind when I left Shawn for blocks of time during airshow season. The truth was, I had missed her terribly. I pretended that not seeing my daughter lost in marriage didn't bother me.

Standing on that stage, I recognized how much my anxiety had dropped to a manageable level after my mom had appeared at the Sheraton Manhattan the previous morning with a bellman in tow. She stood only four-feet-eleven inches when she stretched and recently walked with a metal cane-crutch she called her "pogo stick." She told the bellman, "Put my luggage over there and stay with it."

I was amazed that the New Yorker smiled and did as he was told, remaining a faithful guardian of two mustard-yellow Samsonite suitcases and one matching overnight case. I crossed the hotel lobby to greet her.

"You think you brought enough clothes for two days in New York?"

She looked sheepish, and shook her head. "I know. I know. Your dad said the same thing." She looked me up and down and I felt as if I were being evaluated for a major acting job. Fortunately, I got the part. "Oh Sandra, I'm so excited. Can you believe, New York City?"

The bellman followed us to our room, happy to assist my mom and even appreciative of her meager tip. I was always amazed that people liked my mother, while I found her criticalness and desire to run my life difficult to bear. Still, I had to admit that although my mother was bossy and fault-finding, she was fond of almost everyone. She would listen to them and their stories, never sparing her advice, and in turn, they enjoyed doing things for the sixtyish, semi-handicapped woman.

The bellman placed the bags where my mom directed. Goodbyes over, I closed the door.

She said, "He's from the Bronx, has a wife and three kids, one with cerebral palsy. His mama lives with them, too." She smiled her cat-licking-her-lips grin, "I think that's why he liked me. I remind him of his mama." Pausing only for breath, she continued, "OK, where are we going? Do I need to dress up?"

Her excitement rubbed off on me as we crammed the remainder of the day with every tourist thing we could find. Her enthusiasm buoyed my sagging confidence and, for a while, I felt as great as my Mama thought I was.

All that had come to a halt this morning when a severe case of pre-show jitters drove my assurance underground. Fortunately for my nerves, the show's format was simple. A guest who had an interesting career or accomplishment was introduced along with two imposters. Neither the audience nor the panel knew the identity of the "real" challenger. The panel had less than one minute each to ask the trio a series of questions. At the end of the questioning, they voted on the identity of the real person. The television audience at home played along, guessing who they thought was bogus and who was real.

The bright lights boiled the air around us as we were shown spots on the stage for the opening of our segment. Behind us, the backdrop was of a blue sky with clouds. How appropriate, I thought as my stomach churned. I wished I was flying in that sky. My shoulders felt more tense and rigid than on airshow days. Airshow flying, even riding the wing, was easier than this.

The two women who would pretend to be me were also in their twenties; one a beauty contestant for Miss Staten Island and the other, a wig salesperson with an upper-class accent. They had been chosen for this segment because they had flown in small airplanes, a rarity for people living in the New York City area. I had spent a couple of hours the day before briefing them, answering their many questions while trying to keep it simple. The panel and audience wouldn't be told I was a pilot until after my identity was shared, which made it harder for the panel. A pilot would know more about aviation than a wingrider.

The two challengers' goal was to convince the panel they were me, while my job was to pretend to be someone pretending to be me and therefore, fool the panel and win the game. If we fooled the entire panel, we would divide $500.00; otherwise we would receive $50.00 for each incorrect vote and small prizes from the show's sponsors.

A woman wearing a headset came by and told us that the show was about to begin. She moved us to one side of the stage where we were hidden from the audience. The curtain parted and I heard the familiar theme song as Garry Moore walked out and introduced the panelists. After they settled behind their desk and the audience quieted, he said, "You've heard of the daring young man on the flying trapeze. Well his daring is nothing compared to the intrepid young lady we'll meet in a moment. Look at this film."

I couldn't see the film, but knew it showed me atop the wing of the Stearman taking off from the Sebring, Florida airport. The girl with the headset moved us challengers into position on the darkened stage behind a now closed curtain.

Garry Moore then said, "I've heard of economy tickets, but this is ridiculous." The panel and audience laughed. "She finally did get down off that wing. Matter of fact, she's standing on her own two feet. Let's meet her."

The curtain parted and bright light flooded the stage. The three of us moved forward to our marked positions where the audience and TV camera could see us better. The announcer's voice boomed like God from above, "Number One, what is your name please."

Number One, the wig salesperson with dark hair and about my height, said, "My name is sandi pierce."

"Number Two?" the announcer asked. The curvaceous Miss Staten Island contestant said, "My name is sandi pierce."

"Number Three?" I answered in my Texas accent, "My name is sandi pierce." I saw myself in the monitor to one side of the camera, wearing a red pants suit that covered my white go-go boots. The sleeves of my white blouse with red polka-dots flowed from the vest. My teased and sprayed blonde hair flipped up over my shoulders, just like Sandra Dee's. We continued to stand while Garry Moore read my affidavit and the camera panned to each of us.

He read, "I, sandi pierce, love to ride *on* airplanes. When I say *on*, I mean *on*, not *in*. I am what is known as a wingrider." The film started again on the monitor and showed me on top of the Stearman as it slow rolled and continued into our airshow routine. The panelist's voices blended as they commented, "Oh my God," "I could never do that," along with oohs and aahs from the game show audience.

All the while, Garry Moore continued reading, "At various airshows around the country, I am strapped to the upper wing of a 450 Stearman biplane, and there I stand while the plane executes a series of aerobatic maneuvers. While the aircraft goes through loops, slow rolls, Cuban eights, hammerhead stalls and even flies upside down, my job is to keep smiling and wave at the crowd watching below on the ground. The worst thing I can say about wingriding is that it gets pretty chilly, and very, very windy, but I never get frightened. You see, I have great faith in the man at the controls of the plane. He's my husband. Signed: sandi pierce."

As the theme song played, my two imposters and I made our way to the desk where we sat, ready to stump the panel. Garry Moore said, "That would be a tough act to do the day after you had a fight with your husband."

The commercial break went quickly and Garry Moore opened the next segment saying, "Let's start the questioning with Bill Cullen, who does all his flying inside an airplane."

"And I intend to keep it that way." Bill Cullen, in his fifties, peered at us through horned-rim glasses. I knew this panelist had the most knowledge and could easily trip the imposters if he asked the right questions. In spite of having polio as a kid, he had learned to fly and often talked about airplanes and his love of aviation on the show. He was dressed in camera-friendly colors: blue sport coat, purple shirt, and yellow and purple rep tie.

It didn't surprise me that he began his questions with Number Two; she was the beauty-queen hopeful and looked most like a glamorous wingrider. "Number Two," he said, "Why do they call your Stearman a 450?"

Great question, I thought, but one that I anticipated and had covered in the briefing. Number Two answered, "It's the horsepower of the engine."

I smiled inwardly. Number Two had passed the test. Maybe we would confuse the panel.

Bill's questions continued, grilling first one of us and then another. "Who makes the engine?" "What is a Waco?" Then, he asked Number One, the wig salesperson, "Is the engine a radial or a rotary?"

Oh no, I never thought to discuss rotary engines with the imposters. The Gnome and LeRhone Rotary engines were used in World War I and had cylinders that rotated around the crankshaft. Our Stearman had a radial engine where the nine cylinders were in a circle or radius around the crankshaft, but they remained stationary. Both the radial and rotary were in contrast to the horizontally opposed placement of cylinders on modern aircraft engines.

The silence seemed to last forever as Number One decided how to answer the question. She said, "A rotary engine."

In an instant, one of the imposters had been ruled out for Bill Cullen. Still, I doubted that the other panelists had any idea what he had asked, neither caring nor knowing about radial versus rotary engines. That was about to change with the next question. Bill Cullen said, "Number Two, how often does you husband have his engine overhauled?"

She answered, "Oh, very often, after every airshow."

Oh no, I couldn't believe Number Two's answer. The Pratt and Whitney engine on the Stearman was overhauled every 1,000 to 1,200 hours and such an overhaul cost thousands of dollars. Even cars went at least 100,000 miles between overhauls. Surely, every one on the panel recognized the error of this answer. In a few brief questions, the owl-looking Bill Cullen had ruled out the two imposters. This man was good at his job, while still being charming and smart. The buzzer rang and the questioning moved on to Kitty Carlisle.

Kitty Carlisle was very much the sophisticated New Yorker, dressed in a floor length dress made of gold brocade with a fur-trimmed neckline. Her accent was cultured and her presence on a quiz show didn't quite fit. She began, "I don't care about all those airplane questions. I want to know about the personal equation." She looked over at us. "Number Two, do you and your husband ever fight?"

I couldn't believe it. Kitty Carlisle hadn't given up on the second contestant. Didn't women in New York have any concept of when engines where overhauled? She zeroed in on the family life asking questions more personal in nature. "If you fought with your husband would you feel uneasy going up with him?" "How long have you been married?"

The buzzer rang and next to question us was Larry Blyden. From watching the show, I knew that Larry was a guest panelist not always on the show. He was dressed similar to Bill Cullen, and I guessed him to be a few years younger. He wore a blue sports coat, blue shirt, and checkered tie. He also sported horn-rimmed glasses and started his questioning immediately. "Number Two, what do you do with your skin and hair?" He peppered all of us with questions that we answered correctly. "How fast does the plane go?" "Do you hold your breath?" "How long have you been doing this?"

It was the flaming redhead Peggy Cass' turn. I had seen her in *Bells Are Ringing* at the State Fair Music Hall in Dallas when I was a college student and was in awe of her talent. I couldn't believe I was on the same television show with these famous people. She wore black pants with an orange vest over an ivory shirt. I was no expert on accents, but she sounded like she was from the Bronx or Brooklyn. "Number Three, what did your family think when you took up this kind of work?"

I answered, thinking of my mom out in the audience, "They didn't like it very much."

Peggy Cass said, "I can't believe you've got the guts to do it. Number three, do you glue your feet down?" She continued asking questions about the actual act of wingriding and the imposter's answers became confused. By the time the buzzer sounded, the imposters, the panel, and the audience had little idea how the wingrider stayed on the airplane. At last, Garry Moore asked the panel to vote for who they thought was the "Real sandi pierce."

Bill Cullen, Larry Blyden and Peggy Cass voted for me and Kitty Carlisle voted for Number One. Garry Moore said, "Will the real sandi pierce please stand up." My imposters fumbled around and moved as if they were going to stand while the panel and audience waited to find out the identity of the crazy gal who rode on airplane wings.

Later, Walt and I both would appear on the game show, *What's My Line*, and even fly and be interviewed on *The Mike Douglas Show*. No future television appearance would stir such a feeling of accomplishment as when I pushed back my stage chair on *To Tell The Truth*, and the real sandi pierce stood up.

JUNE, 1972

16

TRANSPO '72

Dulles International Airport, near Washington, D.C.

"There he goes. Up, up, up into the sky. Stuntman and Australian Birdman, Robert Harris Kennedy. Watch as the car tows him into the air." The announcer's voice echoed down the lengthy crowd line.

"Who's the Australian Birdman?" I asked Walt as we made our way down a lane in the Business Center area of Transpo '72.

"Some guy who rides in a chair under a large kite while a car tows him."

I shook my head in disbelief. "How did that kind of act ever get booked here?"

"Beats me."

Acres of Dulles International Airport land had been turned into a transportation theme park. We were part of an elite aerial show, Transpo '72, the first aviation exposition and international transportation exhibition put on by the United States government. It was an honor to have been invited to perform, and give The Flying Pierces even greater recognition in the airshow business.

In front of us, one hundred little prefab houses, called chateaus, stood next to each other, decorated with flags of every state and over sixty countries. We were walking to the one leased by the international corporation, Rockwell, in hopes of watching the airshow from their back deck which bordered the airshow flight line. Military and airline customers sat on those decks, looking skyward, while they were served the best of food and drink by attractive women. Salesmen hovered nearby, ready to answer any questions and press for orders. Bob Hoover, airshow pilot and emissary for Rockwell, had welcomed his fellow airshow pilots to the company chateau.

"Up, up, up he goes." I heard the announcer's voice and looked in the direction of the runway, but the prefabs blocked my view. The announcer continued, "Robert Harris Kennedy is twenty-six years old and is flying a Delta Wing Kite."

Beyond the business centers were exhibit tents filled with samples of monorails and buses and various transportation systems. Military and commercial aircraft sat on display, giant statues spread throughout the grounds. Throngs of people swirled through the public areas, but were forbidden entrance to the chateaus without an invitation from Boeing, Fairchild, Rockwell, or other major firms hosting the airshow parties.

"Oh, no," the announcer's voice echoed across the airshow grounds. The skin on my arm prickled, and a chill passed over me.

"Oh my God! The Australian Birdman's kite has rolled upside down." The voice grew agitated and half-yelled, "The kite IS UPSIDE DOWN."

Walt and I rushed to an opening between two of the chateaus, hoping to see what was happening on the runway.

"He's going to hit…he…he crashed into the ground."

Part of me froze and a dull dread flooded my body. I first heard the siren's wail, and then watched an ambulance pull up to a crumpled mass of kite and tubing that shrouded a body. The man who called himself the 'Australian Birdman' had to be dead, or close to it.

I had never met the stuntman, and had little understanding of why he chose to perform this particular act. What I did know was that only moments before, he had been alive. Alive, and more than likely, full of excitement at performing at one of the largest airshows in the world. Just like me. Had he also walked down the business centers, hoping to find a willing host?

Death is never easy, but for airshow pilots always a curse. Walt and I said little to each other the rest of the day. "Time to fly." "Need help filling up the smoke oil?" Easy words, professional words. My mind, on the other hand, was quite busy talking and reassuring. After all, the "Australian Birdman" was towed behind a car with hand signals that could have gotten mixed up. Anyway, those kites were dangerous, not controlled, like the aerobatics we flew so near the ground. One by one I, the master craftsman, carefully laid mental bricks in a wall of denial about my own mortality.

In spite of rationalization, death had a way of piercing romantic illusions. I only wanted to slink away, regroup my emotions, and move on to the next airshow, leaving behind the image of twisted kite and broken body. Of course we couldn't leave, and we didn't. Instead, only hours after the Birdman died, I hung suspended from the Stearman with the top of my head facing the same runway. I waved to the people eating and drinking on chataeu decks. I waved to the surrounding throngs in the public viewing areas. I was twenty-eight and had powerful defenses. Life moved on.

Transpo '72 had started out with such promise, but so much had gone wrong even before the gates had opened. The first inkling of political trouble came when Senator William Proxmire started criticizing the expense of the giant event. We performers didn't care much about politics or the mega-business deals. We were there to fly our planes for America and the world. Of course, everyone knew that the aerospace industry had the possibility of selling millions of dollars in airplanes. If they were successful, we airshow pilots reasoned, Transpo would become an ongoing event providing international publicity for our airshow acts.

Even though the civilian performers earned little more than expense money, we were happy to be included in this international affair. The sky was filled with planes from the Confederate Air Force, the Red Arrows Formation Team from England, our own Navy Blue Angels, Air Force Thunderbirds, U.S. Army's Golden Knights, and a brand new Army helicopter demonstration team, the Silver Eagles. The Red Devils—Tom Poberezny, Gene Soucy and Charlie Hillard, Bob Hoover, Art Scholl, Bobby Bishop, our wing-act competitors Joe Hughes and Johnny Kazian from California, sailplane pilot Scotty McCray, and many other civilian performers filled out the day's flying activities.

The airshow was a lengthy event, encompassing nearly two weeks time of hot muggy June. A few day's after the Birdman's crash, we were asked to be the opening act for a special guest, Vice-President Spiro Agnew. The Flying Pierces Airshow Team had reached the top of Mt. Everest.

The morning of our flight, we were part of a James Bond movie with Secret Service men swarming around the TCraft and the Stearman. They fitted Walt with a special pocket radio to direct our flight. The Secret Service coordinated our upcoming performance with airshow honchos Colonel Chuck Aly, Transpo flight operations director, and Hank Cloutier, his assistant.

The plan, drawn in fastidious detail, was for Walt and I to take off in formation, with Bob LeBeau, our parachutist and stuntman, clad in his parachute gear perching half-in and half-out of Tinkerbelle. Maintaining formation, we would fly over the parachute landing area and Bob would drop a streamer to check for wind drift. Walt and I would then stage to the north of the field as we climbed to jump altitude. When the secret service called Walt on the radio, we would start the jump run.

After Bob jumped from the TCraft, he would deploy the American flag while Walt and I circled trailing smoke from our planes. Once Bob was on the ground, Walt and I would perform a limited dual aerobatic sequence. Limited because a gaping hole would be in the side of my airplane where the door had been removed for Bob's ease in jumping.

It all seemed logical and well organized. Then, without warning, Chuck Aly shouted, "Get in the air. He's here. The Secret Service says 'Get in the air!'"

We scrambled into our airplanes, roared down the runway and into the sky as if bombs had burst around us. Off the ground, the TCraft, with LeBeau in his parachute gear and half-hanging out the door, fought to gain altitude. Although we had installed a bigger engine, the airplane was still underpowered. The sweltering heat didn't help. Engine noise filled the cabin of the TCraft and wind pummeled my body as it rushed through the opening usually covered by the door. Tendrils of hair whipped my face. The sky, what I could see of it around the bright red jumpsuit of our stuntman looked soupy blue from east coast humidity.

Bob sat sideways on a perch where the front seat used to be with his black jump-booted feet dangling out the door opening. We had removed the TCraft's door for his easy egress and it remained below on the ground. Since we had installed a larger 100-horsepower Continental engine, I now flew the TCraft from the rear seat to keep the airplane properly balanced. My right hand firmly gripped the stick and my left hand rested on the throttle. Both of my legs extended to the rudder pedals, one on each side of what remained of the front seat. The top of my right sneaker brushed Bob's thigh whenever I added right rudder. As the wind blasted my blonde hair, I wished I had thought to wear my wingriding helmet and goggles. Only a red mass of body covered in two parachutes sheltered me. That windbreak, our stuntman Bob Le Beau, would leave shortly.

"Start the jump run, sandi." Walt's voice commanded in my headset. What was he thinking?

"Roger, turning left." I answered professionally, but then said, "Walt, we're not even 2,000 feet."

I yelled at Bob who was in front of me, but couldn't hear my voice due to the wind and engine noise. To get his attention, I pushed my sneakered right foot into his leg. Bob twisted his head, blue eyes questioning mine. His slender face looked even more tanned, framed by the white helmet with his last name in black block letters on the front. His dark brown mustache drooped down his face and I smiled at this former military guy with the long hair.

I made a hand signal to let him know we were on the jump run. He looked at his altimeter and then his black gloved hand pointed to the instrument. He was right, we did need more altitude. Bob knew I relayed instructions from the Secret Service; instructions we needed to follow if at all possible. He lowered his goggles and leaned out the door for a better view. C'mon baby, I coaxed the airplane. Use that new horsepower to get us higher.

Bob, half-dangling in the slipstream like a speed brake, pointed to the right. I put in rudder while keeping the wings level. We had to make compensations for wind drift, but the skidding wasn't helping our rate of climb. Tinkerbelle inched upward as she struggled to gain altitude.

Below us Vice-President Agnew, head probably tilted upward, followed our flight path across the sky. President Nixon was originally scheduled for the airshow but was on a peace-keeping mission to Russia and had sent the Vice-President in his place. Would I get to meet him? Maybe have a picture taken?

Walt's voice, in my headset, brought my attention back to the plane I flew, "TCraft One Two Victor, start the jump run."

I pressed the button atop the control stick and said, "Roger One One Victor, but we're still low."

"Start the jump run," he repeated. I knew that Walt relayed instructions from an ear piece connected to the Secret Service pocket radio he had been fitted with before we left the ground.

We were about to perform for the Vice President of the United States and I was too low and couldn't see where I was going. At least I didn't have to worry about Bob. Only twenty-five years old, he had already served in the military and performed an airshow season with Bill Sweet's National Airshows. It was reassuring that he already had over 2,000 jumps and was only the forty-eighth person to receive Diamond Gold Wings from the U.S. Parachute Association.

Bob motioned right and I again skidded the airplane using rudder so that the wings remained level, but heading us the direction he indicated. He inched his body toward the opening until he sat in the door frame. Turning his head, he smiled and threw me a kiss before he fell forward out of the plane. Left alone with the thrashing wind as my companion, I smiled at the thought of the mock kiss by the departing parachutist while the Vice-President of the United States watched below. Nope Toto, sandi wasn't in Kansas anymore.

I banked hard left, turned on the smoke and began a lazy circle around Bob who now hung under his canopy with a large U.S. Flag trailing behind him. Red smoke from a canister on his boot painted his path through the sky.

I adjusted my throttle, speeding up so that I was opposite Walt on the circle we flew around Bob's descent to the ground. At five hundred feet from the crowd, Walt and I broke away to begin our airshow sequence. Walt dove the Stearman along the runway, rolling the plane with pauses at eight points around the 360 degrees. His slow roll lasted the length of the runway, flying past the viewing area where the Vice President sat, past the people lounging outside the business centers, past the exhibit areas, and beyond the aircraft staging area. As he turned his airplane away from the crowd, I dive-bombed the runway, smoke trailing, and slow-rolled, pausing at each ninety degree point of the roll. No longer aware of the Vice President or my excitement, I concentrated on flying a modified sequence while the wind whipped my hair and my eyes teared.

In spite of a not-quite-perfect performance for the Vice President, my good feelings remained, gradually replacing the sadness of the "Birdman's" death. We crammed Transpo with daily airshow performances, newspaper interviews, a flight in the Goodyear blimp, "America," afternoons hanging out at Rockwell's business center, and wandering the various pavilions.

Things seemed back to normal with the flying exhibitions exciting and safe. Then, the day before Transpo ended, two racers collided going around a pylon during an air race. In spite of the extensive damage to his airplane, one pilot made it back to the runway and landed safely. The other pilot, Hugh Alexander, flying a Cassutt racer, lost a wing, crashed, and died on impact.

We didn't see the actual accident, but the newspapers and television reports were filled with gory pictures. Once again, death permeated the air around the performers. We felt like soldiers in battle watching our comrades die. I didn't know either the "Australian Birdman" or the race pilot, but losing two people in crashes within days chilled my optimism. Weary and tense, the days in the sun, the ongoing parties, and the deaths had taken their toll on me and all the participants. Denial can only go so far. I was not alone in wanting to run away and hide.

Relieved that it was the last day of Transpo '72, I watched Bob open the show with the American Flag Jump accompanied by Jeannie McCombs, who parachuted with a Transpo '72 flag trailing. I smiled to myself as I waved to the crowd from the wing when we landed after the wing act. Thank God, our part of the show was over! Soon, soon we would be able to go to the motel. The next morning, we would pack up and fly to our base in Mentone, Indiana. The thought of being home, even though only a summer home and only for a few days, seemed unbelievably wonderful.

The tension drained from my body as we rushed to the VIP area to watch the final act, the U.S. Air Force Thunderbirds. It was done. The show was nearly over. We could put all the death and destruction behind us. The Thunderbirds would fly, and then all the airshow performers would be honored in a closing ceremony. In the back, a mega fireworks extravaganza designed by Tommy Walker, entertainment director for Walt Disney Productions, would punctuate the end of a long, long airshow.

Rip Blaisdell, Thunderbird narrator and pilot, announced the show as we stood to one side of the VIP area. The name Rip was fitting for the ruggedly handsome pilot with dark hair. His tall frame showed off the blue Thunderbird flight suit that presented a recruiter image of a military fighter pilot. Walt and I had spent many evenings with Rip, sharing airplane stories over beer and laughs. Once, on a dare, Rip had even gone for a ride atop the Stearman's wing.

Walt and I stood looking skyward, watching our buddies, the "Birds," perform. Although we had flown many shows with this particular jet team, the tight formation of the 40,000-pound F-4 Phantoms, combined with Rip's voice and rousing music, stirred my patriotic feelings.

Pushing the tragedies of the week aside, I allowed myself to be swept up in the moment. I thought of the freedom of our lifestyle as we criss-crossed the country. We met such interesting people. How many people got to do what they loved while making a living? Certainly, my father hadn't. I might not be a Thunderbird, but I was an airshow pilot and I had flown for the Vice President of the United States. I was proud to be part of this niche in the aviation world.

Lost in rosy feelings, my attention was drawn away from the Thunderbird formation flying in front of me. I heard a collective gasp from the people around me and down the crowd line. I felt a now familiar knot in my stomach. What was happening?

Confused, I looked to the sky west of the runway. To my horror, I saw a Thunderbird jet spinning toward the ground. A parachute canopy opened above it, and I felt my tension release. Whoever the pilot, he was safe. I had no idea what had happened, only that a Thunderbird had ejected and the pilot was swinging underneath his parachute canopy as his plane spun earthward.

Time slowed as my attention riveted on the small figure under the canopy. I wasn't aware of Rip's voice or if the music continued. I only knew that I willed the pilot safely to the ground. Walt and I were silent as we watched the pilot descend.

The revolving airplane hit the ground and exploded. I jerked, shocked by the noise and violence even from the distance. Orange flames mushroomed up and black smoke obscured the sky. When the blaze settled, the sky was empty. Where had the pilot gone? Did he land safely? A helicopter clop-clopped overhead and made its way to the still burning crash site. Rip told the crowd that medical personnel were on the way to rescue the pilot.

Numbness akin to shock gripped me. Which one of our friends was out there next to that burning mass? Was he alive? At a deeper level, many unacknowledged questions fought to be heard: What about me? What about Walt? Was a crash in our future?

Rip, narration duties concluded, stepped from the Speaker's platform and stood next to me. I could hear him breathing, but aviation sunglasses shielded his eyes. There we stood, three aviators awaiting the fate of our colleague.

Word came that Joe Howard had experienced a mechanical failure, but had successfully ejected from his airplane. Joe, how could it be Joe? We had just seen him earlier in the day. His wife was pregnant with a baby due any minute. Joe, the consummate professional, flew right wing. I flew right wing, and also was about Joe's age. I thought of his pleasant, unassuming smile. With his typical good humor, he had taken the teasing about his wife's pregnancy and how his life would be changed. I looked to the burning crash, thinking of Joe, his pregnant wife, and their unborn child. I thought of Shawn, away in Dallas visiting her Grandmommy and Granddaddy.

The Transpo announcer began a tribute to the performers who had lost their lives during these past two weeks. It wasn't planned, but the lonely sound of Taps echoed across the grounds as the Thunderbird flight team landed without their right wing man. I looked straight ahead, aware of Walt and Rip beside me, but unable to stop the tears streaming down my face.

Concluding fireworks exploded across the runway, and I shuddered as if recoiling from an assault. Walt slipped his arm around me as Rip rushed to be with his teammates. What happened? What had caused the accident? Had they rescued Joe?

Transpo '72 was officially over, but we performers milled around the announcer's area, expectantly waiting to see our fallen comrade step from a rescue helicopter. Finally, the announcer's voice blared over the PA system. Joe Howard had punched out of his spinning F-4. His canopy opened, but then was consumed in a fireball from the jet exploding on contact with the ground. Our Thunderbird hero and friend, Joe Howard, had fallen to his death while we watched the last act of the last day of Transpo' 72.

Silence can feel as if it possesses volume, squeezing all life from the air. Neither Walt nor I spoke as he maneuvered the rental car through the Sunday evening traffic between us and the hotel. Numb, my mind ceased its torturous meanderings. Unable to focus, I even dropped my normal study of Walt and his reaction. It took over an hour to get to the hotel.

In the lobby, Walt mumbled, "I'm going to the bar."

I nodded as I pressed the button for the elevator. I had nothing to say. My words were used up.

In our room, I lay across the bed and stared at the ceiling. The air conditioning prickled the skin on my bare arms, more used to the heat and humidity of summer airshow days. I wanted to cry, maybe scream, but nothing came from my lips. At last, I reached for the phone to call my parents and tell them I was okay. Mainly, I needed to hear Shawn's little voice.

DECEMBER, 1973

17

A GREAT LAKES CHRISTMAS

Dallas, Texas

"When are you going to stop flying airshows?" Mom said.

My hand paused mid-chop over the celery for our traditional cornbread stuffing. It was Christmas Eve and the two of us were alone in my brother's kitchen preparing for the the next day's feast. I resumed cutting the crunchy stalks, but my humming of "Jingle Bells" ceased. Why did Christmas and family so intertwine in my psyche? If within five hundred miles of Texas mid-December, I always figured a way to spend holidays with my family, the downside of previous celebrations escaping my memory. Well, I remembered now.

I tried the ho-ho-ho approach. "Oh, come on. It may be Christmas, but Santa's not bringing you that big a gift." My holiday cheer plummeted into Scroogeville. Mom occupied the head cheerleader position in my life, but she also was my chief critic. Unconditional love, to her, was standing by you while never letting you forget the error of your ways.

"I'm serious," she said, giving me one of her bulldog looks. "So many of your friends have died in airshows. Last year, all those people were killed at that show in Washington, D.C."

My grip on the knife tightened and an understanding of family murder flooded me.

"What about Shawn?" she continued.

Didn't the woman know when to stop? Of course, she didn't. She never had.

"What would that precious child do if you were killed or even maimed?"

I laid the knife on the cabinet and focused on washing celery juice from my hands. She had a point, not that I let her know. It troubled me that something might happen to us and Shawn would be stuck with my mom.

"People, die in car wrecks every day." I said, feeling like an alien explaining myself to a lower intelligent life form.

"Do you even have insurance?"

How did this four-foot-eleven-inch piranha know my weak spots? Of course, Walt and I didn't have insurance. We were young and broke.

"Did you and daddy have insurance when you were my age?"

"Times were different then. Anyway, we weren't doing crazy things like you." She looked pleased, a criminal prosecutor making her case.

"Nothing is going to happen to us." I dried my hands on a green dishtowel with a smiling red Santa.

"I'm sure that's what your dead friends also said." she snapped back.

"Mother." I tried to control the anger seeping from my voice. My shoulder blades felt stitched together like a turkey trussed for baking. "Mother." There, my voice sounded better, "Walt and I are airshow pilots. That's what we do for a living. That's not going to change."

Her look remained steady.

Even though nothing said would make any difference, I continued. "You may not like flying, but I do."

She nodded her head ever so slightly.

I said, "I love flying and I love airshows. Other people think it's wonderful that I'm an airshow pilot. Why don't you?"

Before she could list all her reasons why, I rushed on. "The Great Lakes Aircraft Company wants me to fly their airplane at airshows. That's why I have that new, expensive, biplane parked out at the airport. Their owner thinks I'll sell lots of airplanes for them." I glared at her, but she remained silent.

"That's why I'm here with you this Christmas. Otherwise, we'd be in Florida soaking in sunshine and having our traditional Christmas cookout."

"Sandra," she said. "I know you're a good pilot. I'm proud of you—"

Voice rising, I broke into her placating words. "And why can't you call me sandi? I'm sandi now, not Sandra."

Tears welled in her eyes and I felt even more helpless. I wanted to scream, "Let me be, please, let me be. Can't you just love me?" Instead I rushed out of the kitchen, upset with my mom and disappointed with myself for not handling her better. She had never approved of my flying, so why expect her to change?

The next morning, colorful wrapping paper flew as Shawn tore open a present. Her long blonde hair fell in chaotic curls to her waist and contrasted with her red flannel jammies. Five years old, my baby was turning into a young girl. A giant tree filled one corner of my brother's den with crumpled paper and empty boxes decorating the room. The smell of cooking turkey swirled around us. More observer than participant, I watched the lively Christmas ritual as my nieces, Laura and Polly, also ripped into presents. Norman Rockwell couldn't have painted a more touching scene.

I sat on the floor, close to the action if needed, with Walt's legs secure against my back. A mug of coffee warmed my hands and my body was snug in my fuzzy bathrobe. For one brief moment, I felt part of a television

Christmas special, that is, if I ignored the tension from my husband who was tired of my family and ready to leave, the argument with my mother, and the fact that something seemed off in my brother's marriage.

Shawn removed tape that sealed the edges of the box she held. It had to be a present from my mother who delighted in slowing people down when opening gifts. At last, she liberated a doll from her cardboard prison and squealed, "Oh, Grandmommy, she's beautiful!" My little girl stood cradling her new baby.

"Come here," my mom said. "Your baby is special. Come here, let me show you."

Shawn held her baby close and carefully made her way to her grandmother's side. The two of them studied the doll with her long black eyelashes on blinking lids. How could my mother be so nice to her granddaughter and so maddening to me, her daughter? Would Shawn be as upset with me one day as I was with my mom? I banished the horrible thought.

My sister-in-law, Delsie, sat between my mom and dad on the couch and became part of the exploration of the doll's miniature purse that held a small comb, a barrette, and hair ribbons for her curls. My dad seemed content to watch the people he loved celebrate the holiday.

An excited shriek from my thirteen-year-old niece, Polly, broke into my musing. "It's Elton John…'Goodbye Yellow Brick Road.'" Her sister Laura, seventeen, was mildly interested in the new record album. Polly ran to her dad, who sat in an easy chair, and jumped onto his lap. My brother, Tommy, grumbled and maneuvered his coffee cup to keep it from spilling, but a smile crept onto his face. Nine years older than me, he looked like a model in an ad for fine whiskey, dressed in a heavy robe and with tousled red hair.

Polly slid from my brother's lap to look under the tree for another present with her name on it. Tommy leaned forward, holding his coffee mug in both hands. "Well sis, what's the plan? When are you leaving?"

My mom said, "I don't want her to leave." Walt's legs shifted behind my back. On the couch my dad leaned forward as if to better hear my answer.

I said, "I'll fly out of here in the morning, down to Waco to show Frank Price my new Great Lakes on the way home. Walt and Shawn will follow in the truck."

Tommy asked, "Who's Frank Price?"

Walt said, "He's an airshow pilot friend of ours. Head of the American Tiger Club, a group of aerobatic pilots. Great guy."

Mom scowled, "I wish you'd stay longer."

My shoulder blades inched closer together, but I ignored my irritation. "Mama," I said in the sweetest voice I could muster, "We've been here four days. It took longer than we thought in Oklahoma and I've been gone from Florida nearly a month. It's time to get home."

I thought of my time at the Great Lakes factory in Enid. Even the snug boots and parka purchased from my meager funds hadn't kept me warm against the bitter cold. Maybe it was true that living in Florida made blood thinner. In spite of the grousing, I didn't really mind the cold; my dream plane was ready. Why, now, should I care about my mom? I, sandi pierce, owned a 1920s-designed airplane complete with modern engine, beefed-up wings, and up-to-the-minute parts. Thank you, Doug Champlin, for buying the old Great Lakes production rights and making gorgeous aerobatic airplanes. Thank you for sponsoring me.

"sandi," Champlin had said in his easy-going accent, "you'll get us a lot of publicity, flying at airshows and promoting the Great Lakes. You and Walt are a good team."

Remembering his words, a Cheshire-cat grin spread within and popped out on my face as I imagined flying my new biplane inverted down the runway at airshows.

Tommy said, "What took so long in Oklahoma?"

Walt answered, "Small glitches that ate up time. The airplane made it on schedule from the factory in Wichita down to Enid where they paint and do final assembly. Scheduling was a bit optimistic about the completion date, which wouldn't have mattered but sandi was waiting."

"Out in the cold," I said and laughed at my own drama.

The original plan was for me to fly commercially to Oklahoma, pick up the airplane and stop for a brief visit with my parents in Dallas on my flight home to Florida. Days had turned into weeks, so it was a special joy for Walt and Shawn to join me and all of us spend Christmas with my family. We always struggled financially in the winters. Savings went for necessary maintenance on our planes, shows were sparse, and we lived mainly on deposits for the upcoming season. Fortunately, an airshow deposit had come in time to pay for their trip.

My mother might grumble and I might react to her. Still, it was nice to be home for the holidays. Shawn and her cousins were busy looking at their Christmas loot, my brother had settled back into his chair, and Delsie talked with my mom and dad. My family was happy to see us, but only Walt really understood what flying and the new Great Lakes meant to me.

Last Christmas I never would have guessed I would be the owner of such a magnificent biplane. We had so little extra money, and even with a significant sponsorship from the company, Walt and I could have purchased a home for what the plane cost. It was fitting that I named it Mi Casa. Without financing assistance from Champlin, I would still be flying my TCraft in airshows.

"Hey," my brother said, "What's the chance of getting a ride before you leave?"

My dad leaned forward and said, "I'd—" I saw my mom put her hand on his arm. Daddy leaned back.

"You want to go for a ride, Daddy?" I said.

He shook his head. "Better not."

I turned back to my brother. "Well, we can go. Why don't you fly to Waco with me tomorrow? It's a short trip."

Before Tommy had a chance to answer, mom said, "We could drive down to pick Tommy up. It'd be fun and we'd get to see you a little longer."

That was my mother, exasperating one moment and open to fun the next, even if it involved airplanes.

The following morning, two of the linemen at the Addison airport pulled Mi Casa from the hangar. One of them whistled and said, "She's a beauty."

Bright Texas sun sparkled off the polished silver spinner and propeller, making the vivid red, white, and blue paint glisten even more. The Great Lakes stood a little over seven feet tall with the top wing swept back, giving it a jaunty look. The lower wing jutted out perpendicular to the fuselage. Its antiquated looking gear was from early-generation airplane design. It might have appeared old, but was easy to handle on the ground. Colorful sunburst and checkerboard designs proclaimed "airshow" at first glance. As with the TCraft before, my name was upside down in large letters on one side, and right side up on the other.

Walt, Tommy, the two linemen, and I stood silently, holding disposable cups filled with steaming coffee, in awe of the beauty before us. We were pilots in an aviation Louvre, absorbed in our version of Da Vinci's *Mona Lisa*. Mi Casa was the finest of airshow airplanes and I, her lucky pilot. Shawn, bundled in a too-small winter coat, played happily with her new doll over to one side. TCrafts, Great Lakes, or Stearmans made no difference to her. They were only parts of her parents' grown-up world.

It was winter and my Mona Lisa was open cockpit. Tommy and I bundled in parkas and gloves for the upcoming chilly flight. He settled into the front cockpit and I slid down into the rear where the pilot-in-command flew. The plane fit me perfectly, neither cavernous like a Stearman nor snug like a fighter plane. I felt like Goldilocks climbing into a "just right" bed.

My feet reached the rudder pedals and the stick pulled comfortably and completely back into my lap. The Great Lakes fit me without pillows or even rudder pedal adjustment. In front of me, the panel was filled with flight and engine instruments, vivid white letters and numbers standing out against their black faces. Underneath them, the aviation radio was mounted to one side.

Seat belts, helmet, and goggles on, I yelled, "Clear Prop," and quickly scanned the area to make certain Walt, Shawn, and any other interlopers were out of the way. As the propeller slowly rotated and the engine came to life, my gaze darted to the oil pressure gauge.

Most of flying is about habits, habits you start to learn as a student pilot. Yelling to warn people you are about to start the engine, checking for oil pressure as soon as an engine catches, using checklists, and scanning the sky for traffic are just a few of the many things instructors drum into their students' befuddled brains. Pilots take to the air in many different airplanes over the course of their careers, and these ingrained habits carry forward, no matter the size or speed of the airplane.

Frosty air blew over the windshields and snaked around our shoulders. We rode in an airplane convertible in the winter where turning the heat up full blast had little impact on the temperature.

In the cold, dense air, the Great Lakes leapt from the ground in less than six hundred feet. What a contrast to the airliner I had ridden to Oklahoma.

Downtown Dallas stood etched in the crystal morning light. In my childhood city and carrying the only person from my family to ever fly with me, I was proud of being an airshow pilot, proud of my Great Lakes, and basked in my brother's imagined praise. It didn't matter that a cold front was moving in and the temperature dropping. It didn't matter that America was in the midst of an oil crisis or that Vice-President Spiro Agnew, for whom we had performed at Transpo '72, had resigned. The Arabs and Israelis may have killed each other during the Yom Kippur War only months earlier. All was well in my little world of biplanes and airshows. My eyes misted and I questioned whether tears froze during winter in open-cockpit airplanes.

"Hey, Tommy," I said over the radio intercom. "How ya doing?"

"What a view." Tommy's voice was easily understandable in my headset. "This is spectacular. Any chance I can fly?"

"Of course, I'll talk you through some turns." I didn't know how many years it had been since my brother had piloted an airplane, but that morning, he was the Red Baron and I was his flight instructor.

As we neared Waco, the airport tower reported wind gusting at 35 knots; not a good condition for a tail wheel airplane that on the ground tended to weathervane into the wind. My fingers covered with heavy gloves suddenly felt wooden, and a chill spread through my insides. I had only a few hours of flight time in this type of plane. The thought of landing in such high wind sapped my confidence. It didn't help that my brother was a passenger and that Papa Tiger would be watching.

Since airplanes must come down, high winds or not, the tower suggested I land on a taxiway facing into the wind. They said, "Great Lakes 506 Golf Lima, cleared to land on taxiway in front of Frank Price's hangar.

No other reported traffic."

Fortunately, the Waco airport had been a World War II base with wider taxiways. With the wind at our back, the plane zoomed across the ground on downwind leg. A turn to right base leg and the strong wind hit our side, blowing Mi Casa away from the airport. Another ninety degrees to final approach and we were ready to land on the taxiway. Frank's hangar stood off to one side in the distance.

It took more power than normal to counteract the howling Central Texas wind. At times, we seemed to hang suspended in the air. Then we sailed over the fence, over the runway that was angled to the taxiway, and slowly decreased the power until the Great Lakes settled onto the taxiway on its main gear. With forward pressure on the elevator with a little extra power, we taxied, tail wheel in the air, until we neared the turn to Frank's hangar. Finally, with the power back, the tail sank to the asphalt and I planted the stick firmly into my lap.

With the plane facing the wind, taxiing wasn't difficult. That wouldn't last. I turned onto a smaller taxiway and gusts bombarded the fuselage from the right. The airplane's nose turned windward. I put the wing's aileron down into the wind to spoil the lift, used rudder to compensate, and hoped we wouldn't bolt into the nearby grass. At some point the wind would be greater than my ability to keep control but, with so few hours in the airplane, I didn't know when.

I noticed Frank and another man half-jogging across the ramp toward us. Frank grabbed a handhold on the right wing, his friend the other side. My tension eased. Two men were hanging on the lower wing and we weren't going anywhere we didn't want to go.

"That's a relief," my brother said over the intercom.

My "Yep" didn't convey what I really felt.

In front of the hangar, Frank motioned for Tommy to take his place holding the right wing and I shut the engine down. Frank pushed the hangar doors open enough to maneuver the Great Lakes into a bare spot and then closed the doors.

The World War II hangar rattled and banged, dust floating over Frank's flying museum of great airplanes. An original Great Lakes used for aerobatic instruction was nearby with an old T-50 Bamboo Bomber, like the one the television Sky King piloted, was tucked into one corner. The Bucker Jungmeister Frank had flown into Austin when I was a student pilot, sat beside Mi Casa.

Our new group of pilots stood admiring the biplane as if it were a new baby. Frank said, "So, this is the new Great Lakes." We remained silent as he walked around the plane, studying it in detail.

Smiling, Frank said, "They've done a good job on this Great Lakes." He looked at me, "She belongs here with the other Tiger Club airplanes."

Papa Tiger understood. Mi Casa belonged, and so did I.

MARCH, 1974

18

BIPLANES AND FRIENDS

Sebring, Florida

One spring day, four of us airshow pilots stood on the concrete ramp of the Sebring airport watching *The Great Waldo Pepper* movie being filmed. An eighteen-wheeler truck towed a World War I Jenny biplane, strapped on top of a flatbed trailer, up and down a far taxiway. Savannah Lee, Bill Lumley, Walt, and I stood with our mouths agape like country folks visiting the big city. We were caught up in movie-making and enthralled with the possibility of seeing stars Robert Redford or Susan Sarandon. Savannah, whom we had met at an aerobatic contest two weeks earlier, and Bill had stopped at the Sebring airport on their way to visit us in Avon Park.

Living in a world of men had its privileges. I flew airplanes men enjoyed flying, had adventures men enjoyed having, and told stories men liked to hear. Still, a part of me missed having women friends in my life. Women friends talked about feelings and expressed concerns without expecting solutions. I could gripe about Walt without someone thinking I was coming on to them. My women friends were scattered and few. We performed occasionally with National Aerobatic Champion, Mary Gaffaney, who was older and always encouraged me as a mentor but wasn't a close friend. Grace "The Ace" Page, who flew a cub comedy act in shows, was also older but a close friend. Unfortunately, she had moved to California. I wanted a girl friend nearer to my age, and if she was obsessed with flying, so much the better.

"Can you believe they're towing an airplane on a flatbed?" I said.

Walt nodded, engrossed in all the activity across the ramp.

"Unbelievable," Savannah said.

I smiled at her, incredibly happy to have met this woman aerobatic pilot who was my age. Her shorts did show a lot of leg and she was hanging all over Bill Lumley, but hey, no one's perfect.

The March day was pleasant, no gnats, even though Florida had begun its transformation into tropical summer. Walt and I had flown my Great Lakes the fifteen air miles to Sebring from Avon Park, our winter base. Shawn was back in Avon Park, happily playing under the watchful eye of Laura Gossick, owner with her pilot husband, Don, of the Avon Park Flying Service. Bill Lumley's highly modified aerobatic airplane, a De Havilland Chipmunk, rested on the Sebring ramp next to my plane.

Savannah's gaze traveled over my Great Lakes that sparkled in the toasty March sunshine. A vivid blue sky dotted with white puffy clouds was the perfect backdrop. I knew she was impressed.

"I'll take you for a ride later, if you like," I said. She grinned and murmured her approval.

The billowy clouds were the reason that *The Great Waldo Pepper* movie crew had come to the Sebring airport. The movie had been filming its flying sequences off of Zuehl Airport near San Antonio. Papa Tiger Frank Price, world renowned airshow pilot Art Scholl, along with the Hollywood stunt pilots of Tallmantz Aviation, had been creating aviation magic in Texas. Weather and sky had changed, and the movie was behind schedule. In an act of desperation the production crew found a location where clouds were nearly always in the skies, Central Florida.

"How are they keeping the Jenny on the trailer?" Savannah asked. She was tall with long straight dark hair, and tan legs that seemed to extend forever from blue shorts partially covered with a white T-shirt that said *International Aerobatic Club.*

Walt kept his eyes focused across to the distant taxiway that looked more like a runway. He said, "I think they have cable lashing the Jenny's wheels to the trailer. Look how the fan on the small trailer in front is blowing wind over the airplane."

Directly in front of the trailer with the Jenny was a smaller trailer. The little trailer was filled with several people, a large movie camera, and a fan. The trailer caravan was pulled by a truck tractor. How Hollywood! The crew filmed the sequence from the smaller trailer, making it appear the Jenny was flying through the air. The conglomeration moved slowly up and down the taxiway.

"I can't wait to see how this looks in the movie." I said.

"I can't wait to see how Redford looks. Have you seen him?" Savannah asked.

"We thought we saw him," I said. "The other day we stopped by to invite Frank Tallman to dinner." I paused to see if Savannah knew about the owner of Tallmantz Aviation, the Hollywood stunt flying company built by Paul Mantz and Frank. She nodded and I continued, "We got to know Frank at Transpo '72. Anyway, Walt and I came up to the movie area over there behind the rope." I pointed over to our right where a mini-movie studio was set up. "Redford was sitting right there in one of those chairs, wearing his pilot costume, and reading a newspaper." I grinned, like a teenage groupie.

"Really?" said Savannah, fellow groupie. It was great sharing idle chit-chat with someone on the same wavelength as me. Some women do not like other women and prefer the company of men. I was not one of those women.

I nodded at Savannah and punched Walt on the arm to get his attention.

"Ouch," he said, never taking his gaze off the action out on the taxiway.

"Tell her what happened."

Walt remained silent, so I said, "Redford stood up and walked toward us." Savannah and Bill leaned slightly toward me. I said, "He got nearer. I couldn't believe it. He was coming over to talk to us."

"Wow," she said, listening to my every word.

Walt looked up. "Yeah, wow. All at once, Frank Tallman's voice called out, 'Hey, you two.'"

Savannah and Bill looked confused.

"It was Frank Tallman in a Robert Redford mask," I said. Walt turned his attention back to the action on the taxiway. "The Tallmantz pilots wear Redford masks in the air so it looks like Redford is flying the…"

Walt broke into my story, "Look," he said. "Look, on the left wing out by the strut. Someone is kneeling, holding on to the strut." We turned to see what he was talking about.

"It's a girl," he continued. "See her dress blowing. That's why they have the fan."

"I bet she's a wingwalker in the movie," Savannah said and looked at me. "Like you, only she's not far off the ground. Suppose that's Susan Sarandon?"

"Probably," I said and smiled at Savannah, happy to be with a woman who flew, who understood flying, who even understood the joy of flying upside down. Savannah was single and totally engrossed in aerobatics. She owned a Super Decathalon and had been competing in aerobatic contests around the United States and flying a few airshows. I relished her friendship.

"Amazing?" Walt said. "They have men under the airplane on either side. See, there on the skids. There's a guy on each side, pushing and then pulling the wing up and down." He shook his head. "Make it look like it's riding the air currents flying through the air."

The Sebring airport had been a B-17 bomber base during World War II. Around us spread the 1940's barracks and army buildings interspersed with modern facilities for airplanes and an industrial park. Concrete and Florida palm trees completed the picture. The giant old base had become the site for a sports car road race in 1950, the first endurance race held in the United States. The new race ran over the taxiways, ramps, and streets of the airport and the "Twelve Hours of Sebring" became an international event. In fact, where the movie company was now creating their piece of sky was actually part of the course where sports cars raced. I never had heard of a sports car race being run on an airport. *Waldo Pepper* and crew were bringing another excitement to this sleepy area of Central Florida.

The four of us left the movie set, and flew back to Avon Park. On the short flight, I flew the Great Lakes in formation close to the Chipmunk's right wing. Below us, blue lakes of various sizes scattered amidst the acres of neat rows of green citrus trees spread in all directions. This central part of Florida was 150 feet above sea level and considered the highlands area. My heart felt as warm as the tropical air in which I flew. What a great life I had with my dream Great Lakes, a dashing husband, a wonderful daughter, and now a potential woman friend who was an airshow pilot. I planned to invite Savannah to come back and visit.

A week later she did return, buzzing the Avon Park airport in her Super Decathlon. Walt, Savannah, and I hit it off immediately, as if we had known each other for a long, long time. We laughed and joked together, sharing flying stories and critiquing each other when we practiced our airshow routines every day. Shawn even liked her.

The days of her visit multiplied and although Savannah would say she was going to leave, there was always a reason to stay. I didn't want her to go. I enjoyed her company and at last, Walt and I decided to include her act in our Flying Pierces lineup. We could sell her solo act as part of our show. Girl pilots always were of interest to sponsors.

It wasn't unusual to ask a third person to join our airshow. In the past, stuntman Bob Le Beau had parachuted and done the car-to-plane transfer as part of our airshow group. Hank Burden had joined us for one season offering barnstorming passenger rides in his 220-horsepower Stearman before and after our air shows. Hank had even shared an apartment with us at our summer base in Mentone, Indiana. Tom Monterastelli was our favorite mechanic and flying buddy, an active participant in our team. He had even gone to work flying fire ant contracts in the big bombers.

We had enjoyed having other people as part of our group, only this time it would be a girl. Part of me questioned whether that was a smart thing to do, but the three of us were having so much fun together that I dismissed the idea. Savannah was thrilled to become a solo act in our airshow and pitched in on maintenance, marketing activities, and playing with Shawn.

In April, we moved the whole operation to Mentone, in northern Indiana, in preparation for our summer season. We had chosen to base there several years earlier. The town was located within five hundred miles of the majority of airshows in the United States. Once settled, we were ready for the major part of our 1974 airshow season.

Our first outing was not an airshow, but a visit to Galesburg, Illinois and Jim Leahy. Jim owned an original Stearman and was the founder of the newly formed National Stearman fly-in. We had flown in their airshow in 1973 and both planes were booked for this year's September show. We wanted Jim to meet Savannah and also hire her to fly. Jim planned an impromptu fly-in for us and our mutual friend, Tracy Pilurs, who drove down from her home in the Chicago area.

Our Flying Pierces flight of three zoomed over the Galesburg airport with Walt in the lead, me in my normal position tucked in close on his right wing, and Savannah just as close on his left. Shawn rode in the front seat of Savannah's Decathalon which was warmer than my open-cockpit Great Lakes. We circled and descended down the main runway.

"Smoke on," Walt said. Three trails of smoke popped on and we dove earthward and rushed down the runway, smoke puffing a trail behind us.

"One out," Walt said. The Stearman pulled up and out of our formation, made a sharp turn to the left and entered the traffic pattern for landing.

"Two out," I said and pulled up, following Walt onto downwind leg.

"Three out," Savannah said, pulling up and turning in behind me.

What fun! A three airplane formation was even better than two. I saw Tracy and Jim leaning against her red convertible watching us and talking as we taxied in.

Jim was an aviation enthusiast who paid for his hobby with his electrical contracting business. He was medium height and slender with an athletic build, like a biker or runner. His dark hair was thinning and I thought he had probably worn glasses all his life. He was older than me, but I wasn't certain by how much, maybe early forties.

The flying marathon began shortly after our arrival. First, Jim and Walt flew Jim's Stearman while I took the Decathlon up and then Savannah and Tracy flew my Great Lakes. Shawn played happily on the ground, entertained by whoever wasn't busy in the air. First round of flying finished, it was time for lunch and sharing of stories.

That afternoon, I was surprised when Walt offered to let Jim fly his Stearman. 'Ol Smokey was a single seater and the only way Jim could go for a ride in it was as pilot-in-command. Walt never let anyone fly his airplane, including me. Jim then flew 'Ol Smokey, I soloed Jim's Stearman, and then Savannah, again, took up my Great Lakes. Before two days were finished, I had made seventeen flights in four airplanes, taking many of Jim's friends up for rides in my Great Lakes.

We spent the night at the Holiday Inn, a large part of it in the bar, regaling each other with flying stories. We discussed getting up early for a dawn patrol flight over town, but fortunately, good sense prevailed and we decided to meet Jim at the airport at 8:30 rather than 5:00 A.M.

The next morning, I left Walt and Shawn in the room and joined Tracy in the coffee shop. She looked up from her newspaper and motioned for me to join her. "Hey, kiddo," she said and gave me a once over. "Stayed up a wee bit late last night?"

"You know how pilots are. Why did you leave so early?"

She half-snorted, "Early? It was 10:00. That's my bedtime. This old lady goes to bed so she can get up and feel wonderful in the morning."

"You're not old," I said and looked at her closely. She had gray hair, but her face had few lines. No, she wasn't old, just older.

"Old enough to be your mother," she said.

I ordered breakfast and noticed Tracy had set down her newspaper and was staring intently at me. Never one to hold back her thoughts and opinions, I wondered why she now hesitated. After the waitress left, I said, "OK. What's up?"

"sandi, I feel like a mother to you." I nodded but remained silent. She continued, "I just feel like I need to say something." I felt myself tensing. What did she need to tell me? She seemed to gather her energy and the words burst out of her. "You need to get rid of that girl. She's going to be trouble."

I was confused. What was she saying? "I don't understand. Savannah is just a pilot with our airshow. That's all."

Her words came stronger and powered with certainty. "Never bring another woman into your marriage. It's bad business, for the marriage and your airshow team."

"Whatever are you talking about, Tracy? Savannah is my friend. I really like her. We all get along well. We've had people travel with us before, Bob LeBeau, Hank Burden, and Preston Ewen."

"You're just too optimistic, kiddo. Listen to me, I'm older. Can't you see the way she hangs on the guys, including Walt? I know what—." Tracy's words were stopped by Savannah's voice a few feet from us.

"Good morning. Can I join you?"

I hoped she hadn't heard our heated discussion. In spite of Tracy's surprise announcement, the three of us had a pleasant breakfast. Tracy and Savannah were talking airplanes when I left early to go back to the motel room.

Later at the airport, Savannah pulled me aside. She lowered her voice and said, "Do you know what Tracy said to me after you left?" I shook my head no. "She said…she said she would ruin me in the aerobatic world if I did anything to hurt you and Walt."

I was stunned. Tracy must have been serious about her warning to me. I looked closely at Savannah. Was Tracy seeing something that I had missed? I said, "Tracy usually means what she says."

Later that day, Walt and I flew in Jim's Stearman. It seemed strange that Walt had me practice take offs and landings since I had soloed Jim's Stearman only the day before. After the flight, Walt said, "How would you like to solo Ol' Smokey?"

I was shocked. Walt's Stearman was big and heavy on the controls. We used it to make our living. I can't say I never thought about flying it, but it seemed unnecessary and perhaps a bit foolish.

"Of course, I would love to fly your Stearman," I said quickly before fear engulfed me.

April in Illinois was still cool and I wore a heavy jacket and gloves in the open-cockpit biplane. The first challenge was getting enough cushions behind my back to put me close enough to the rudder pedals, but still give me full-stick movement. I also needed cushions underneath me to raise me high enough to see out of the airplane. Walt was six feet tall and my five foot two and one-half inches height meant that I looked directly at the instrument panel level and could see little outside of the airplane.

By the time I had the proper cushions, my initial excitement had turned to panic. What if I couldn't fly the airplane? What if it was too big for me? What if I lost control on landing and ground-looped? What if…what if… what if? I knew Walt was offering me something that he did not give lightly.

It was time to fly and Walt started zipping up my jacket. I whispered, so the others wouldn't hear, "Are you sure I should do this?"

He touched my shoulder. "You flew Jim's Stearman just right, even with wind across the runway. This is the same airplane, only bigger engine." He turned to Shawn who had walked over to be part of the excitement. "Your mom's going to fly 'Ol Smokey. What do you think about that?"

Shawn smiled. "Cool."

Ol' Smokey was bright and shiny and my Superman, Walt, flew it. And now, my six-year-old daughter looked up at me with admiration, even thought what I was doing "cool." The biplane might be big and brawny with nearly three times the horsepower of my Great Lakes, but it had two wings and an engine like any other airplane. I knew I could fly it.

Walt smiled his lopsided grin as he said, "What? Is my courageous aviator, rider of wings, cheater of death, scared? No way, you'll do great." He gave me a gentle push towards the airplane. "Anyway," he said, "do you think I'd let you fly it if I was the least bit worried?"

The Stearman stood high off the ground and I had to jump to get up on the lower wing. Nothing new there, since I jumped up on the lower wing every airshow before the wingriding act. This time, though, I swung my right leg over into the pilot's seat and lowered myself into the huge cockpit which swallowed me.

At least Walt's parachute felt familiar, since a similar one rested in my Great Lakes. The similarity ended there. I grabbed the gargantuan control stick, happy my hand was able to fit around the contoured handle. The seat cushions raised me to Walt's height and his view of the world. My gaze moved upward to the center section where I normally perched during the wing act. How did it feel to fly an airplane with a person on top, to be responsible for their safety while doing low-level aerobatics?

Walt called out instructions for starting the engine. Ka-boom, the engine backfired, then popped. My hands moved fast on the throttle and mixture, and all nine cylinders roared to life. The chug-chug, chug-chug, chug-chug of the radial engine was even more enjoyable to hear from inside the cockpit while the faint smell of oil hung around me like fine perfume.

The Stearman began feeling more like an airplane than the shrine I had made it. It was bigger than most of the equipment I flew, but, I realized it was mainly bigger in my head. I lined up on the centerline of the runway, added power, and felt all 450 horses of the Pratt and Whitney engine roar to life. I was off the runway in a flash. I held the plane down close to the ground to gather speed. The controls felt much heavier than my Great Lakes and required a great deal of forward pressure on the stick to keep the flight path somewhat level. I reached over and flipped the smoke switch on. Near the end of the runway, I pulled up to what I hoped was a ninety-degree vertical line. I then lowered the nose for climb out and felt the effect of power as I roared to altitude.

Beneath me, the flat fields of Illinois spread in all directions. The chilly air was a tonic for the flush of heat that burned inside of me. In the air, Ol' Smokey seemed a more normal size. I made turns, climbed, held various speeds, and did all the things pilots do to discover how an airplane flies.

High over the ground at five thousand feet, I lined up along a section line that ran into the distance. Frolicking through a loop in the sky, the fields disappeared from my view. My Great Lakes was the Mama biplane and Walt's Stearman the Papa with much heavier control pressures.

Confident, I picked a point on the horizon, lowered the nose to accelerate to 120 miles per hour needed for a slow roll. The stick pressure was heavy and I was unable to hold full aileron to keep the airplane rotating. Instead, I found myself flying inverted with thousands of feet of air between me and the corn fields below. I grabbed onto a piece of fuselage tubing and to one side of the cockpit, using it as a lever to push on the aileron. The plane slowly rolled back to upright.

How did Walt do it? His right arm must be super strong to fly this airplane with such precision low to the ground. I played with the airplane, trying different strategies to keep full aileron so that I could perform a reasonable slow roll. Cuban eights, hammerhead turns, snap rolls, were all much easier than having to hold a sustained aileron necessary for a precision slow roll.

Time came to return to ground and my tummy did a flip-flop. Tail wheel airplanes fly the same in the sky as planes with nose wheels, but on landing become very different beasts. The Stearman was a big tetrahedron prone to swing into the wind once it touched the runway. Swing too far and I might lose control, going round in a circle. If lucky, a ground loop could be simple with the only hurt to my pride. At the other extreme, the wing could scrape the runway or even take out taxi lights. I shuddered remembering the Atlanta aerobatic school's Stearman up on its nose in the ditch.

None of these options appealed to me. I wanted a good landing, a landing appropriate for the aviator I considered myself to be. After touchdown, I had no idea how good or bad my performance was. I hadn't ground-looped or bounced the airplane like a basketball down the runway. Filled with gratitude, I was on the ground with Walt's plane in one piece.

Taxiing back to my waiting fans, I saw Jim's wide grin. He gave me a thumbs-up. Next to him, Tracy glowed as proud as a mama. Shawn stopped playing with her dolls and waved. Savannah's look was more complex. Was her smile trying to cover envy? That was understandable. If the situation had been reversed, I could imagine me being envious.

Walt sported that uneven grin that I so loved. I felt like Superwoman, the perfect mate for my Superman. Nope. Tracy had to be wrong. I had nothing to fear from Savannah.

SUMMER, 1974

19

TIGHTENING THE FORMATION

Milwaukee, Wisconsin

"Let's go get a bratwurst," Walt said. He was dressed in his airshow day uniform, a white short-sleeved shirt with a small American Flag over the left pocket and his name over the right.

In Wisconsin, most airshows had grilled "brats" instead of hot dogs, something I had never eaten growing up. "Yum," I said. "Let's go. Don't want to miss the Harrier performance. I loooove," I elongated the word, "to watch it fly."

I slipped my hand into Walt's and smiled at the way my red, silver, and blue wingriding outfit shimmered in the Wisconsin sunshine. This was our third year at the Milwaukee Air Age. They adored The Flying Pierces and we adored them. They had hired only Walt and me, so Savannah took the opportunity to visit a friend. It was nice being alone this weekend. She was a good enough pilot and the media did feature her as I had thought they would but, and it was a big but, things had changed. Whatever topic the three of us discussed, more and more it was Walt and Savannah on one side, with me on the other. I had lost my friend and I didn't know why.

Walt accused me of jealousy and he was right. Had Tracy been correct in her assessment of Savannah? Walt reassured me there was no reason to be concerned, but still, I wanted her gone. In our arguments, he blamed me for not trusting him. Still, it wasn't unusual to come upon them a little too close together for my comfort. Was cheating on the man-I-loved's mind? It didn't seem possible with all we shared and how we felt for each other, but I remembered how both of us were married to other people when we met.

Enough of such irritating thoughts. My world radiated beauty. I held my man's hand as we went in search of a Wisconsin brat sandwich.

People crowded the airshow grounds. Kids sat on daddies' shoulders while mommies lotioned their children's exposed surfaces. We wove our way around the lawn chairs, blankets, and camping stools to one of many red-white-and-blue colored concession stands with flags fluttering on the corners. The beer line was long, but only a few people stood ahead of us in the sandwich line.

The announcer's voice echoed around us, "Folks, you won't believe our next act, the Hawker Harrier. You've heard of Flash Gordon. Well he had nothing on this air machine. The Harrier is a single engine fixed-wing aircraft with vertical take off capability. That's right. It'll lift off vertically in front of you."

As if to emphasize its power, the Harrier's engine noise welled and overrode the announcer's voice. I looked toward the runway and saw a fighter aircraft raise straight up, appearing above the people's heads. The camouflage-painted airplane hovered above the ground as if suspended from some invisible crane in the sky.

The Marines were demonstrating the Hawker Siddley Harrier at airshows across the country. Airshow pilots, along with the crowds, were totally amazed by its ability to stop on a dime and turn three hundred and sixty degrees, then in the next minute, take off and accelerate like a fighter plane. A fairly small airplane, it looked like something from the movie "Star Wars" with air intakes for the engine rounding out on each side of the fuselage.

Along with the crowd, we stood mesmerized by the Harrier demonstration. We dabbed mustard on our brats and rushed toward our airplanes, parked between the crowd and the flight line, for a close up view of the exciting performance. It was a perfect place to watch the Harrier that was positioned on the other side of the runway over a grass area near the center of the crowd line.

The announcer's voice rippled from the speakers down the crowd line. "Look! The Harrier is bowing to you." We stopped mid-crowd to observe the nose of the Harrier tip forward as if to bow to the crowd. The airplane's unique ability to pivot and tilt came from a series of rotatable nozzles and vectored thrust from the engines. The airplane hovered about one hundred feet above the ground. It tipped its nose forward. Then without warning, it crashed. The ground shook around us, and the plane burst into flames.

People screamed. Children cried. The announcer's voice rose in pitch, but I couldn't understand what he said. Startled, Walt and I stood still in the midst of the chaotic drama around us. My mind raced, trying to figure out how one moment the jet was in the air, and the next, an orange and black fireball raged on the other side of the runway. I couldn't bear to think of the pilot.

Suddenly, I remembered our own airplanes parked close to where the Harrier had crashed. "Walt," I said.

He looked down at me with a tired face that seemed to sag.

"Are our planes safe?"

Taller, he had a better chance of seeing what was going on. After scanning the area as best he could, he said, "The crash is pretty far away. They should be okay. Come on. Let's get over to our planes."

We elbowed through the agitated audience to the gate in the snow fence that separated the crowd and show planes. The guard at the gate stopped us, but we saw that our planes were undamaged. I thought of the young Harrier pilot we had talked to at last night's airshow party. Across from us, airport firemen put out a raging fire that had been a magnificent jet fighter. I crossed my arms as if I could protect myself from what I saw before me. The thought of burning to death in an airplane wasn't pleasant.

"Thank God Shawn is in Dallas with mom and dad," I mumbled. Walt nodded.

In a few minutes, the announcer's voice boomed over the speakers. "Folks, you won't believe this, but the pilot was able to eject before the plane crashed. That lucky Marine is on his way to the hospital now."

A roar went up from the crowd as if a gladiator had bested the lion. Fate had given up a thumbs-up to one brave young man. My eyes misted as relief surged through my body. How could anyone survive such a crash? Later, Life Magazine would have the crash on the cover showing an orange-black fireball and a body in an ejection seat flung away from the plane.

The airshow went on after thirty minutes and we performed our acts as usual. Airshow life continues in spite of accidents. Walt and I were no different than other pilots who became proficient at stuffing difficult images to some far-away compartment in their psyches while telling themselves, "It'll never happen to me."

We left Milwaukee on Monday morning, rushed back to Mentone, read our mail, washed clothes, picked up Savannah, and prepared to leave for the next airshow in New Bedford, Massachusetts on Tuesday morning. It wasn't that we denied the accident; we were just too busy to think about it.

Tuesday morning, our flight of three airplanes took off for Massachusetts. Around us, the weather had turned sour with grayish-black clouds hanging low, tattered rags over the bare Indiana farmland. We zigzagged through the subdued sky searching for better weather. Light rain streaked across the Great Lake's windshield which restricted the already limited forward visibility. I flew, tucked close to Walt's right wing with Savannah on his left. Walt hunched forward in his cockpit, peering intently into the sky ahead. His job was to keep us away from hidden radio towers and other aircraft as he navigated a railroad track underneath us that led in the right direction.

Normally, with clouds and visibility this low, we sat on the ground waiting for better weather, but Massachusetts was many miles away. Walt had delayed the take off for over an hour as he paced the Mentone airport office, coffee cup in hand, waiting for better weather. He, as team leader, was responsible for keeping us safe and on course. Savannah and I gave our input but, like most formation pilots, followed where led, doing our best to stay in position.

Once in the air, the three of us recognized that we it would be safer to land and wait for better weather. Instead, our brave little flight of three gaily painted ships poked around low-hanging clouds hiding occasional thunderstorms. Getting to the airshow on time was a professional requirement. Sweeping aside my apprehensions, I concentrated on maintaining the Great Lakes' position in the formation. I thought only of keeping the Stearman lined up between the flying wires of my left wing, and once again, banished unwanted concerns.

In spite of the bad weather, it was great to be back in the air. Visions of an exploding Harrier faded as I flew that morning. The beauty of our formation, partially suspended in gray mist with black-green ground passing beneath us, captivated my senses. Our three peacocks winged their way through a ghost sky as we continued eastward, now following an interstate highway.

Flying formation requires trust in the leader and other team members. For a controlling person like me, it was a lesson in patience and learning about areas of responsibility. The weather? Not my job. Keeping away from radio towers and approaching aircraft? Not my job. My job? Keeping the Stearman in that "sweet spot" between my flying wires. What freedom.

A quick fuel stop, and we were back in the air. By mid-afternoon, the clouds and visibility had improved. At ease in the better weather, I relaxed and stole glances at the cars and trucks on the interstate below us. I glanced over to the Decathalon off Walt's left wing. Savannah had moved closer to the Stearman in airshow formation rather than cross-country distance. At airshows, we tightened the formation, but traveling to and from them we maintained a greater distance.

It was strange. Did Walt tell us to tighten up? Maybe I missed his command.

I slid closer to Walt's right wing matching Savannah's distance. No longer able to look to the highway below, I had to keep my attention pinpointed. In my peripheral vision, I saw the Decathalon inch closer.

What was going on? Why had she tightened her formation?

Gone were my tranquil feelings. I was angry and challenged. I slid closer, matching her distance from Walt's wing. At this closeness, I had to remain fully concentrated to maintain position and be safe. I kept waiting for Walt to say something over the radio. We couldn't keep flying this close and not risk hitting him.

My shoulders tensed until I felt a burning sensation across my upper back. I had to relax and not think, moving as the Stearman moved. I could hold a relaxed focus for a while, but then the strain returned. My muscles cried out for release in my shoulders and between my eyes. Even my hands hurt.

Still, I didn't intend to chicken out. If Savannah wanted to see who could fly the closest formation, she had better watch out. I inched nearer to the Stearman's right wing and said outloud, "Okay hotshot, beat that."

I didn't know if Savannah moved two inches closer. I only focused on keeping my view of Walt's head between my flying wires.

Walt's voice finally broke the silence. "All right, gals, loosen up. Franklin, Pennsylvania is ahead. We'll spend the night there."

I gratefully eased into loose formation and stretched, trying to unknot my shoulders. A dull ache signaled the beginning of a headache. I wished for an aspirin, but that would have to wait until we landed. A soak in a hot tub was going to feel great tonight.

Although exhausted from the strain of such close formation flying, I knew something was going to have to be done about the competitive relationship that had developed between Savannah and me. If this kept up, at least one of us, if not all, was going to be hurt.

At the motel, I lay fully clothed across the cheap blue-and-green print bedspread that covered one of the double beds. Two small blue canvas travel bags lay on the oatmeal colored carpet. Walt had escaped to the bar as soon as we checked in. Outside the window, a light drizzle began in the gray sky. I heard television sounds and an occasional drawer slamming from Savannah's room next door.

I pushed myself up from the bed and took off my jacket, not certain what I should do. If I confronted her, Walt would be angry. If I failed to confront her, it might be dangerous for all of us. I needed to move quickly, since Savannah could join Walt in the bar before I had a chance to talk to her. Feelings churning, I knocked on her motel door.

"Who's there?" she said.

"It's me, sandi."

She opened the door. "What's up?"

"I'd like to talk a second. Something happened today that concerns me."

I strode past her into the room. She hesitated, but finally turned and followed. I went to the far double bed, moved a small canvas suitcase, and sat on the end of the bed. She plopped across from me onto the other bed.

"Savannah, although we probably do need to talk about what you're trying to do with Walt, I didn't really come here to discuss him. It's the flying that bothers me." I saw her puzzled look, and questioned whether she was pretending confusion.

"Whatever this competition you and I are doing is getting in the way of the team's flying."

"What are you talking about? Walt's your husband. You two are my friends."

I shook my head at this Alabama girl and thought of Scarlett O'Hara. I said, "You can pretend what you want, but today you started flying extremely close in formation. I'm sure you noticed that I came up just as close, in fact, moved even nearer."

"So that's it," Savannah said. "The formation flying got to you. I was practicing, that's all. Maybe we should tighten up the airshow formation a little."

"That's exactly what I mean," I said. "You don't realize the danger you put us in today. The weather was bad. We were tired. I look up and you're eating Walt's wing."

Savannah jumped to her feet, seemed to hesitate, and then turned to look at her hair in the mirror. "You're such a worrywart. We flew along just fine, no danger. If there was a problem, Walt would tell me."

I stood up. "Continue to fly as you flew today, always pushing to show me up, and one of us will be hurt."

The color rose in her cheeks and she turned to face me. "You're overreacting. I was just practicing my close formation."

I wished the door would slam as I left, but it swished closed. I marched to the bar where I joined Walt. He agreed to talk to Savannah about her formation flying.

The next morning, Savannah and I talked easily as if we were friends once more. On the remainder of our eastward journey, she maintained a safe distance in formation. Maybe we could return to the friendship and fun of our time in Florida.

Along the way, we briefly visited Leo Loudenslager, fellow airshow pilot and aerobatics competitor. I noticed Savannah using her southern charms on him, also. We checked weather before leaving Leo, planning to spend the night in Danbury, Connecticut. In spite of all the bad weather, we would make it to New Bedford the next morning in time for the press rides and interviews.

Walt, Savannah, and I took off from Sussex as a flight of three with smoke puffing. The further east we flew, the more mist formed in the air around us until the visibility dropped to less than three miles and instrument flight conditions prevailed. The Flying Pierces Airshow Team was caught in foggy East Coast weather that hadn't been forecast.

I struggled to keep my emotions in check. Enough, already. Flying airshows, Walt and I lived a life with occasional danger and I had been able to handle it, but since Savannah, it all seemed too much for me. We followed an interstate highway beneath us that was choked with evening traffic. Rolling hills disappeared in the clouds on either side of the highway as we neared Danbury. We dropped closer and closer to the traffic as we attempted to stay underneath the thickening cloud cover.

Savannah and I were glued to Walt's wings, following wherever he led. In my headset, I heard him talking to Air Traffic Control who said our location on the radar was eight miles from the Danbury airport. The weather was below Visual Flight Rules minimums, so they gave us a Special VFR, allowing us to land legally. "If we can find the airport," I said out loud and let out a gallows laugh. No airport lights were visible in the weather that was driving us close to the ground.

The headlights of the cars were lanterns illuminating the landscape of a darkening evening sky. My breathing became quicker and I felt my rising panic, all the while staying tucked close to Walt's right wing. The Great Lakes was open-cockpit and mist bathed my face, beading on the windshield. We had to get on the ground, otherwise, we might fly into one of those gently sloping hills on either side of the freeway.

I called on the radio, "Walt, we need to land."

"The airport is only three miles away," he said. "We should see it any minute."

I glanced briefly ahead and saw only mist, gray mist obscuring what I knew to be ground. My throat constricted and my heart beat more rapidly. What could I do? I was a formation pilot and the decision wasn't mine. Was I required to follow my leader into the ground? I felt the copper taste of fear in my mouth.

I pressed the microphone button on the stick and spoke into the boom mike in front of my lips, "Walt, I think I'm going to land on the grass next to the freeway."

He immediately said, "It's not level. You'll wreck, maybe flip over on your back."

I started to answer when he said, "There's a graveyard, there to the right."

I glanced quickly right and saw a fenced area with crosses and trees.

"It's on the map," he said, "Off the end of the runway. We're at the edge of the airport." I heard the relief in his voice. He said, "Turning right, now."

Our formation of three turned slightly to the right and flew into the mist. Walt radioed the tower who cleared us to land on a runway we could not see. Walt slowed the formation down and we began a slow descent. In a few moments, runway lights appeared.

Walt called, "I'll touch down. sandi, you come in next on the right side of the runway. Stay as close as is safe. Savannah, you take the left side of the runway. Stay behind sandi."

I touched down on the runway to one side of the Stearman, careful to remain behind him. I saw Savannah's airplane in my peripheral vision, not far away on the other side of the runway.

Walt led us to the ramp, where I taxied the Great Lakes in beside him, and shut off the engine.

I sat for a moment in my open-cockpit dream airplane, feeling the fog on my face. My breathing slowed. I was numb, unable to make sense of what had just happened. Later in the bathroom of the fixed base operation, I realized that I still wore my helmet and goggles, which I always left in the airplane.

20

BLUE ANGEL SKIES

Lexington, Kentucky

The sleek Blue Angel TA-4 Skyhawk jet glistened in the Kentucky sunshine. I couldn't believe it. I had finally finagled a ride with a military jet team, something I had been trying to do for the last five years. I had wanted this ride for a long time.

At one time, both the Thunderbird and Blue Angel jet teams gave rides to the media, celebrities, and local dignitaries for promotional purposes. Since I didn't fit into any of those categories, I had to be creative if I wanted to fly with one of the teams. I thought I would be able to go up with The U. S. Air Force Thunderbirds, until a movie star appeared on the Johnny Carson television show and spoke negatively about her ride. Suddenly, all promotional flights with the Birds stopped.

A sympathetic Thunderbird crew chief had snuck me into an F-4 and let me taxi it to the ramp after the New Orleans airshow. It had been a production worthy of a spy movie with me donning an olive drab flight suit and slipping into the cockpit of the fighter. I had placed the Thunderbird white-with-red-and-blue-trimmed helmet on my head and imagined flying such an airplane. For a pilot who wanted to fly the F-4, driving it on the ground to the hangar was interesting, but not very satisfying.

Finally this day, I was to fly with John Patton, the Blue Angels Narrator.

My excuse? I had written several stories for aviation magazines and of course, I "needed" to write a story on the Blue Angels. As part of the media elite who usually provided positive press coverage for the team, my flight was scheduled for the Lexington Airshow.

In keeping with my basic personality, I was once again conflicted, feeling both anxiety and excitement about my upcoming flight. What if I embarrassed myself? I imagined the Blue Angels' narrator traveling around the country saying, "My God, who let that gal fly in airshows?" At last, I told myself that who cared what anyone said, I was going to fly with the Blues.

The day was airshow perfect with puffy white clouds meandering across an aqua sky that covered fields of deep blue-green Kentucky grasses. As a light breeze stirred the windsock beside the runway, I noticed Savannah looking at me in a way that I interpreted as envy. Most pilots would have been envious, but it felt good to see her watching me as I prepared for my flight with the Blues. My anger had been building at the way Savannah flirted with Walt. He kept telling me not to worry, but I didn't like the way they acted when they were near each other. She and I did little talking these days, focusing on business and idle chit-chat. I wasn't proud of the fact that I went out of my way to do little things that would irritate her, things that Walt wouldn't see.

Walt helped me put on the Blue Angel jump suit with various military patches. The legs had to be rolled up as my height was shorter than normal members of the team. I felt my husband's pride as he prepared me to blast off with the Blues. He kissed me goodbye and said, "Go get 'em, Tiger." I snuck another look at Savannah and was happy to see her watching. I gave her a thumbs-up which she ignored, and then walked to the sleek blue jet with yellow trim that was painted in the team's official colors. Excitement overcame concerns as I hopped onboard the two-place version of a very popular military attack plane. The first modern military fighter I flew became number sixty-four on the list of airplane types I had flown.

The A-4 Skyhawk was compact, standing only fourteen feet high, with swept back cantilevered wings that gave it a sporty appearance. Wing tip to wing tip was twenty-seven and one-half feet. A canopy covered both pilot and passenger, and air intakes were on either side of the fuselage, pushing air into the single powerful turbojet engine. No wonder pilots lovingly called it a hot rod. I imagined myself one of those brave Navy and Marine pilots who had flown this attack workhorse in the Viet Nam war, glad my life wasn't in such peril.

John Patton climbed into the seat in front of my instrument panel. In a few moments, it lit up with various colored lights. His voice came through my head set. "You ready, sandi?"

I pressed the mike button on top of the stick and answered, "Ready."

John talked to ground control, then the tower, as he taxied to the end of the runway and turned into the wind. He ran down the take off checklist, calling each item out loud so that I could follow. Lining up on the runway, he added power and we blasted off. I began to understand the aviation phrase, "Climbing like a homesick angel." Encased in a clear canopy, John and I zoomed heavenward gaining over eight thousand feet per minute with only sky in front of us. I turned my head and saw the airport below, falling away as if in a dream.

At ten thousand feet with only Kentucky horse farms and lush grass below, John said, "You've got it. Keep it level and practice some turns."

I eagerly gripped the stick in my right hand and searched for the artificial horizon on the instrument panel, then said, "Roger."

I looked outside the front of the airplane, trying to decide where the

nose belonged in relation to the horizon when flying level. I glanced back
at the artificial horizon on the instrument panel, and saw that the nose of
the airplane was not level. I pushed the stick forward to lower the nose. The
altimeter read 12,000 feet. One moment of inattention and we had climbed
two thousand feet. After some practice, I was able to keep the TA-4 flying
straight and level for a few minutes.

John said, "OK, try some slow rolls."

"I'll do a point roll," I answered. Now was my moment of truth.
Would I show my flying ability to my Blue Angels hero or would I disgrace
myself? I decided to do more than a garden-variety slow roll. I'd impress
him with a crisp point roll where I paused at every ninety degrees of the
roll. Accustomed to my Great Lakes that required heavy pressure on the
stick when rolled, I pushed hard on the TA-4 stick and rolled left, briskly
stopping at the first ninety degree point with the airplane perpendicular to
the ground far below. John's helmeted head bounced off the left side of the
canopy. I had over-controlled the airplane and his head had jerked to one
side, making contact with the canopy. I pressed the mike button. "Sorry,
John."

"No problem," he answered.

I grinned, knowing that pilot story would pass over beers in the future.
"That woman's a tiger—she bounced my head off the canopy."

The next slow roll I simply moved, rather than pushed the stick to the
left. We pivoted quickly around the horizon. After a few rolls, John said,
"OK, I'll show you a loop."

He lowered the nose of the airplane, quickly accelerating to entry speed.
Up we went into a loop that seemed to take forever. I was accustomed to
flying loops in my Great Lakes that peaked five hundred feet above the
beginning altitude. In the TA-4, one simple loop covered several thousand

feet.

John said, "OK, you've got it."

I lowered the nose of the airplane, pulled up, and looked to the side to see the horizon as I normally did. I watched the plane pivot and turned my head back forward, expecting to see the ground in my windshield. No ground appeared and my stomach lurched. I was barreling through the sky and had lost my frame of reference. We flew quite a few moments before the ground reappeared. Later, I would learn to look at the artificial horizon that worked while upside down in military jets. It was the best way to maintain my reference to the ground.

We looped and rolled across the blue-green countryside. Later that afternoon, John rode with me in the Great Lakes. He had never flown an open-cockpit biplane. I had nothing to fear. Life was good, and I loved it.

SEPTEMBER 8, 1974

21

THE CRASH

Naval Air Station – South Weymouth, Massachusetts

I moved my shoulders to release the tightness, a tightness that I had come to identify with Savannah. Along the crowd line, people searched the sky for the opening parachutist. The first strains of the National Anthem cascaded down the line of speakers. Also turning to look skyward, I placed my hand over my heart. The American Flag unfurled below the parachutist and my patriotic heartstrings tugged. This good feeling meant the nagging sadness that threatened to drag me into an abyss had momentarily lifted.

We were part of a large airshow at Naval Air Station – South Weymouth, a southern suburb of Boston. Bob Bishop in his Bede Microjet was scheduled to fly along with The Red Devils' Charlie Hillard, Tom Poberezny, and Gene Soucy. The Red Devils had become the top of the airshow best combining champion aerobatics with airshow excitement. Savannah, Walt, and I flew solo acts scattered amidst the afternoon's performances. The Wing Act and The Red Devils Formation would lead up to the grand finale, the Navy's Blue Angels.

The day before, the Naval Air Station had filled with record crowds enjoying the impressive aircraft in the buttery sunshine with a tinge of fall in the air. Our media coverage was spectacular, but my spirits remained low. Too many things had happened this year: too many accidents, too many close encounters with the ground, and way too much Savannah. As an antidote to soothe my negative thoughts, I reminded myself of all the good things the year had brought. Our years of hard work were paying off with more airshows, more publicity, and more national recognition. I smiled, remembering my flight with the Blue Angels, a dream fulfilled. And there was Shawn, no longer a baby but with an upcoming sixth birthday. We could easily make it back to celebrate with her. She was in the first grade and remained with friends in Indiana so she wouldn't miss school.

Best of all, something had shifted. Savannah had announced she was leaving The Flying Pierces at the end of the season. I didn't know why. My only certainty was that Walt and I had weathered some storm. He was still nice to Savannah, but removed in a way that I understood. I took it to mean he was back in love with what really mattered to him—airplanes, his Stearman in particular. I never doubted that Walt loved Shawn and me, but we would never win over his love of flying. Was that why I felt so down?

The anthem came to a close as I sauntered down the ramp toward the planes. Ol' Smokey stood tall and proud with my Great Lakes tucked close. Savannah's Decathalon sat on the other side of the Stearman, at a distance. The matching paint schemes of the Stearman and Great Lakes glistened in the sunlight with our upside-down billboard-sized names running down the left sides.

I was telling myself what a perfect couple we were, when I noticed Savannah talking to Walt on the far side of the Stearman. He seemed engrossed in searching for a tool in his canvas bag. He pulled out a wrench, turned from Savannah, and knelt next to the large left tire of the Stearman. She leaned toward him and continued talking.

Jealousy struck and quickly turned to hatred, flooding my body like a cold winter dip in the ocean. I wanted her gone. Now! No, Savannah didn't fit my cozy little romantic view of my life. Calm down, sandi. Be magnanimous. After all, you've won. You aren't leaving. She is.

"Hi, there," I said.

Savannah jumped slightly and straightened away from Walt who kept working on his tire, oblivious to both of us.

"Oh, hi sandi," she said. "What's up?"

"I was talking to a reporter from one of the local community papers near here. He interviewed me and I suggested he do a story on you and Charlie Hilliard. You're the newest and Charlie's the most experienced airshow pilot at this airshow. It'll make an interesting story."

Savannah's expression softened. "Thanks, I'll talk to him after I fly."

I crossed to my Great Lakes before I said something more, something I would regret. Arranging stories was part of my job. It didn't mean I liked Savannah or wanted to help her out. Holding back my anger and hurt, I refrained from saying the words I longed to fling at her and at Walt, too. Fuming, I pulled a red shop rag from my tool bag and, with great energy, began to wipe the smoke-oil residue from the belly of the Great Lakes.

The three of us were staying with Ted and Myrt Strong, friends we had met at Oshkosh and owners of Strong Parachute Company who sponsored us with parachutes. They had opened their New England home to us, filled with loving, cats, and good food. The glamour of staying in hotels in our travels had lost its allure and we relished the opportunity to visit with buddies in their homes.

The night before, we had spent the evening enjoying each other and a good meal. We had gathered in front of the television to watch a documentary about motorcycle stuntman, Evel Knievel. Myrt and Ted were parachutists and pilots. They understood people who thrived on sports requiring skill and more than a little daring. I snuggled next to

Walt on the sofa as a lively discussion took place during the commercial breaks. Did crowds come to see people get hurt at airshows or motorcycle demonstrations or were they rooting for the performers to beat danger? We all agreed we believed that crowds rooted for us to live.

At the end of the Kneivel show, Savannah stretched and said, "I want my life to be a blaze of glory."

"Not me," I responded. "I want to die an old woman whose heart stops beating right after making love to the man I love." I looked at Walt and everyone, including Savannah, laughed.

"I'm tired," I said and stood up. "Keep notes Savannah, so I won't miss any deep philosophical truths. I'm going to bed."

Now polishing the Great Lakes, I questioned whether I should have stayed until Savannah went to bed as I had done so many times before. Maybe I should have hauled Walt off to bed with me.

A voice called, "Got time for a picture?" I turned to see a man in his thirties with a camera and press pass hung around his neck. He repeated his question. "Got time for a picture?"

I smiled my best PR smile. "You want me with the Great Lakes or the Stearman?"

"Both," he said. "I'm writing a story for a regional magazine."

I wiped the oil from my hands and picked up my long silver gloves that matched the red and silver sparkling outfit I wore. He snapped a posed picture of me in front of the Great Lakes. In the background, the sound of Savannah's engine started as she readied for her solo act. The photographer and I moved over to the Stearman and began the familiar media dance.

Underlying all the questions was the unspoken, "What's a nice, normal looking gal like you doing in this swashbuckling business?" It might be 1974 with the feminist revolution in full blossom, but people couldn't believe I rode outside the wing of an airplane. Not a joiner, I still felt a vital part of the women's movement. Airlines searched for qualified women pilots, girls dreamed of flying military jets one day, and I hoped they were inspired by my airshow flying.

Would a woman ever fly with the Thunderbirds or Blue Angels? I speculated while posing in front of the Stearman. I leaned over the tail and smiled for the camera. In the background, I heard the growl of Savannah's engine as she lowered the nose to gain speed for her first maneuver.

"Can you climb up on top of the wing and let me take a couple of pictures?" the reporter asked.

"Sure," I said and hopped to the lower wing. My hand reached up and grabbed the center section and in seconds I was on top of the airplane, leaning against the back brace. The silver glove glittered in the sunshine as I waved my arm. The announcer's voice echoed down the crowd line, "And now, twenty-eight year old Savannah Lee will zoom skyward into a hammerhead turn. Just above a stall, she'll flip downward, snap-rolling toward the earth."

The hammerhead turn with a snap-roll was early in Savannah's airshow sequence. I knew there was time for schmoozing with the reporter before filling the smoke-oil in my airplane, time enough to be ready for my solo act scheduled three acts after Savannah's performance. Walt came up to the Stearman, but stayed out of the photo session.

The reporter yelled, "Just one more time, wave at the crowd."

I raised my arm and heard a collective gasp reverberate down the crowd line. Could a heart beat stop? I pivoted on the wing to see what was happening. The sky was empty, and for one moment, the image of a B.F. Goodrich television commercial parodying the Goodyear Blimp crossed my mind. In the commercial, the sky was empty and said, "Here's our blimp.

We pass the savings on to you."

Time seemed suspended as I searched the empty sky. Where was Savannah? Behind me, the din grew. People yelled and pushed against the crowd lines. I heard the clang of fire engines and lowered my gaze to the runway below the show line where an inferno blazed. It looked like an airplane. Confused, I slid down from the wing of the Stearman.

Walt stared at the fire, and mumbled, "Savannah. It's Savannah."

No! He couldn't be right.

Gene Soucy's mom, Pegge, had come to watch her son perform and stood nearby on the ramp. She crossed to me and wrapped me in her arms. I blurted out, "I wanted Savannah gone. She caused trouble in my marriage. I wanted her gone."

Mrs. Soucy held me tightly and for one moment, I felt as if everything was all right. Compelled to watch, I pulled from her arms and turned. Walt stood a few feet ahead of me, and beyond him in the distance, lay a crumpled mass of airplane. The fire had been put out.

A military car drove up the ramp, stopping in front of our airplanes. The door popped open and the Commander of the Naval Air Station, the same Commander that Savannah had joked with on press day, motioned for us to join him in the car.

Now he wasn't smiling and his voice was grim. "We can't do anything out here. The firemen are handling it. We'll go to my office. Better communication there."

The silence in the car was oppressing. No one brought miraculous news of Savannah's survival. I knew she was dead. The car sped us to his office, far from the flight line.

In the Base Commander's office, an aide offered us a drink and I said, "Not until after we fly."

The commander's voice was uncompromising. "You are not flying today."

OK, then bring me a bottle of something, something I can drink very fast that will blur the memory of the fire on the runway, the past year, and all my feelings. Instead, I said, "In that case, I'll have a scotch and water." I rarely drank hard liquor, but hoped for a quick extinction of my present reality.

Walt and the Commander discussed notifying Savannah's next of kin. On the surface, everything appeared normal, but pain covered the room. It spilled out of Walt's eyes, which were pinpoints in a contorted mask. Did I look as devastated as I felt? An aide left the room to see if he could locate Savannah's home telephone number in Alabama.

I thought of my mother. What if mother heard about this? I said, "May I use your phone. I need to call my mom and dad to let them know I'm okay." I pulled in a deep breath as I thought of having to share this news. "The national news might announce a woman was killed at this airshow and they won't know it wasn't me."

Our naval boss, now very much in charge, motioned to a phone at the back of the room. With molasses movements, I dialed my parent's phone number. Were they sitting watching television on a Sunday afternoon? Had they gone to church earlier in the day where long-time friends might have asked, "Where's Sandra this weekend?" My dad would have taken on that proud-father look and said, "She's flying up near Boston."

As I waited for one of them to answer, I knew that mom had always suspected she would get a call about *my* death, not Savannah's. She answered.

I took a deep breath and said, "Hi Mom, it's Sandra. How are things in Dallas?"

I hesitated to tell her of the accident, listening as she said something, but not really paying attention to her words. At last, I said, "I have bad news. Savannah is dead. She crashed during the airshow here in Massachusetts." No reaction. I rushed to fill the silence. "I didn't want you to turn on the news and hear or see footage and think it was me. We had lots of media here."

Mom finally spoke. "Did Shawn see it?"

"No, thank goodness. She's in Indiana staying with friends."

"Well, that's a blessing." My mom who never was at a loss of words, now held her tongue. Was it shock or was she finally learning some sense of prudence?

"I need to go now. I just wanted you to know I was safe. I love you."

Her soft words covered me like a down comforter. "Your dad and I love you very much. I'm sorry about your friend. Call me tonight when you get to the hotel."

Walt stood next to the Commander's desk with a telephone at his ear. His face was long and infused with sadness, a sadness from which I couldn't tear my gaze. He said, "No, Mr. Lee. We don't know what happened. I didn't actually see her crash." He listened a moment and then said, "Let me give you to the people who know those answers." He held the phone to his chest and in a lowered voice spoke to the Commander. "He wants to talk to someone about getting her body home."

22

TAKING A FRIEND HOME

The next day we met with the National Transportation Safety Board. We knew the airplane and understood aerobatic flying, so they asked us to assist them in determining the cause of the accident. The twisted hulk of Savannah's airplane was stored in a hangar at the base. I had an intense pain in my stomach when I saw the mangled charred mass. Although crumpled, it was still recognizable as a Decathalon. Stuffing my feelings and distaste for the job ahead, I said hello to the NTSB Official who had been assigned to this accident.

He thanked us for helping him and shared that they were nearly certain Savannah had been killed on impact, seconds before her airplane exploded into a fireball. Eyes filled with tears, I wanted to run from the room, screaming and crying. Instead, I turned away from the airplane's remains and breathed deeply. Walt was visibly moved by the wreckage, yet, he was able to get into the investigation as if he hoped beyond hope, something had been wrong with her airplane.

So many accidents are attributed to pilot error. Most aviators hope that accidents happen as a malfunction rather than a lack of ability or lapse of judgment on their part. Parts are fixable, while ability and judgment are more difficult to correct.

One by one, the inspector ruled-out possible causes of the crash. "There was plenty of fuel," he said, "no loss of engine power due to running out of fuel."

The inspector shied away from looking at me. He asked Walt, "Can you think of any reason why she didn't recover from the downward snap-roll?"

"I questioned whether there was control malfunction, either the elevator not working or something causing it not to work," Walt replied in a near-scholarly voice, devoid of emotion.

The two of them began following the control systems, checking to see if the steel-braided cable that connected the stick with the elevator was intact and properly installed. It was. They followed the rudder pedal connections in the same way. They looked to see if the rear seat belt had somehow gotten entangled with the stick, in the rear seat where the passenger or instructor usually rode. At first, they thought they might have discovered something, but again, the inspector was able to determine that nothing had impeded the control stick's movement.

Walt and the inspector were at the rear of the airplane and, not being a person to sit idly, I moved to what remained of the cockpit. Leaning inside, I saw strands of Savannah's long brown hair on the instrument panel, held in place by dried blood. Bile rose in my throat and I moved away. "I'll be back in a minute," I said, rushing from the room.

When I returned, the NTSB inspector handed me a charred piece of Savannah's watch. Had the straps been burned or torn from her arm? I turned it over and again saw strands of her hair matted to its back. I put it in my purse wishing for all of this to be over.

At the end of the investigation, nothing structural was found that could have caused her accident. The official report was "Pilot Error," stating that she more than likely started a maneuver too low for recovery before impacting the ground.

The next day, we left on a commercial flight to attend Savannah's funeral. Her body had already been flown home on the Monday after the accident. Lost in our inner worlds, Walt and I had little to say to each other. The Lee family was gracious, but distraught. Walt attempted to answer their questions without knowing what to say. We didn't know why she had flown into the ground while doing a maneuver we had seen her perform countless times. More than likely, something had caused her to start her sequence lower than normal.

That evening we went with the family to the funeral home. Subdued lighting and soft religious music provided the backdrop for Savannah's casket in the viewing room. Yellow roses hung from the top of her closed coffin to the floor, amidst a room overflowing with colorful floral sprays and arrangements. The sweet smell of gladiolas, mixed with carnations and roses, enveloped me like a choking fog. I wanted to run away; away from the funeral home, from the accident, but mainly from my guilt and remorse.

Small groups of mourning relatives and friends clustered around the room. Air heavy with sadness, the moaning sounds came in waves, breaking over the quiet murmurings. Walt, head in hands, sat on a chair next to Savannah's mom. He began to weep. Leaning near, Mrs. Lee comforted him. The family minister, wearing a suit with a black collar, placed his hand on Walt's shoulder and spoke to him. I couldn't hear his words, but knew he offered condolences.

People wandered up to me, discussed Savannah or some aspect of the accident, and then drifted away. Unable to stay any longer, I escaped to the restroom, determined to flee the quicksand of the room, the sticky sweet smell of the flowers, and the soft sad Southern accents. Emotions more under control, I returned to my duty. On entering the room, the first thing I saw was Walt, once again, hunched over crying as Savannah's mom patted his shoulder.

It felt like too much. Why did he break down again? Why did no one pat my shoulder and tell me it would be okay? I decided I would leave, take the rental car and let Walt do whatever it was he had to do. It was obvious that didn't include me. Instead, I stood still, knowing that I would never be forgiven if I left. Attempting to control my rising panic, I took deep breaths. Sorrow masked with a smile, I did my best to comfort the family with small talk and pleasant memories of their loved one. All the while, I snuck furtive glances at my usually stoic husband and his overwhelming grief.

A constant stream of friends appeared, stayed awhile, and then left. I heard women crying behind me while one man, who paced the room, turned to me and said, "You folks are crazy. Why would anyone go fly a damn airplane upside down? I don't get it."

His voice boomed through the silent room. I looked at him and questioned if I was crazy. How to explain the joy I felt in the air? I wanted to share how my problems faded away when I was busy in the cockpit. I wanted him to know how peaceful it was to fly, how rewarding to overcome the challenges of the sky, how much I was in love with the world of aviation.

Searching for words beyond my reach, at last I said, "Airshow pilots love flying. We thrive on the challenge of aerobatics and thrilling crowds. Life is hazardous; we all die before it's over."

He turned away, not understanding.

Though it seemed an eternity, we spent only two hours at the viewing. Silence hung between Walt and me on the return to our motel, my restless mind filled with images of burning airplanes and gasping crowds. Finally, sheer exhaustion forced me into a troubled rest. When we awoke the next morning, there was only time to get ready before the drive to Savannah's home and the waiting family.

We rode with the Lees to the funeral in a black Cadillac limousine. Savannah's mother tried to ease the tension with chit-chat, but no one was interested in conversation. My feelings tumbled one upon the other, grief mingling with horror and fear. On the surface I smiled pleasantly, but observed Walt with apprehension. What did his intense grief mean?

We finished the day and its difficult requirements. That night, Walt and I sat in a bar at the Atlanta airport, waiting for our connecting flight to Boston. We felt bloodied, hewn down by emotion, lack of sleep, and the unreality of our life since Sunday afternoon. We were tired, but also liberated from the sorrow of the past few days. We had buried Savannah, cried our tears, comforted the family, done our duty, and were now alive and free.

Guilt still lurked around me, and I assumed Walt felt the tumultuous churning of unresolved emotions also. For the moment, liquor and laughter kept us pushed far away from gruesome reality. Our words spilled out, one upon the other, breaking the death silence that had so strained us. We shared impressions of Savannah's family, the friends, and the funeral. We couldn't talk enough, and as we talked, we drank. I chugged Kahlua and Cream while Walt put away beer after beer.

During one break in the conversation, I asked, "Isn't it time for our flight?"

"You're right. Time to get going." Walt struggled to his feet and we wandered toward the boarding gate. Enroute, we discovered our flight had been delayed an hour.

"More time for a drink," I said.

"Great idea."

We hugged each other, went to the bar, and ordered another round. Finally, we boarded our flight and fell asleep before the plane reached cruising altitude. The Navy sent a driver and car to pick us up when we arrived at Boston in the middle of the night. We went quickly to our room, shutting the world behind us.

Walt shed his clothes and was in bed by the time I stepped into the shower. I joined him in bed, tossing and turning, as troubled thoughts and feelings that had been kept at bay intruded. The longer I lay, the more upsetting my thoughts became. I watched in horror as I remembered images of Walt and Savannah together, interspersed with burning airplanes and close calls that I had experienced. I twisted from side to side, moved closer to my husband, and then away. Unable to take the tension any longer, I shook Walt.

"Walt, are you awake?" I said.

He mumbled, "Just barely."

"I need to know something."

"Go ahead."

"Did you go to bed with Savannah?"

There was silence, and then, he said, "Yes."

I had expected him to answer no, then to drift off to a more secure sleep certain of at least one thing in my life. My heart beat faster. "You went to bed with Savannah?"

"Uh-huh."

Perhaps some part of Walt needed absolution, to come clean and bare all. Perhaps with his defenses worn down, his honesty simply slipped out. Maybe it was the liquor. Whatever the reason, he was now awake and I sensed him waiting for my reaction.

Cascades of emotions swept across me. The thought passed through my mind that I was glad I had taken a shower, as if being clean would make it all easier. My being was in overload and I was unable to sort out the implications of Walt's confession.

Shocked, my body took over and demanded sex. We joined not in love, but some primitive possession rite. I wanted to make him mine again and block the images that kept intruding. Hurt, angry, I demanded physical proof of his love.

Walt covered my face with gentle kisses, seeking absolution for his confession. All the emotion of the past days flowed into the sex act. I reacted to his gentleness with force, my body an instrument of anger. In the cave of a room, no sound save animal noises beating out an ancient rhythm, my body reclaimed him. Exhausted and temporarily absolved, he returned to sleep.

I lay in the silence, shrieking inside while distressing thoughts and feelings ravaged my mind. Finally I got up and groped my way in the dark to the bathroom. Door closed, I hit the light switch and scooped cold water into my hands and onto my face. If only I could wash the hurt and pain away.

Back in bed, my fatigued body sought sleep, but I was unable to quiet my mind. Once again, I rose. This time, I dressed and went outside.

The night was moist and a half moon cast a muted light over the Officer's Quarters and surrounding grounds. Tense, I started to run, full-out running, running to burst my lungs and blot feeling. I had wanted Savannah gone, and now she was.

I was alive and she buried in a Southern cemetery. My fate had brought me a husband and daughter, something she coveted but didn't have. I thought of her mom and dad and their sorrow, sorrow from which I had at last fled. As each step pounded the earth beneath me, conflicting emotions pounded my psyche. When my body could go no further, I stopped to catch my breath.

I paused, but the inner turmoil coalesced around my real concern. Did Walt love her? Was that why he cried so? Was my entire life a farce, some romantic illusion created by my mind? I tried to avoid the feelings that ripped me apart, but my emotions would no longer obey.

Instead, they exploded like an atomic blast. In the middle of the night on the tennis courts of NAS – South Weymouth, I began screaming. Chilling animal sounds of pain tore from my throat and echoed off the nearby trees. I felt like they would go on and on, never knowing an end.

I could hear myself screaming in the distance, as if the cruel sounds came from someone else. Part of my mind assumed the Naval Military Police would come soon and take me away. I hoped they would give me drugs and let me crawl into some corner alone. Was I having a nervous breakdown, whatever that was? I hoped so. Anything would be better than the insanity of my world.

I screamed, yet my mind still tormented me. Would nothing stop my mind?

Then, with great clarity, a thought struck. I'm a pilot. Mentally ill people aren't allowed to pilot airplanes. The FAA would take away my medical certificate, probably my licenses, and never give them back. In a flash of insight, I knew I couldn't survive my current situation without flying. With the consequences of my actions squarely facing me, my screams stopped as if turned off by an automatic switch.

Whimpering, I sank to the ground. And like all the Scarlett O'Haras before me, I decided to think about it another day. I limped back to the room without seeing anyone.

The room was dark with Walt's low snoring as background music. He slept while I had been screaming my head off. Angry, I wanted to pound him awake, but I was too tired to do anything but crawl into bed.

Before dropping into a dead-sleep, I wondered why I was the one who cried while the man in my life slept?

23

WESTWARD TO THE STEARMAN FLY-IN

The next morning I was like a zombie in an old horror movie, dead but still walking, or in my case, flying. I was tired, emotionally exhausted, and feeling hopeless in the face of my life. It was Thursday and we were late for our next airshow, the National Stearman Fly-in, at Galesburg, Illinois. It didn't matter that neither Walt nor I belonged in the air. We had an airshow to do. One goal alone filled my mind. Get to Galesburg where Tracy waited. Maybe she could help me sort out my messed-up life. Of course, it wasn't as messed up as Savannah's. I shuddered at my dark humor. In five days, I would be thirty years old and I didn't feel like I wanted to endure one more day.

We left South Weymouth in loose formation, this time a formation of two planes. Flying my usual place on the Stearman's right wing felt comfortable until I remembered that only one week before Savannah had been on the other side. That twisted heap of chromoly steel and fabric, stored in the hangar at NAS South Weymouth, would no longer fly in formation with any other airplane, nor would its pilot.

The New England countryside, breathtaking on our inbound flight, now slid beneath my wings unnoticed as thoughts in my mind circled like vultures fighting over a carcass. A broken record played over and over with images of my jealousy mixed with little passive-aggressive acts of unkindness toward my, now martyred, team mate. Why hadn't I just told her to leave? Why had I been in such denial, so wanting to believe Walt when he had said, "Get your jealousy under control. Nothing is going on."

In fact, what strange quirk in my personality had brought Savannah into our marriage in the first place? I thought of Tracy's early warning about her. Why hadn't I listened? Cut through the bull, kiddo, I imagined Tracy saying, bottom line, Savannah was a relatively inexperienced airshow pilot. You know the first two years are some of the most dangerous for airshow pilots.

But why? Why was I alive and Savannah dead?

I stared at Walt, tucked into the Stearman cockpit, face forward, protected by his sleek Plexiglas windshield. Was he running his own version of guilt and grief? I knew he would never talk to me about it, and in that moment, I didn't care.

I was angry. Mad at the world, mad at Walt, mad at Savannah, and mad at myself. My stomach ached. Screams wanted to burst from my throat. I slid out of formation and called Walt on the radio, "I'm going to do a loop."

Silence, and then an emotional voice answered, "You shouldn't be doing aerobatics with your plane loaded."

True enough, but I didn't care. I needed to do something, anything to get rid of the energy swirling my brain. I lowered the nose to get the airspeed necessary for a loop. It crossed my mind that the front seat had my travel bag secured under the seat belt. It might hold firm, but could come loose and get caught in the controls.

As I pulled into a loop, I heard Walt's voice in my headset, "Be careful!"

Up I went, arcing around a circle in the sky. I heard noises of tools shifting in the baggage compartment. No sound came from the front seat.

I began a slow roll and remembered that negative g's would make my

luggage move more. I put in full left aileron and did a barrel-roll around the
horizon, keeping positive g's on the airplane throughout the roll.

The physicality of the aerobatics helped for the moment, enough to
skim the top off my imploding energy. Searching the sky, I saw Walt slightly
ahead and to one side. I radioed, "Catching up and back into formation."

This time there was silence from the Stearman.

Our flight of two wended its way across Vermont, New York,
Pennsylvania, and Ohio while I remained acutely aware that I needed to
talk to Tracy. Walt and I would land, say little as we gassed up or grabbed an
airport sandwich, and take off again.

On one such stop, I knew that I had to talk to someone or I couldn't
keep going. I tried Tracy's number in Chicago, but no one answered. I
searched my mind for someone to call, but my only close friend had just
been killed in an airplane. I didn't want to admit the affair to our men
friends, and I didn't want to talk to my parents about what had happened.
At last, I remembered the kind minister from Savannah's funeral who had
given me his card that dreadful night at the funeral home.

I had the operator call his church number and charge it to our home
phone, but there was no answer. I then gave her his home phone number.
This time, a man's voice answered, "Hello."

"Pastor, this is sandi pierce. I met you at Savannah's Lee's funeral. My
husband, Walt, and I flew with Savannah."

"Yes, sandi, I remember you. This is amazing that you reached me. It's
my day off and my family and I were going out the door when the phone
rang."

"I'm sorry I'm bothering you, but I needed to talk to someone." The
words rushed from my mouth, as if I couldn't speak fast enough. "I think
I'm going crazy and I'm flying to an airshow. Walt and Savannah were

involved with each other." I couldn't make myself say the word affair.

A moment of silence on the other end and then he said, "I knew something was wrong when he was so upset." His voice was kind, reaching to me over the phone. "How are you doing, sandi?"

"Not well," I whispered.

"Are you thinking of hurting yourself?"

"How did you know? I just want to die. I don't want to live. The pain is too great. I can't take it. I don't know what to do."

He spoke soft southern words that soothed my soul. We talked of my daughter waiting in Indiana, of my love of flying, of people's inadequacies, and the resilience of the human spirit in spite of pain and distress.

At last, he said, "Do you really not want to live?"

"Not really die. I just want the pain to go away. I want things to be like they were before Savannah came into our lives. I just don't want to hurt."

"Is there any way you can get out of this upcoming airshow?"

I thought of canceling the show and how upset Walt would be at the suggestion, and the effect it could have on our business. "No. I don't think that's much of an option."

"I'm a long way from you, sandi. You need to find a counselor, a pastor, someone who can look out for you as soon as you can."

"My friend, Tracy, is waiting for me at Galesburg." Even over the phone line, I could sense his relief.

"That's good. You have my phone numbers, but I'm hard to catch. I want you to promise me that you won't do anything to hurt yourself without talking to me first. No matter how long it takes to reach me."

Part of me relaxed as I said, "I'll do that."

As I hung up the phone, I saw Walt coming out of the office of the fixed base operator. He said, "Who were you talking to for such a long time?"

"My mom," I said and walked away.

On the rest of the journey to Galesburg, I remembered the pastor's kind voice and understanding words. The Great Lakes, with its familiar cockpit snug around me, felt comfortable. The drone of the Lycoming engine was unbroken, the double wings provided reassuring life, and the air flowing across the windshield was diverted from my face. If only people were as predictable as airplanes.

Even so, I fantasized flying off into a slow fade on the horizon like Robert Redford had done in *The Great Waldo Pepper*, away from the hurt and shattered dreams. This was real life, not some romantic notion, and I had to contend with airplanes that crashed and blazed, friends that betrayed, and a ruptured relationship.

We flew with little radio contact, alone in our separate airplane worlds. When the sun dropped on the horizon, we parked on the nearest airport, fueled the airplanes, pulled out our travel bags, and took a courtesy car to a nearby motel. Walt went to the bar, I to the room. Our communication stopped flowing as if the Army Corps of Engineers had constructed a dam between us overnight.

Saturday morning, we crossed the Indiana countryside. The urge to land and be with my child was nearly overpowering. We had missed Shawn's sixth birthday. I wanted to hug her and tell her how much I loved her. Nothing else seemed important. Yet, we flew on to Galesburg and the National Stearman Fly-in where we had an airshow to fly. I felt so alone, but then I had felt alone ever since Savannah had occupied Walt's attention. At least before, we all had pretended nothing was different. This time, there could be no play-acting. I struggled to remind myself of my lifeline to the pastor in Alabama.

Saturday afternoon, we finished the last leg of our journey. The

Galesburg municipal airport lay amid fields of corn in the distance. Only five months earlier Savannah, Walt and I had flown into this same airport with Jim and Tracy on the ground watching. This day, Jim and Tracy again awaited our arrival, but now we were a flight of two, and I seemed frozen.

We flew over the airport to check the wind sock and flight pattern. The ramp was full of Stearman biplanes with original paint schemes and resembled a World War II flight training base. Below us, some of our most devoted airshow fans looked overhead to watch our flight.

Walt owned the plane these aviators idolized. Ol' Smokey had begun as a trainer, but now had a 450-horsepower engine in place of the original 220 Continental engine. I followed the roaring Stearman in a plane many of the Stearman aficionados had never seen, Champlin's new version of the classic Great Lakes.

The sun sparkled off our sunburst-and-checkerboard paint schemes, deepening the reds and brightening the whites. We were the "American Dream," at least to these adoring aviators. We were airshow pilots who flew great equipment and received media coverage. Celebrities in our field, we signed autographs and handed out pictures to amazed fans. Best of all, we crisscrossed the United States and Canada in open-cockpit airplanes and people paid us to do it.

These Stearman lovers imagined lazy mornings at airports drinking coffee and telling pilot stories in place of business suits and offices or factories. The fact that we were married and had a cute daughter with long blonde curls made the fantasy even more appealing. These aviator bankers, lawyers, electricians, and postmen shared the airshow illusion Walt and I also held dear, but one that recently had been difficult for me to live. Everything had changed in a moment. I, who had been so certain of my life and its direction, now felt adrift with my world tilting on its axis.

We made our usual airshow arrival, zipping down the runway, close to the ground with smoke trails following our path. Each of us pitched up 90 degrees, zoomed heavenward, and turned to enter downwind leg of the traffic pattern.

After we had parked, I saw Jim Leahy walk across the ramp to greet Walt. I unbuckled my seat belt and parachute straps, resting my red-cloth helmet with black goggles and Dave Clark headset over the stick. I wasn't in a hurry to leave my security blanket for airshow talk and condolences about Savannah.

I heard a voice call my name and looked to see Tracy walking toward me. "Hey kiddo. You taking a nap in there?" She wore her usual purple colors, this time a violet sweatshirt and lighter slacks.

"I could use one." Quickly getting to the ground, I hugged her. "It's so good to see you," I mumbled as tears formed in my eyes.

"Hard time these last few days?"

I nodded, hoping that this woman, my friend and mother-figure, had answers I so needed. She, who had survived the loss of friends and the love of her life, airshow hero Harold Krier, in airplane accidents must know something I didn't. In spite of those things, she still loved airplanes and life. Perhaps she would share her secrets and help me understand.

Walt and Jim sauntered our way. Jim grabbed me in a ferocious bear hug, and said, "All is well, even if you think otherwise." I adored Jim and wanted to be pleasant, but with nothing left to give I simply laid my head on his shoulder.

"Walt," Tracy said, "I'm taking sandi to the hotel. We'll get you two checked in."

He looked as relieved as I felt.

"sandi," she ordered, "Get your bag. Let Walt bring the others when he comes."

I climbed into her red convertible and sank into the leather seat, head back and eyes closed, grateful it was too cool to have the top down. "I'm sorry," I said. "I'm so exhausted I feel like I can't take another thing."

She patted me on the arm. "I know, sandi, I know. You just rest now. We'll get you a room, you can take a hot bath, and the world will be better."

"Promise?"

She patted me again. "I promise."

She checked us into the hotel and waited in my room while I showered. Comfy in a snuggly robe, I sat on one bed with pillows propped behind me. She relaxed in an easy chair a few feet away.

"Is there a party tonight?" I asked.

"There is," she said, "but you don't have to go."

"Walt will want me to go."

"So?" she replied.

She was right. Walt might want me to pretend everything was the same, but something very significant had happened. We had to deal with it. The words tumbled out of my mouth. I described the shock of the accident, the NTSB investigation, and our participation as family in the funeral. I recounted Walt's affair with Savannah and my jumble of feelings. I told her about finding Savannah's hair on her watch and the way I thought my heart would split watching Walt's grief at Savannah's death. She nodded, asking occasional questions.

I hurt too badly to share how I felt unlovable, as if no matter what I did, I couldn't hold a man's love. I didn't tell her how my self-esteem had plummeted the last few months, while Savannah and I competed for Walt. I didn't reveal how I felt like delicate crystal close to shattering.

The soap opera of my life spewed out and Tracy in her wisdom sat and listened. When it seemed that there were no more words and the emotions had quieted, she broke the silence. "How did it feel when you got back in the Great Lakes?"

I thought a moment before I answered. "Strange at first, but after a while I felt secure in my airplane, even protected. Nothing had changed. Push the stick forward and we went down, pull back and we went up. It was very concrete and somehow comforting to know that some things in life are fixed." A pause, and then, "Why aren't relationships that easy?"

She half-snorted. "You're asking a woman who's been divorced many, many years? I don't know the secret of relationships. However, I know a good one when I see it. You and Walt have something special."

Yeah, right. It looked pretty tarnished to me. I thought I was starring in a Hollywood romantic comedy and, suddenly, it had turned into a melodrama. I didn't remember Savannah's part being written in the love stories I enjoyed. An image of her burning airplane crossed my mind.

"What's wrong?" Tracy asked.

"I was thinking of Savannah's crash."

"You worry about dying in an airshow?"

"Not really," I said. "I worry more about Walt getting hurt. I don't think I'll die in an airplane crash." We looked at each other.

"Of course," I continued, "I doubt that most of our airshow friends expected to die in their airplanes."

Was Tracy remembering Harold and his death alone in some Kansas farm field? I rushed on, "I can't understand what happened. Savannah had done that maneuver so many times. It wasn't difficult." I sighed, remembering the ways I had done little things to make her life miserable. "She seemed sad lately, a little down. Do you think she might have killed herself?"

Tracy's eyes became fierce, reminding me of an eagle zooming in on its prey. "Don't romanticize her. She didn't kill herself. She screwed up and crashed. Savannah was fairly new to the airshow business and she goofed. It's as simple as that."

"She was a natural, Tracy." Did I sound as whiney as I felt? "I've had to work so hard to learn to fly like I do. She seemed to do it with no effort."

"Kiddo," Tracy said, "I'm sorry you're hurting. Your friend betrayed you, and then went and died at an airshow in front of you. That's tough, but I think the record speaks for itself. You're alive and she's dead."

I heard her words, but they made little difference.

APRIL, 1975

24

AIRSHOW LIFE CONTINUES

Bartow, Florida

Who am I? The question troubled my mind. I inched the Great Lakes closer to the Stearman's wing, maintaining cross-country formation distance. Shawn rode in the front seat of my biplane. Did she sense the distress in her parent's marriage? For years, I had thought of myself as an airshow pilot, but was that still true? Walt, the Superman who loved me, wanted me to be his Superwoman, but the role didn't fit anymore.

Green citrus trees flashed underneath us. In the front cockpit ahead of me, I saw the top of Shawn's little head covered in a red cloth helmet. I couldn't see the black goggles that masked her face, and could only imagine her blonde braids peeking out the bottom of the helmet, bobbing as we rode the undulating currents of sky. I leaned forward, keeping Walt's plane in my line of sight as my left hand reached under the instrument panel and groped the side of the front seat until I felt Shawn's arm. I gave her a pat and quickly straightened, never taking my gaze off the Stearman. Her small head turned to look back, but I knew she couldn't see me, only the back of her seat. I pressed the microphone button on the top of the stick in my right hand. "How're you doing up there?" I said. Her hand shot up and she gave me a thumbs-up signal.

Shawn was a special gem; a sapphire or maybe a ruby, wrapped in red, white, and blue airshow clothes. One thing I knew for certain, I was a mother. I might not be the mother I wanted to be, like Ozzie's Harriet, Rick and David Nelson's mom on television, but I loved my daughter and wanted only good things for her. The thought of my other daughter, living with her father and step-mom crossed my mind. I only wanted good things for her also. Did I deserve all these bad things that had happened to me?

Whatever. Being a mother was one identity I lovingly embraced without question. Yet, I was more. I knew people in their thirties often questioned the decisions they had made so far in life, but somehow Savannah's fiery death and Walt's involvement with her had flung me into an existential crisis that seemed bigger than merely a life transition. Somehow, my sense of self had encompassed only exterior things. It was easy to think of myself as a Texan who lived in Florida during the winter months and in the Midwest during airshow season. I was a Christian who strived to be good, but broke the rules and ended up with deep guilt. I tried to be a good daughter, but had moved far away from my family.

I flew airshows, but what did that really mean? Was I so full of ego that I had to impress others with my daring, or more an adventurer like Lindbergh, or a seeker like Jonathan Livingston Seagull? I didn't know, and I was sick of trying to figure everything out.

I did know that I had another brand-new Great Lakes. This one came complete with four ailerons, one-hundred-and-eighty horsepower, and the same shiny Flying Pierces paint scheme. I smiled as I applied pressure to the stick, adding a touch of aileron to maintain my position next to Walt's wing. Thank you, Great Lakes Aircraft Company; thank you for creating such a responsive airplane. Doug Champlin had come through for me again, making certain I was flying the latest model. The additional horsepower and extra roll-rate made the plane easier to fly and able to outperform the earlier model. At least that part of my life was definitely airshow-pilot-heaven. I might be a mostly broke airshow pilot, but I was extremely lucky to have this marvelous airplane.

Walt and I flew north from Avon Park to Bartow, Florida for an April event, a special airshow, hired by my hero, Richard Bach. I had read all his aviation books, drinking them in like a traveler finding water in a desert. His words captured many of the feelings I had about flying. My favorite was his bestseller, Jonathan Livingston Seagull, which had made him a household name. Tracy Pilurs also talked about Bach, her writing mentor, "the great man," for hour after hour.

Bach now lived forty miles north of us in a pilot fantasy house on the Winterhaven airport. He had hired us to fly in his airshow at the nearby Bartow airport. I fancied myself to be like Jonathan Seagull with a passion for learning and flying, pushing myself to the limits, and overcoming fear on a regular basis.

In spite of the Florida sunshine, my darling daughter, my spectacular airplane, and the thought of finally getting to meet Richard Bach, I felt more like a ship that had run into an iceberg than Jonathan Seagull. I was upright, but certainly not stable. On the surface things appeared the same. Business was good with more airshows than ever. I still waved at the crowds and smiled for the cameras, telling reporters the same aerobatic romance story, but I spent many restless nights trying to find sleep. Walt and I continued to spend most of our time in each other's company, avoiding the subject of Savannah and discussing little but business. I had no idea what he was thinking or how he felt. I was certain he felt my anger, anger that covered a well of hurt that overpowered me at times.

How could he have risked our relationship, our business, our family?

Did Walt love me or only want me as an airshow partner? It was difficult to separate fiction from truth in our relationship. I loved flying, the freedom I felt, the challenge of the moment, but was it worth it to continue to risk my life flying airshows? With Shawn now in school, should we be staying in one place and give her a life like other kids? Only my love for flying and the first grader in the front cockpit remained the same. Who was I really? The questions swirled until my head began to ache. I'd need an aspirin when I landed.

When we had returned to Florida last winter after Savannah's death, I followed the Alabama pastor's guidance and found a counselor who supported my self-discovery. The counselor I chose was in Tampa, a two-hour drive from the airport in Avon Park. I hurried to my weekly group sessions and hated to return home to Walt. Watching people die had taken a greater toll on me than I had realized. I was alive while so many respected others were not.

The counseling gave me a chance to stop and look at my life, to heal and hopefully move on. I was discovering my true responsibilities. If Walt was in a down mood, I learned that it wasn't my fault, but his responsibility. If my mother criticized me, that was hers with which to deal, not mine. These were mind-boggling concepts for me to ponder. Could it be, unlike Atlas, I could shrug the world off my shoulders? The counselor encouraged me to stay alive and provide food, shelter, and love for my daughter. He suggested life ran smoother when people kept their commitments or renegotiated them. Above all, I needed to take time to nurture and support those I loved, including myself.

I found it difficult to imagine the world as a place where people were in charge of their own feelings. No matter what Walt's action, my job was to take care of my own happiness. It just didn't seem possible. Some part of me felt not good enough, not as capable or as good-looking as I needed to be. I had been taught to try harder to make things perfect for the man in my life, to please him. If anyone was discontented around me, part of me felt it was my fault, that I had done something wrong or could at least do something to make things okay. Now, I was learning that it wasn't my job to fix the world. I was only responsible for my attitude and my life. I thought again of Jonathan Seagull and wondered if that was what he meant by "not limiting ourselves."

I heard Walt's voice over the radio. "180 Golf Lima, Bartow's ten o'clock and about three miles. Let's descend and make a pass down the runway. Change to Unicom."

I flipped the intercom button to radio, and said, "Roger, 180 Golf Lima."

Back to intercom, I called Shawn in the front seat, "Honey, we're going to make a pass down the runway at the airport. We'll have smoke on and then we'll land. You OK?" Her hand came up, slowly this time. I knew she didn't enjoy flying in the front cockpit all alone since she wasn't tall enough to see what was happening.

Maybe I was a selfish person, only thinking of my wants and not my child. Maybe if I were a smarter business person, we wouldn't run out of money in the winter. Maybe if I were thinner, things would be better with Walt. I followed the Stearman as we roared down the runway, happy to brush aside my mental "maybes" for the real world of formation flying. Sure, there were some negatives about being an airshow pilot, like we could get killed and we didn't have enough money, but at least I didn't have to think about anything else when flying.

Sliding the Great Lakes closer to the bottom wing of the Stearman, the world fell away with my only concern keeping my view of Walt's head

between my wings in the "sweet spot." Puffy white smoke covered the
land behind us. The Flying Pierces had arrived at the Bartow airshow. As
I unhooked Shawn's seat belts, I saw Richard Bach in the distance, but we
wouldn't meet until the next day.

Airshow day was typical for Central Florida, sunny and warm with
scattered puffy clouds. I swatted the gnats away from my face as I cleaned
my airplane. Shawn followed her dad as he prepared the Stearman for
the day's work. He was dressed in dark blue pants, white shirt ablaze with
colorful patches and embroidered logo of the Flying Pierces on the back,
trailed by his daughter with a blue baseball cap pulled over her blonde
braids. Colorful red ribbons were tied on the ends. She wore a patriotic
T-shirt and her already-tanned child legs jutted out of red shorts. Walt
paused as he studied something at the tail of his Stearman. He said, "Shawn,
get me a Phillips-head screwdriver."

She quickly moved to the olive-drab canvas tool bag behind the plane,
searching through the pliers and wrenches and found a screwdriver. She
looked intently at the end and said, "Daddy, which one is a Phillips?"

Walt kept working on the Stearman, but answered, "It doesn't have the
straight end."

Satisfied, she brought him the requested screwdriver. Shawn loved her
daddy, how could I think of separating them? Surgeon Walt took the tool
and screwed a loose panel tighter while his nurse assistant watched her
beloved daddy work. Was there some truth to our press release persona?
Maybe, contrary to popular romantic movies, being hurt was part of being
married.

Later in the afternoon, I stood in front of the Great Lakes while Walt
flew his solo routine. Shawn had gone for a cold drink with a friend of
ours. In the background, the announcer's spiel filled the air. "There he

goes, Ladies and Gentlemen. Your fellow Floridian, Walt Pierce, pilot extraordinaire. See how close his top wing is to the runway. He could nearly reach out and touch the ground under his head."

As I watched my husband perform, in my new counseling mode, I searched to find my true feelings. In spite of all the accidents I had seen, I was surprised that I felt only pride in his performance mixed with some anger at his past behavior, some sadness, but no fear. Nope, it wasn't fear I felt. Instead, I observed a colorfully painted classic biplane, piloted by a man whom I had loved enough to risk all, perform in a vibrantly blue sky. My eyes misted and I was aware that I was too sentimental for my own good.

I looked down the sparse crowd line. With so few spectators, getting paid for the show might present more problems than the day's flying. I heard someone nearby and turned to see Richard Bach standing next to me. A nod from me, and an inclined head from him. Though we hadn't been introduced, we knew each other. sandi pierce was the airshow pilot/ wingrider he had hired to fly his show, and he, Richard Bach whose picture graced magazines and books. He stood tall, slender with full dark hair and a black mustache. A few years older than me, he looked the part of the fighter pilot he had once been.

We stood in silence, watching the Stearman perform its intricate sky ballet. Bach seemed enveloped in a quiet calmness. Shy or merely confident, there seemed be no need for spoken words from a man who wrote them so beautifully. We were two observers, caught up in the beauty of Walt's performance. At last, Bach looked at the sparse number of spectators and said, "It's like a family picnic."

I laughed. "That's right, Richard. There aren't enough spectators here to pay for the show's expenses. Looks like you've given a gift to the folks of Bartow."

I longed to share other words with him. How did Jonathan Seagull keep from feeling the sadness that had taken residence in me? How could he find happiness in being alone? I wanted to ask my aviation philosopher why someone who loved flying as much as me seemed to be pulled in another direction. His books meant so much me, but my thoughts remained my own. Richard Bach was strong and silent while I felt young and intimidated. I had never thought of myself as shy, but perhaps I was. Was this another unrecognized facet of my personality?

Instead of sharing my thoughts, I absorbed the warmth of the April sun and felt the Florida breeze tickle my skin. There were so many things about myself and life I had never considered. In silence, we stood side-by-side, two lovers of airplanes and flying. Our gazes followed the Stearman as it looped and rolled with the sun sparkling off its polished struts and spinner. Many decisions faced me, but for the moment I would make none. I imagined myself leaving my problems behind as I frolicked across the endless azure sky in the big biplane with only a trail of fluffy white smoke marking where I had been.

FEBRUARY, 1976

25

SKY KING

San Diego, California

My friend, Myrt Strong, and I sat in a circular booth in the motel coffee shop in Chula Vista, the nearest acceptable motel to Brown Field and the Mexican border. Breakfast odors filled the room while teardrop slivers of oil hung suspended in the air. Today, I reminded myself, today I will not tear into my husband in front of other people. I knew it wasn't good for our marriage, but something inside of me wanted to rip Walt to shreds.

I slid a red felt-tip pen from a box filled with colorful hues, then hesitated, questioning whether the black or purple pen would be better. Nope, red was perfect. The medium-sized pen felt good in my hand, just the right mass with a tip spewing volcano-crimson between the lines of an intricate dragon on the page in front of me. A kid for a moment, I was a creator coloring the world as I wanted. I had purchased the book and pens two months earlier in Ft. Lauderdale and colored my way through the pages across the southern United States.

We flew a winter tour with a new group, The Great American Airshow. Flying airshows in winter anywhere other than Florida was a new experience for us. Weather, always unpredictable this time of year, had been kind until we reached Southern California. Houston had been chilly, but with good crowd turnout. Tucson was its usual, warm and sunny. We arrived in

San Diego where radio stations played, "It Never Rains in California" as the unremitting wet stuff sunk our spirits and prospects for a financially successful airshow. As performers, we would get our money, but our promoter, Bob Yde, had a harried look on his face.

A woman on a mission, I colored with focus.

Myrt said, "Don't be selfish, sandi. Share your book."

She had joined us for our winter adventure, battling cold temperatures and wind in the open-cockpit front seat of my Great Lakes. Walt, Savannah, and I had been staying at her home the weekend of the crash at South Weymouth.

"Myrt," I said and continshued coloring, "why am I so mean to Walt?"

Myrt paused in her coloring to look at me, "Are you serious?" When I didn't respond, she continued. "Only a saint wouldn't have felt a wee bit of anger."

I drew heavy violent strokes of color coming out of the dragon's mouth. "It's been over a year. Shouldn't things be back to normal?"

Finally, I looked up at my friend. Living through that trauma had deepened our friendship and Myrt had been a Godsend on this trip. She had eased the burden of travel by helping keep the airplanes clean, toting bags, making the entire airshow group laugh. She also passed peanut butter crackers to me as we flew cross country. I would be tucked off Walt's right wing in loose formation as we meandered across the vast expanses of countryside and Myrt's hand would appear under my instrument panel offering a cracker. To perform this feat she had to half-turn in the front seat while snaking her hand under the instrument panel, all the while wind whipping down her back.

Myrt picked up a teal colored pen and said, "You're over it when you're over it." She reached for the coloring book. "C'mon, share with a friend."

"Hey, watch it." I said as I protectively covered my dragon art. "I'm the daredevil sandi pierce, the fearless woman airshow pilot and wingrider." I raised my body up. "To paraphrase our intrepid announcer Kirby, er, I mean SKYYYYY KINNGGG, I am the equivalent of Charles Lindbergh, Evil Kneivel, Debbie Reynolds, and of course, the famous flying rancher's niece Penny rolled into one person." I referred to former movie personality Kirby Grant, aviator and star of a favorite childhood television show, *Sky King*.

"Yeah, right," said Myrt and made a grab for the book. I moved it her direction and watched as she added a few strokes that brought the dragon into greater focus. Myrt was an artist and her coloring showed subtle hues and shading while mine was reminiscent of child's play. I smiled when she picked up the yellow pen and went to work on the dragon's eye.

Beyond us, people sat at scattered tables eating breakfast, some with families, and others alone. The coffee shop was nice enough, in spite of the overpowering smell of frying bacon. Around us sat emaciated, hairless people with turbans and hats, people who sought life from Laetrile treatments in Tijuana. Their sadness and mine permeated the air and seemed to grip me.

Myrt began penning green streaks in the dragon's now yellow eye. "That's some evil eye," I said.

She laughed, "We need some strong mojo to keep from catching something in this restaurant."

Thank God for Myrt and her humor. I didn't know how I would have stood this trip without her friendship. The waitress brought coffee and took our order, and we colored as if our only purpose was to fill the book before the end of the tour. We still had Las Vegas, Las Cruces, and a final show in Dallas before heading back to Florida.

"Can I join…" I looked up and saw Walt hesitating. "…you two artists?"

"Sure, Superman," I said, surprised by the sarcasm that dripped from my comment. Superman had always been a loving term of endearment for my husband. I noticed Myrt's startled expression and saw Walt's body pull back, as if hit by an imaginary blow. He slid into the booth, next to Myrt.

My anger seemed to pop out at the most unexpected times. In the past, my gaze would lovingly fall on him and my words would bath him in love. Now, I could barely stand to look at him. Even so, I had vowed I would be nicer and I planned on living up to that promise.

Fifteen months had passed since Savannah's death and since then, my feelings had run the gamut of emotion—from hurt to self-doubt, at last settling into anger. I was pissed at Walt and also at myself. Gone were my romantic illusions, gone was my security of feeling movie-script loved. His actions had forced me to look at my life with new vision. I had enough therapy to know I wasn't taking responsibility for my life and was blaming Walt. I didn't care. Part of me wanted him to be miserable, to suffer like I suffered. This was not a good thing, especially for a husband-wife airshow team. So, I had colored my way across the county, expressing my emotions in vivid reds, blacks, purples, and greens.

I also watched my former hero with an eagle-eye, aware when he talked with women at airshows, alert when he was friendly to a gal bartender, and mistrustful of time he was away. The more suspicious I became, the more he withdrew. I had turned into a bitch and I loathed this part of me. I spent the first nine years of our relationship pleasing him, now I decided to only please myself. Decision by decision, I asked myself what I wanted to do, not what Walt had in mind. I was freeing myself from my Pygmalion, but I had gone overboard in the opposite direction. Even though I did as I pleased, I wasn't happy. I had no clue how to be an equal partner in a marriage.

Confused and in turmoil, part of me wanted out of the marriage while another part did not want to change my life and possibly, my career. Why couldn't we go back to the way it was before Savannah? I longed for the warm cocoon of romantic illusion. What a mess.

"Hey Walt, wanna color?" Myrt asked. She was good at including people in whatever fun she created.

Walt read his menu and mumbled, "No artist here."

Not much of a husband either crossed my mind. Stop that, sandi. Your attitude doesn't help. Maybe my mom was right; maybe I did belong in one place with my daughter. Before leaving Florida on this winter tour, we sent Shawn to Dallas to attend school and stay with my mom and dad. They enjoyed having her with them, but my mom didn't hesitate to tell me I was wrong to pull her out of her Florida school with familiar friends and teachers. Even though I argued, I knew what she said was true. While I had agreed to go on the airshow tour, even wanted to go, I was angry at myself for choosing a life that lacked stability for my child. My stomach ached when I thought of my little girl in a strange classroom. I was an awful mother, that's probably why my life was shit. I longed to be home with Shawn in the proper school and me in my therapy group, even though I doubted I would ever be the happy person I had once been.

I looked up and saw Kirby Grant ready to slide into the booth next to me.

"Can I join you?" he said.

"You can join us anytime," I said, happy to be distracted from my negative thoughts.

Kirby was an aging version of the man I had watched on television. He wore his airshow-day costume, cowboy-businessman suit with fringe on the jacket, silver tips on the western shirt's collar, bolo tie with sterling silver slide, and polished boots. His handsome face was wrinkled, surrounded by blonde hair gone gray. He carried extra weight, but still was tall and movie-star attractive. I thought of this man, not as Kirby Grant, but my Uncle "Sky," and I felt like his niece, Penny.

"What'd you order?" His full voice boomed. I smiled and remembered the television announcer say, "Out of the clear blue western sky comes Sky King."

No wonder Bob Yde, our airshow promoter, had hired Kirby as a personality announcer for this bicentennial celebration airshow tour. Yde had been in promotion most of his life, bringing a touring company of *Jesus Christ, Superstar* from England to the United States. He had decided to give airshows a try and booked Sky King, The Flying Pierces, the formation team of Jim Holland and Lindsey Hess and parachutist Bill Wilkinson. He named the new adventure "The Great American Airshow." America's grown-up kids now enjoyed seeing "Uncle Sky" at the local airport. The three of us at the table were no exception.

Walt looked at Kirby and said, "Did you miss the old Bamboo Bomber when the show was brought back?" Walt referred to the classic-looking Cessna T-50 with a tail wheel that Sky King flew on the television show as he chased the bad guys and ran his Arizona ranch. In the second television version, Sky upgraded to a modern Cessna 310.

"You know, that was my personal airplane. Good ship. Wasn't really made of bamboo, but had a wood wing. Also wasn't a bomber." He smiled. "Those radial engines were sweet-sounding and the cabin was roomy."

"Jacobs engines?" Walt asked.

"Yep, same as on the Cessna 195. Of course, they didn't let me do as much of the flying as I wanted. Insurance people always poking around." He shook his head as if he couldn't understand the business world. Kirby had over six thousand hours of flying time and was as hooked on airplanes as the rest of us.

Our waitress brought a menu for Kirby and then scurried away. Kirby put on his reading glasses to study the menu. Walt looked at me. "How did the formation go for you yesterday?"

I laid down the red pen and pretended I was the woman I used to be. Maybe that would help keep my anger under control. I shook my head. "Not good. I couldn't catch up." Visible relief spread across his face at the tone of my voice. I saw his muscles relax and his eyes take on a detached thinking-about-a-problem-mode that originally I had found so charming, but now irritated me.

Walt referred to a formation flight where Jim and Lindsey joined us in the air to circle the opening parachute jump. The four of us in our bright, circus-colored planes followed the jumper's descent with trails of smoke. After the jumper made a stand-up landing in front of the crowd, each of us would zoom to stage center for an introductory maneuver, quickly followed by the next airplane doing a different maneuver. The four planes then formed to one side of the field with Walt flying lead, Jim and Lindsey on either wing, and me tucked into the slot position slightly below the Stearman's tail.

It sounded like a great idea, four peacock biplanes in formation roaring down the runway before pitching up for landing. In reality, my Great Lakes was slower and had less horsepower than the others. Most of the time, I played catch up with the formation, not exactly Thunderbird jet-team precision.

Kirby put down his menu and followed our conversation. "I remember learning to fly formation…" he started to say, but was interrupted by the waitress who came with breakfast for Myrt and me and an order pad for the guys. Kirby smiled his best television smile at the waitress. "I'll take the special with sausage."

Walt glanced up. "Bacon and eggs," he said and went back to his inner world of airspeeds, power settings, and positions in the sky.

"I need to join up with you earlier," I said, and took a bite of bacon, happy that I wasn't biting his head off.

Walt leaned over Myrt, towards me. "That's what I was thinking. You trail closer in the flag jump. I'll throttle back until you're tucked in behind me."

I nodded, visualizing how it would take place in the air and said, "Cut the power a little as we descend down the runway. I can't keep up." We smiled at each other, knowing we had a plan. If only living with another person was as easy as solving flying problems.

Kirby put his reading glasses in his pocket, content to listen to our pilot talk. Myrt, with a Cheshire-cat grin on her face, took a bite of toast. It was a smirk that said, "I told you so. You two are perfect for each other. You'll make it through this."

Under the table, I kicked her shin.

APRIL, 1976

26

CRUMPLED WINGS AND DREAMS

Sarasota, Florida

"Need any fuel?" Walt said as he looked at me, his basset-hound eyes
underlined in folded circles of skin. He had been drinking too much beer,
getting too little sleep, and looked the worse for it. The incessant tension
had taken its toll on both of us. Well, at least, that was going to change.
Shawn and I were moving to Tampa and I intended to file for divorce, that
is, if I didn't back out.

As tears welled in my eyes, I shook my head and turned to my Great
Lakes. Part of me resisted leaving Walt, only wanting things to be like they
had been before Savannah. That was not going to happen. Something
fundamental in our relationship had been shattered.

Finding a job as a flight instructor at the Tampa Downs Airport had
been easy. The fixed base operator had even agreed to give me time off to fly
airshows during the summer months. Shawn would have a normal school
life without the ongoing tension so present in our home. Of course, she
wouldn't have her dad. What would that mean to her life?

Doubts dive-bombed my mind. What would my world be like without
Walt? Would we get along better not married? I hated change over which I
had so little control. Very aware of the downside of this new arrangement,
I hoped we would fare better than the Sonny and Cher comedy team did

after their divorce.

In the background, Kirby's voice echoed down the crowd line, "Folks, get ready for a thrill. The Flying Pierces, Walt and sandi, are about to take to the air. They may look like many married couples, walking hand-in-hand gazing into each other's eyes…"

Yeah, right. Lately, we had been throwing eye-daggers at each other. Did Kirby know we were divorcing? It didn't matter, the Great American Airshow was scripted and that day's airshow was the final performance for our little band of aviators. While Walt's and my separation had seemed inevitable, the Sarasota airshow felt like a funeral with everything taking on a sentimental poignancy. This was the last press conference promoting us as husband and wife. In a few minutes, we would take off for our final formation-aerobatic routine as a married couple. I sighed, glad that Shawn was off with Jim Holland's wife, Helen, instead of watching me drizzle tears.

In my maudlin mood, it seemed fitting that she was eating lunch with Helen. So many airshows ago, Helen had booked us for our first wingriding flight at the Beaufort Water Festival near Hilton Head Island. On that hot South Carolina day she had also taken care of Shawn, a toddler in a stroller, while Walt and I flew. Our lives had intertwined in such significant ways.

Kirby continued the commentary. "When Walt and sandi go flying, they climb into separate biplanes, hers a Great Lakes and his a Stearman, both relics from bygone days."

The Stearman roared to life. Quickly, I flipped on my master switch and turned the key in the starter. The engine caught and I moved the mixture to rich, jockeying the throttle to keep it running smoothly. Walt gave me a thumbs-up to signal he was ready to taxi. He moved into position behind me as I led us, s-turning our way to the end of the runway. With no room for my sappy musings, I focused on the upcoming dual flight.

I flew lead, Number One, in our dual aerobatic sequence, since the Great Lakes was a slower airplane with less horsepower, so it was easier for Walt to fly formation on me. He had the extra power to catch up.

"One's ready," I said over the radio.

"Two's ready."

I taxied onto the left side of the runway. Walt followed, slightly behind and to the right. "Adding power, now," I said, as I pushed the throttle forward.

The Great Lakes shot forward and I was in the air with the Stearman charging into position off my right wing. I kept the nose of the Great Lakes low, building speed and staying close to the ground. We rushed down the runway, until, finally at the end of the concrete, we pulled up vertically and soared skyward with the two planes operating as one. We would never do this again as husband and wife. Was I making the right decision?

"Smoke off," I said, and lowered the nose of the Great Lakes to a normal climb attitude.

Up we went into a Cuban Eight maneuver, the two planes synchronized in a sky ballet. On to the Hammerhead Turn.

"Hammerhead," I said. "Pulling up now."

Back came the elevator until the Great Lakes rocketed vertically. Savannah had pulled up into this maneuver on that fateful day in Boston. My head pivoted left so that I saw the left wing make a ninety-degree angle to the horizon. Did she intuit what was about to happen? Probably not. Wait…wait…wait…close to a stall and then, kick full left rudder. Whoosh, our flight of two now plunged earthward. What happened in Savannah's cockpit that day? Did she know she was about to fly straight into the ground? I pulled the nose of the Great Lakes back to the horizon, establishing a straight-and-level flight line. The airspeed slowed slightly and

I said, "Loop. Pulling up now."

We flew our dual act as we had flown in practice and at airshows so many times. I wished for a moment that we had the money to practice more. The planes were expensive, fuel was expensive, and living cost so much. We made good money, but it quickly disappeared, much like my airspeed as I pulled up into an Immelman with Walt glued to my right wing. Could I make it financially on my own?

"Trailing position," I said. "Now."

"Moving, now," Walt said, and disappeared from his position on my wing. He had moved, slowing until he followed behind me. I wished for a rearview mirror.

"Trailing now," he said.

We executed a series of slow and point rolls across the airshow flight line. Walt trailed, mimicking my actions within a few seconds. I slow-rolled, point-rolled, snap-rolled and always, after a few beats, he began the same maneuver. At the conclusion of this sequence of rolls, I continued my same heading as he flew a half-Cuban Eight turnaround. Smoke off, I circled at one end of the airshow flight area. I watched as the Stearman pulled up into a loop in the front of the crowd and then snap-rolled at the very top. The airplane recovered inverted, and completed the remainder of the loop. His maneuver left a heart shape of smoke in the sky and I knew that at this moment Kirby told the crowd, "Walt has left a valentine for his darling wife."

Walt radioed, "Two hundred feet, circling."

I looked to Walt's side of the airport and saw a puff of smoke that he gave as a locator for me to see his plane. "Two hundred feet," I said and turned my smoke switch on and off.

"Contact," he said.

"Contact," I said. "One turning, now."

"Two turning, now," he said.

I swung the Great Lakes so that I lined up on the left edge of the runway. Lowering the nose to accelerate, the Great Lakes moved closer to the ground. The Stearman flew a line over the opposite edge of the runway. We approached each other, separated only by a few feet of runway. As we neared the center of the crowd line, I was certain Kirby's voice was filled with fear as he said, "Walt and sandi are on a collision course. What are they doing, playing chicken? Who will waver first?"

He didn't know how true his words were, for Walt and I had been on a collision course since I had met him. I lived in a dream world and Walt occupied another world, one I didn't understand even now.

"Rolling left," I said. "Now."

As our two planes met in the center of the airshow area, we rolled away from each other. From the ground, it looked like we had nearly collided and the crowd gasped in relief.

I waited for Walt to join me at my end of the airshow area for our last maneuver before landing. The Stearman closed in on me, but stayed out of formation until I had slow-rolled to inverted. The Great Lakes pulled negative g's and I fell from my seat, resting on the two seatbelts that held me securely inside the airplane. It still felt like I'd fallen a mile. I eased forward on the elevator to maintain altitude while correcting for a slight right crosswind. "Two join," I said, very aware even after all my hours in an open-cockpit plane that nothing was between me and the ground.

"Two joining, now," Walt answered. From the periphery of my vision I saw a darkness. The Stearman had slid into position. My concern was maintaining level flight and keeping the wind from drifting our formation over the crowd. The air was bouncy, undulating with afternoon heat and coastal breeze.

We neared the end of the runway. I said, "One out, now."

I pushed further forward on the stick, raising the nose up forty-five degrees for an inverted pitch-up. I then slow-rolled to upright and positioned myself for the downwind leg to landing.

"Two out," Walt said, as he pulled the Stearman up vertically.

The landing remained. My thoughts returned to my move to Tampa and the changes that lay ahead. Before I had a chance to announce the command to turn off the smoke, Walt said, "MAYDAY. MAYDAY. Something's happened to my wing."

Without thinking, I added full power and pulled the Great Lakes's nose into a climb, turning away from the crowd. What was going on? Time slowed, each moment an hour. Please God, don't let anything happen to him.

The Stearman made a shallow turn, trying to get into better position for landing. Would he stall and crash in front of me, in front of Shawn? I flew toward him, still a long way from the end of the runway. What could possibly be wrong with his wing? I had been so angry, but please, let him be okay.

The radio fell silent. All watched paralyzed as the drama unfolded.

I was closing on the Stearman when Walt broke the silence. "My right top wing panel has lifted outside the N strut. It folded back over the wing. It's still flying. I'm headed for the runway."

Too far away to see his shortened right upper wing, my heart pounded like a train engine chugging uphill. Horrible accidents I had seen flooded my mind. I prayed our daughter wasn't watching.

His upper wing could tear from the airplane. Then the bottom wing would collapse. I shuddered at the thought of him smashing to the ground.

The airport fire truck waited beside the runway, an ambulance, lights flashing, parked next to it. I tried to push out images of Savannah's flaming airplane surrounded with firemen. Nausea gripped me.

The Stearman inched slowly across the land separating it from the runway. Walt maneuvered the airplane at a lower than normal speed. Anything to keep the damaged wing intact. Please, God, let him make it! Please, let him make it! Make it to the ground.

The Stearman crossed the edge of the airport. Would the wing fail now, with the Stearman nearly down? Ol' Smokey sailed over the lights off the end of the runway. Low enough now that if the wing failed, Walt would probably survive the crash. At last, he touched down on the runway.

"I'm on the ground," Walt spoke in the calm voice of the test pilot he had once been, but I knew his emotions were churning.

I flew to one side of the Stearman and saw part of the wing panel folded back over the remaining top wing. That he made it back to the ground was a miracle. Numbness spread through me as I attempted to push away tears and nausea. My body instinctively flew the airplane, turned to downwind, called the tower, and adjusted power without conscious thought.

"180 Great Lakes, cleared to land," the control tower said.

"Roger, 180 Great Lakes," I answered mechanically and lined up for final approach. The disabled Stearman sat parked to one side of the runway. Walt was next to it, surrounded by a crowd.

Habit took over and I landed on one wheel, my usual airshow landing. The other wheel plopped down and I taxied to a spot away from the crowd encircling Walt and his Stearman. I sat in the cockpit of my Great Lakes, anesthetized from the tension, my mind a blank screen.

Then, the tears began. I cried for my failed relationship and shattered dreams. I wept for Walt's betrayal and Savannah's death, for all the deaths and people I admired. The prop rotated to a stop. I wasn't aware that I had shut off the engine. I wanted to get out, to run to Walt, to understand what happened, but was unsure if my tears would stop. I closed my eyes to shut off the world and the tears ceased, but thoughts bombarded my consciousness.

An idea coalesced from the myriad of images in my mind. Had it been twenty minutes later in the airshow, had I been on the wing during the wingriding act, Walt and I would both have been killed. The disabled Stearman could not have generated enough lift to continue flying with me standing outside the airplane. Reality hit me like a blow to my stomach.

"Mommy, Mommy." I opened my eyes to see Shawn running towards me with Helen following. Shawn seemed happy, oblivious to what nearly had happened.

"Did you see Daddy's airplane?" she asked.

I lumbered out of the Great Lakes, hugging my daughter close to me, very grateful to be alive.

"Helen bought me a coke and I didn't see Daddy fly." I shot a grateful look and mouthed thanks to Helen's somber face.

"I'll leave you two now," Helen said and quickly left.

"Thanks, Helen," I yelled to her retreating back.

Shawn, oblivious to her dad's accident, continued to jabber about her day as we walked over to the Stearman. She ran into Walt's arms and waiting hug. His fatigued face was streaked with sweat. He and I exchanged a look of relief, but said nothing.

Close up, the Stearman looked worse than it had in the air. Several feet of the right-upper-wing's outer tip had lifted and folded over the remainder. The bolts holding the N strut to the wing were no longer fastened at the top to the wing.

"Walt, those bolts aren't holding anything. How did you keep the wing from lifting off?"

He smiled, white teeth peeking from an ashen face. "I flew very, very slow and very, very carefully." His voice tapered away.

Certainty, at times, comes in a flash, a gentle nudging from another place. In that moment I knew I would not be killed at an airshow, for another future awaited me. It was a strange perception, as if someone had whispered, "Not that direction. Over here" and pointed to an obscure unknown path. How could it be? I was an airshow pilot, an aviator, with little desire to do anything else. I wasn't looking for a new life. I remembered Jonathan Livingston Seagull's life changing, and being told that one school had finished and it was time for a new one to begin.

New life or not, I was confident that my wingriding days were over. I smiled as I recognized how happy my mother would be.

"Walt." His eyes met mine. "You need to find another wingrider. I think I just hung up my silver boots and gloves."

He nodded, showing no surprise.

Shawn dropped from his arms and said, "Mommy, can we go swimming at the hotel?"

I hugged her. "You bet. A swim in the pool sounds great."

So many events had brought me to this point in my life, some happier than others. Just as I had the first time I climbed on top the Stearman's wing, I pulled together all the courage I possessed, and took Shawn's hand firmly in mine. We stepped forward together into an unknown future.

1989

El Paso, Texas

"Hey, Mom," my daughter said. "It's Shawn."

"Hi, Sweetie. Enjoying Florida?" I cradled the phone between my shoulder and ear, moving a stack of papers to one side of my desk, the better not to be distracted. I didn't want to miss any of the conversation with my nearly twenty-one year old daughter. She had been visiting her dad, searching for a direction in life.

I listened as she rambled on about sunshine and tans while I looked at the large oil painting across from my desk. It had been such fun to wander the El Paso Museum of Art to pick out the decoration for my office. Knowing that I was a pilot, one of the curators had shown me a beautiful impressionistic oil of two biplanes crossing the English Channel. It nearly filled one wall of my office, and I loved it.

"How does Suzie like being mayor?" Shawn asked.

"She's at home in this job." I said referring to Suzie Azar, my flying buddy and new boss. I had been Suzie's campaign manager for her mayoral race. With the help of many volunteers and Susan Hatch, political adviser and friend, Suzie became the first woman mayor of El Paso. Unable to resist, I followed her into city government as her Executive Assistant for Economic and Marketing Development.

"Do you like whatever it is you're doing better than that management training stuff?" Shawn had never understood my work teaching team-building for business and nonprofits.

"You know me. I enjoy new challenges."

"So, what's next? Running for office?" Shawn asked.

"I just got this job." My daughter knew me too well, a restless Spirit who enjoyed exploring new horizons. "Actually, I'm thinking of going back to school and getting my Masters Degree in counseling when this is over."

"You've been doing that for years without the license." I imagined an indulgent smile crossing her face. I missed her terribly.

"Enough about me. What are you doing? Have you discovered the meaning of life? How's your dad?"

She paused before saying, "I have something to tell you." Her words then tumbled, one upon the other. "I rode the wing. I'm going to be Dad's wingwalker. We're going to fly airshows and I'll walk on the wings of the Stearman. I'll have a neat spandex jumpsuit."

My heart seemed to hesitate. The silence extended as I attempted to digest what my precious baby had said. "Your Dad put you up on that wing?"

Anger at Walt seeped into my words. How dare he? OK, Sandi, slow down. You get to fly airshows and ride the wing, but your daughter doesn't?

"Yep," Shawn's confident voiced enthused. "I even climbed out of the cockpit and made my way out to the N strut on the lower wing." Memories of airshow accidents flooded my mind.

"Hmm," I said, buying time as I pieced together words, words that I hoped would not alienate. Courage, Sandi. A little self-coaching couldn't hurt.

"I guess 'what goes around comes around.'" I laughed, and Shawn joined in.

"It's so much fun," she said, "and Dad says I'm really good. He's been looking for a wingwalker, and now I'm it. And Mom…" she paused, "…I'm using my full name, Shawn Dell, only spelled like the chandelle."

Walt, how could you do this? Then again, how could you not?

"Well, *Chandelle*," I said, pushing down fear that now churned with my anger. Focus, Sandi. Focus on her joy. "Tell me about the first time. I was so scared, were you?"

"Sure, but it was great fun. It's so gorgeous up there. Dad says 'I'm a natural. Just like my mom.' Me, can you believe it? I'm Dad's wingwalker."

I listened as my daughter, the woman, shared more excitement than I had ever heard from her. Please God, keep her safe.

"Shawn, er I mean, Chandelle, why didn't you talk to me about this before you did it?"

"Oh, Mom. You would have tried to talk me out of it. Anyway, we're talking now. Be sure and tell Stan and the guys, especially Will. And don't forget Grandmommy." She referred to my husband, Stan, and his sons Will, Steve, and Mike, clustered around her in age.

"Who could forget Grandmommy?"

"Guess she won't like it, huh?"

"Well, Miss Chandelle Pierce, wingwalker and daughter extraordinaire, we all do what we gotta do." I took a deep breath and pushed aside my concerns. "So, tell me about the harness that holds you onto the airplane." We spent the next thirty minutes, talking as one airshow performer to another.

After we hung up, I stared at the picture of the impressionistic biplanes in a sunny cloud-filled sky across from my desk. So many years ago, only two years older than Shawn was now, I had set out on my own grand adventure. Airplanes had taught me about freedom and responsibility. In spite of tremendous self-doubt, my passion for flying made me persist beyond all obstacles. So much had died around me: friends, respected mentors, and a love with its romantic illusions. Still, from the ashes of my sadness and sorrow had arisen a phoenix of knowing. The education was painful at times, but I had learned that humans are more like dolphins playing in the ocean than bodies that perish. I discovered loving was much bigger than any limited story we might create. And most importantly, I realized that while some fear is appropriate, so much of it is merely the excitement of moving into the unknown. I did have anger at her dad for putting her on the wing, but how can you stay mad at the person who taught you to fly?

If Shawn wanted an airshow life, then I would be brave and support her choice. I picked up the phone, dialed a familiar number and heard my mom answer. In spite of living in El Paso for many years, her seventy-nine-year-old voice still dripped with Dallas. I smiled at the thought of her, amazed at how much I loved and adored this woman who had done her best to protect me every step of my life.

"Hi there," I said. "I just talked to Shawn in Florida."

"Oh, Sandra, how is she?" I chuckled, knowing she would never call me Sandi.

"Well, Mama, bet you can't guess what our baby is doing."

OCTOBER 23, 2009

Parris Island, South Carolina

Light from the car diffuses the early morning fog as our family cheering section gathers to celebrate granddaughter Meagan's graduation from Marine Boot Camp. Our motel is in Beaufort Bay, located minutes from the base.

The moist air swirls around me as I think back to a morning so many years ago when I rode from Beaufort Bay to Hilton Head Island for my first ride atop the Stearman's wing before performing at the Beaufort Water Festival. I remember the exhilaration of parachuting into the salty water of nearby Beaufort Bay during that airshow. My mind time-travels to early morning preflights on the PV-2 in similar fog at nearby Savannah and Charleston. I taste the remembered sweetness of a peach under a tree next to my TCraft after the engine quit. That highway where I landed is less than one hour from here.

I brush aside my memories as I see Meagan, so like her mom at that age. She stands tall in her uniform, fit, lean and focused.

Surrounded by those I love. I smile at Walt and his wife, Betty, who smile back and then at each other. We are so fortunate, Walt and me. Both of us had lessons of youth to learn and we did.

Filled with joy in my life and pride in granddaughter Meagan, I hug my dearest Stan and think, "Thank you, Walt, for teaching me to fly."

THE END

Note: Savannah Lee is not the character's real name.

FLYING PIERCES AIRSHOWS

We flew more airshows than this, but some details have gotten lost over the years

Before 1971

Odessa, Texas
Sayre, Oklahoma
Seiling, Oklahoma
Fulton, Missouri
Hattiesburg, Mississippi
Beaufort, South Carolina
Andrews, North Carolina
Calhoun, Georgia
Cedartown, Georgia
Rome, Georgia
Marietta, Georgia
Lake Altoona, Georgia
Huntsville, Alabama

1971
26 Performances

Avon Park, Florida
Memphis, Tennesee
DuPage (Chicago), Illinois
Cleveland, Ohio
Milwaukee, Wisconsin
Chicago Lakefront, Illinois
Mason City, Iowa
Oshkosh, Wisconsin
Naples, Florida
Mt. Vernon, Illinois
Batavia, New York
Osceola, Wisconsin
Bloomington
Westovia

1972
47 performances

Sarasota, Florida
Bartow, Florida
Avon Park, Florida
Ft. Myers, Florida
Winterhaven, Florida
Athens, Georgia
Transpo '72/Washington, D.C.
Aurora, Illinois
Burlington, Wisconsin
Waukesha, Wisconsin
Salisbury, Maryland
Beaufort, South Carolina
Milwaukee, Wisconsin
Oshkosh, Wisconsin
Sauke Prairie, Wisconsin
Mt. Vernon, Illinois
Nashville, Tennessee
Cleveland, Ohio
Plainview, Texas
Washington, Pennsylvania
Columbus, Ohio
Selmer, Tennessee
Davenport, Iowa
Naples Florida

1973
46 performances

Miami Air Races, Florida
Avon Park, Florida
Tallahassee, Florida
Monroeville, Alabama
Sanford, Florida
Washington, Illinois
Naval Air Station/Albany, Georgia
Athens, Georgia
Ashland, Kansas
Sheridan, Michigan
The Mike Douglas Show/Kent, Ohio
Lexington, Kentucky
North Springfield, Vermont
Thunder Bay, Ontario, Canada
St. Louis, Missouri
Lake Charles, Louisiana
Anderson, Indiana
Huntingburg, Indiana
Goshen, Indiana
Oskhosh, Wisconsin
Sauk City, Wisconsin
Mentone, Indiana
Naval Air Station/South Weymouth, Massachusetts
Nashville, Tennessee
Cleveland, Ohio
Lewistown, Pennsylvania
Galesburg, Illinois
Quincy-Taylor, Missouri
Venice, Florida
Kissimmee, Florida
New Orleans, Louisiana

1974
33 performances

Naples, Florida
Washington, Illinois
New Bedford, Massachusetts
Walkill, New York
Lexington, Kentucky
Eldorado, Kansas
Kokomo, Indiana
Portland, Tennessee
Hudson, New York
Anderson, Indiana
Milwaukee, Wisconsin
Oshkosh, Wisconsin
Endicott, New York
Winnipeg, Manitoba, Canada
Pittsfield, Illinois
Pekin, Illinois
Baraboo, Wisconsin
Naval Air Station/South Weymouth, Massachusetts
Galesburg, Illinois
Charleston, Illinois
Gardner, Massachusetts
St. Petersburg, Florida
Melbourne, Florida
Sebring, Florida

1975
52 performances

Ft. Pierce, Florida
St. Petersburg, Florida
Freeport, Grand Bahamas
Avon Park, Florida
Bunnell, Florida
Bartow, Florida
Lexington, Kentucky
Fairmont, West Virginia
Charleston, West Virginia
Naval Air Station/Corpus Christi, Texas
Eldorado, Kansas
Flanders, New Jersey
Kokomo, Indiana
Dallas, Texas
Mt. Pocono, Pennsylvania
Oshkosh, Wisconsin
Chicago Lakefront, Illinois
Hartford, Wisconsin
Nashville, Tennessee
Galesburg, Illinois
Ottawa, Ontario, Canada
Latrobe, Pennsylvania
Vincennes, Indiana
Washington, Pennsylvania
Naval Air Station/Jacksonsville, Florida
Avon Park, Florida
Sebring, Florida
Melbourne, Florida
De Land, Florida

1976
35 performances

Ft. Lauderdale, Florida
Houston, Texas
Tucson, Arizona
San Diego, California
Las Vegas, Nevada
Las Cruces, New Mexico
Dallas, Texas
Jacksonville, Florida
Sarasota, Florida
Jackson, Mississippi
Owensboro, Kentucky
Oshkosh, Wisconsin
Latrobe, Pennsylvania
Hartford, Connecticut
Lake Charles, Louisiana
New Orleans, Louisiana

1977
30 performances

Ft. Lauderdale, Florida
N. Perry, Florida
Tampa Downs, Florida
Walterboro, South Carolina
Little Falls, Minnesota
Oklahoma City, Oklahoma
Greencastle, Indiana
Oshkosh, Wisconsin
Meadville, Pennsylvania
Marion, Indiana
Dyersburg, Tennesee
Lakes Charles, Louisiana
El Paso, Texas
Venice, Florida

1989
Chandelle & Walt Pierce
Wildcats Airshows

Daytona Beach, Florida
Solberg, New Jersey
Bridgeport, Connecticut
Sussex, New Jersey
Connellsville, Pennsylvania
Altoona, Pennsylvania
Latrobe, Pennsylvania
Kissimmee, Florida

Walt Pierce continues to fly Ol'Smokey.

www.barnstormerWalt.com

AIRSHOW SAFETY

Flying low-level aerobatics at airshows is a very demanding endeavor requiring skill and practice. In the 1950's, rules were instituted to protect spectators at airshows across the United States. No spectator since that time has been hurt by an airshow performance accident at any U.S. airshow.

Airshow aircraft fly over a flight line at least 500 feet away from the crowd and high-speed aircraft perform on flight lines 1,500 feet away. Airshow pilots must demonstrate skill levels and are monitored to maintain their low-level airshow waivers. The Federal Aviation Administration has an Inspector at each airshow who holds daily pilot briefings and stops the airshow if rules are violated and safety could be compromised.

Rules now require certain levels of experience to parachute at an airshow or participate in an aerobatic competition.

The Experimental Aircraft Association, the International Council of Airshows, the International Aerobatics Club and other aviation organizations work closely with their members and the Federal Aviation Administration to improve safety in all aspects of sport aviation through forums, workshops, training and continued focus on safety.

Acknowledgments

Many thanks to my beloved buddies, John Roger and John Morton, who continually light the way. So much gratitude for my hubby, Stan, who has loved me through thick and thin. Thanks to my family, especially Will, poring over the manuscript and sharing encouraging words. Great logo and book-design, Steve. Wendi, special thanks for helping make this happen! Thanks Gloria Kempton, Tom Bird, Margarita Velez, Phyllis Caves, Ruth Drayer, Shellie Faught, Karen Powell, Mary Bradley, Zanna Dobbs and the Lincoln County Writers' Association. Special kudos to Shaughn Marlowe for gracious editing. Thanks for a great website, Bill Yorston.

Thanks to all my friends who kept the faith and my aviation buddies who love to hear flying stories. Thanks, Steve Lambrick for the loan of your special Stearman. Thanks to the Experimental Aircraft Association and the Smithsonian Institute for help with research.

In spite of all the encouragement and support, this work is totally from my viewpoint. I'm sure others will remember things I may have forgotten or interpret the events from a different perspective.